'A well-balanced and accessible  ʜhensive overview of current research and policy in cellent guidance and useful practical strategies on hᴏ improve e-safety for children, young people and prof wɪ̣ᴇr community. It is an extremely valuable addition to the field of cyberbullying and e-safety.'

— *Nathalie Noret, Senior Lecturer in Psychology and Director of the Unit for Child and Youth Studies Faculty of Health and Life Sciences, York St John University, UK*

'Adrienne Katz has gone beyond her already impressive research into and experience in the field of cyberbullying and the effects it has on children and young people with this new book. She looks here at what advice we can give to young people, as professionals, that will really work, and that young people can understand and use to protect themselves against cyberbullying. The book gives an insight into what young people really feel about this type of bullying, what they want us as professionals to do about it, and what is the most effective way of protecting them against it. They want to be more involved in the strategies to reduce cyberbullying, and to be consulted during the process.

This book answers the important question, how can we give young people the freedom to enjoy technical communication, whilst keeping themselves safe? It is a compelling read and a must for every school's bookshelf.'

— *Val McFarlane, Director, Bullying Intervention Group, UK*

'Based on extensive practice and research, this book provides you with easy to follow approaches to engaging young people with effective e-safety education and to successfully tackle bullying issues in the school community. The author skilfully engages young people to advise on how we can "nudge" them to adopt safer behaviours when using communication technologies. Young people's voices and case studies give us insight into experiences faced by youth in today's technological age.

Bullying through the use of new technologies is a phenomenon impacting on young people 24/7. Using Cybersurveys to find the "digital self" of teenagers, the author describes the trend in the use of mobile communication devices to hurt and humiliate, with young people de-sensitised to shocking messages online. This insightful and practical guide explores what cyberbullying is, how it affects young people and what to do to prevent it, as well as how to respond if it happens to you (or someone close to you)!'

— *Mohammed Bham, Chair of the National Association of Principal Educational Psychologists, and Anti-Bullying Lead at Solihull Council, UK*

'This is a comprehensive and priceless resource for all those who share the passion and dedication of the author to prevent and tackle cyberbullying and educate our youngsters with regards to e-safety. It provides insight into the virtual world of our young people and the realities of the impact that cyberbullying can have on their lives.'

— *Graham Tilby, Head of Safeguarding, Dudley Safeguarding Children Board, UK*

'At last a really good, practical, down to earth book about the menace of cyberbullying. Written by an expert in the field, this is an innovative guide for teachers and educators in a time when technology has moved from "share the computer" and "get off the phone" to a time when young people have the world at their fingertips – both the good and the bad. Talking to young people about their experiences, how they want to use their electronic devices, how they can enjoy and use them with confidence and purpose and how they can avoid being both the bully (sending unkind messages to schoolmates and others) and the victim (the receiver of an unkind messages) is as much an educative process as teaching a child their times tables. The difference is that while the times tables remain constant, what we taught them last year/month/week about the smartphone may well be out of date already.

This book contains good advice for teachers and educators to help young people think about the power they have at the push of a button. I am sure that this book will be a seminal work on cyberbullying.'

— *Carrie Herbert, MBE, Chief Executive, Red Balloon Learner Centre Group, UK*

CYBERBULLYING
AND
E-SAFETY

CYBERBULLYING AND E-SAFETY

What Educators and Other Professionals
Need to Know

Adrienne Katz

Jessica Kingsley *Publishers*
London and Philadelphia

Kind permission has been given by Kipling Williams for the quote on p.84.
The advice for teachers steps on p.152 are reproduced with the kind permission of the ATL.
Material gathered by the Reach project has been quoted with the kind permission of the charity EACH.
Permission to use the example of an Acceptable Use Policy (AUP) in Chapter 11 has been kindly
given by Alan Harding of Birch Hill Primary School and the Association of Teachers and Lecturers.
Permission to use items Adrienne Katz developed for the BIG Award has been kindly given
by Val McFarlane and Vicki Cheetham of the Bullying Intervention Group (BIG).

First published in 2012
by Jessica Kingsley Publishers
116 Pentonville Road
London N1 9JB, UK
and
400 Market Street, Suite 400
Philadelphia, PA 19106, USA

www.jkp.com

Copyright © Adrienne Katz 2012

Library of Congress Cataloging in Publication Data
A CIP catalog record for this book is available from the Library of Congress

British Library Cataloguing in Publication Data
A CIP catalogue record for this book is available from the British Library

ISBN 978 1 84905 276 4
eISBN 978 0 85700 575 5

Printed and bound in Great Britain

For Lola, Scarlet, Jake, Jesse, Lily and Louis
and your safe digital futures.

ACKNOWLEDGEMENTS

To Katriona Lafferty, Rebecca Calnan and Toni Bretell – this is where your inspired work with young people has taken us. To Lindsay Newton – thanks for inviting me to work in Dudley in the first instance; and to the Dudley Safeguarding Children Board for agreeing to undertake the survey. I would like to thank Jonathan Charlesworth of the charity EACH (Educational Action Challenging Homphobia) and his colleagues for permission to quote from material gathered for the Reach Project, and many valuable discussions, creative contributions and comments. To my colleagues, Val McFarlane and Vicki Cheetham of the Bullying Intervention Group (BIG), grateful thanks for permission to use some items I developed for the BIG Award. To Lorna Jackson and Emma Bond: my gratitude for the use of the Cybersurvey data in your county. To Alan Harding of Birch Hill Primary School and the Association of Teachers and Lecturers (ATL), my thanks for your kind permission to create an example of an Acceptable Use Policy (AUP) inspired by your policies. To Diane Le Count, thank you for undertaking first a pilot and then a full wave in Essex. To Birmingham Bullying Reduction Action Group, Solihull's Mohammed Bham, plus Jo Brown and colleagues in Oxfordshire: I am indebted to you for making the first year of the survey so successful.

CONTENTS

PREFACE

So, why did I write this book? It was smartphones that did it. They caused me to re-appraise. Suddenly it seemed that what we were telling young people was out of date. Their social behaviour changed so dramatically in the new, always-connected world and yet e-safety messages stayed the same. It was like giving a dial-up message in a WiFi world.

I worked for 14 years at the cutting edge of dealing with bullying of all types and, more recently, the delivery of e-safety messages to children and young people. I've helped to develop British government guidance on bullying, I've delivered anti-bullying training to local authorities and schools, served as a regional adviser for the Anti-Bullying Alliance (www.anti-bullyingalliance.org.uk) and explored the issues with young people in schools, colleges, the justice system and children's services. There is no doubt that for young people and adults alike, cyberbullying is a gamechanger. It hurts people in new and deeper ways than traditional bullying and there is a relationship between the two types of bullying that is reinforcing and mutually sustaining.

With the arrival of smartphones, cyberbullying itself has changed gear. Mobile phones with cameras had already produced a major change in cyberbullying behaviour when they became widespread a few years ago, but now we have moved to a world of constant internet access, GPS location devices and Bluetooth (see Appendix 1 for definitions) and Apps, which even allow companies to harvest personal information from a children's game. Clearly this raises challenges for keeping children and young people safe online. There is no longer simply a family computer in the living room to think about. Every child has access to a handheld device, and if not their own, then someone else's. And the safety filter on that phone may not even be set. While the new technology offers infinite exciting opportunities and a future in which digital boundaries will only be further erased, the time is right for a re-think about e-safety advice.

Evaluation has always been part of the work of anti-bullying practitioners – questioning whether or not we have made a difference. Yet there has been little routine evaluation of the impact of the e-safety education pupils have received, or even whether girls and boys responded differently. E-safety education has traditionally been delivered in a 'top-down' way: experts speak, trainers are trained and then the children are told what to do.

When taking a step back and thinking about what kind of e-safety education is needed for the present day, I decided that it made sense to consult the recipients of cyberbullying. We needed to know what they thought of the advice and whether it changed their behaviour. With the help of inspirational colleagues I set up the Cybersurvey as an online tool to collect pupils' views. In the first year, only 40 per cent of students said they always followed the e-safety advice they had been taught, despite the majority saying it was 'good' or 'very good'. Age and gender threw up interesting messages while some pupils seemed especially vulnerable.

At the same time, my day job involved advising teachers about complex cyberbullying cases they were struggling to deal with. Monday mornings began with a flood of calls from schools about bullying on Facebook involving under-13s, problems on Little Gossip, or some other risky behaviour that had happened over the weekend.

These cases often involved a child or young person who was vulnerable in some way. Combined with the cyberbullying, they often had poor e-safety practices or understanding. I soon realised that although the majority of young people were resilient and coping well, we needed a more finely tuned approach to e-safety delivery for certain young people.

The Cybersurvey data helped define three tiers of support: universal, targeted and intensive. Through this strategy it would be possible to provide the extra support and advice that certain vulnerable young people need. We could pre-empt some problems and pick up those who were being persistently victimised. It could deliver more to children with special needs and those who did not understand or absorb the e-safety advice. If we saw the needs of the child first, we could tailor a response and develop appropriate resources.

This book explains the evidence that led to this proposed new approach, and my hope is that it will start a new conversation about how this might become a reality.

Chapter
1

YOUNG PEOPLE IN THE NEW CONNECTED WORLD

As I write this, 60 per cent of British teenage smartphone users confess to being 'highly addicted' to their mobile phone; 47 per cent even use it in the toilet.[1] Fashion in the ownership of these devices seems driven by young people, with almost half of all teenagers owning a smartphone compared to almost a quarter of adults. In fact, in 2010, more UK children had a mobile phone than a book.[2]

In a short time, perhaps by the time you read this, there will be a new generation phone or device capable of being all things to all people. But our lives have changed fundamentally because we can access the internet through this small personal handheld phone. Connecting to the internet is now personalised, private and mobile. Where once dial-up was expensive and time online was limited, in many countries access to the net has become cheap enough for individuals to stay connected indefinitely, and packages come with unlimited data included in the tariff. Cheaper rates have meant that mobiles have become accessible for children.

The change has been rapid – the volume of mobile data transferred over the UK's mobile networks increased 40-fold between 2007 and 2010. And young people cannot imagine a world without these trusty companions. 'I'd die without my BB,' said Keisha, referring to her BlackBerry when I interviewed a group of girls, who all agreed. So reliant are they, some even feel they do not exist if they are not 'on' all the time, and they say they cannot sleep until the last message or tweet has ceased. 'I sleep with it under my pillow,' said Aisha. A school nurse described teenagers' mobiles as 'a body part', so attached are they to their phones. Fear of being without a phone even has a name: 'nomophobia'.[3] This change has been described as 'transformative' in the same way that the shift from fixed line dial-up to broadband was in the early years of the 21st century.

The major shift in this fast-changing scenario is that young people prefer to access the internet for personal use via their phone or handheld device rather than through a shared computer at home. Tablets and even games consoles offer internet access. With a device in their hand anywhere they go, young people are not nagged to 'get off the computer' or to share it with other family members, and can keep their interactions private. All their contacts are carried with them wherever they are. They can access Facebook and thus their entire social world. The phone is the enchanted gateway – through it they can access information for living, travelling and learning. Their music, movies and games are on tap. They manage relationships, reputations and recreation.

But while this opens up exciting and innovative possibilities, we are increasingly aware of the threats of cyberabuse and cybervictimisation, as well as other risks embodied in content and contact with ill-intentioned people.

This book explores these threats and how educators can address them, whatever screen they appear on. It outlines how e-safety education could evolve and progress, targeting the very needy in new ways.

Bullying is, of course, not new. Cyberbullying is a behaviour which takes advantage of any available digital tool for communication, whether online, or via calls, texts or images. But the major change of the past two years is that advice on internet safety needed to change the moment individuals could access the internet anywhere using a small personal handheld device.

The rapid development of technology in the past decade has been accompanied by tremendous adult concern and even panic about the risks facing our children. So it seems that the right place to begin this exploration is to consider how the internet influences the behaviour of young people.

MEANING OF THE SELF ONLINE AND THROUGH DIGITAL MEDIA FOR TEENAGERS

The way we see ourselves has changed utterly now that we can 'advertise' and even amplify our chosen version of the self via the internet. Reflected back from our profiles, we see ourselves as we want others to see us. But sometimes we see a devastatingly hurtful view of ourselves posted by others. Imagine what this means to children and teenagers who are still finding their identity and seeking approval from peers. Does this 'digital self' influence behaviour?

Our chosen version or versions of ourselves?

Digital media almost require that users show off. There is our verbal skill in our ripostes and jokey messages and our photos, so carefully chosen perhaps to show we are party animals, sexually attractive or holiday jet setters. There is what we say in our social networking site (SNS) profile and our huge list of friends – all 'proving' we are really popular. For adults it is a huge temptation to show off the self, or the *version* of the self you wish to display. For young people, it is doubly so. It is their reputation management.

It suddenly seems deadly boring to text or type a message that shows no sense of humour, or one that doesn't use text speak, symbols or emoticons. What does it say about us? How dull to simply type out what you mean to say. Instead, most people treat this version of themselves as a gr8 personal advert. But young people can take it further. They can even swear in a new secret language – reminiscent of those secret languages we invented in my 1950s childhood when computers were unknown. Which adults can decipher 'sofa king great'? It puts users into their own cool club of insiders and excludes all others. This sense of insiders and outsiders is one of the crucial factors in cyberbullying and is helped along by the nature of digital communication.

THE ENDLESS 24/7 AUDIENCE

Consider that huge audience out there. Posting and tweeting provide 15 seconds of fame many times a day. Audiences vary and we might have multiple identities. Nobody need know you are thin or pimply. Everyone is suddenly equal 'out there' and free to roam. If you are under 13, never mind – young people have learned to lie about their age online as much as the ill-intentioned older person who wants to groom children and pretends to be 14.

Experiment and risk bring excitement, and no group craves this more than teenagers. The internet can be liberating and thrilling for many. It can be a lifeline for the isolated and lonely. But the possibility of anonymity or concealed identity brings another dimension.

INHIBITION IS GONE

People do and say things that they never would consider face to face in an offline situation. Some actions seem to be provocative – aiming to shock or hurt. In other interactions, the sender hopes to be accepted by the group because she is funny or daring. It is this display of 'skill' that leads many teenagers on to ever flashier displays, more shocking and ostensibly 'funnier' with each round.

Critical appraisals – 'Did you see what she was wearing!' – quickly escalates to 'She's a slag' or 'He's so gay.' Exponentially they increase in nastiness as others join in, and the fact of 'othering' someone puts the author into an 'in' group.

The shock value of each round of insults has to be ramped up as teenagers become desensitised to the language because it is used around them all the time. An example of this can be found in a small 2008 UK survey, 'Teasing, Taunting, Touching: What is OK?' for a BBC television programme, Panorama (broadcast in January 2011). One in five of the respondents said they were often called 'gay', 'slut' or 'slag'. Around a third said this was 'never OK' but more than a third said it was 'mostly OK' and a further 22 per cent thought it was 'sometimes OK'. Twenty-three per cent had received jokes or threats about sexual assault or rape on an SNS, but only 4 per cent had told anyone about this.[4]

An Associated Press (AP)-MTV poll in 2011 reported that US teenagers text as they speak and use discriminatory slang including words like 'slut', 'fag' or 'retard' to sound cool or funny, not to express hateful feelings towards a group of people. Only 44 per cent said they would be extremely offended if they saw someone using the inflammatory 'N' word online or in a text message.[5] Yet there are significant minorities who are hurt by this demeaning language. In the AP poll 65 per cent of women said they deemed 'slut' deeply offensive if aimed at them specifically.

The coarsening of language when these words are used regularly on screens means some people give little or no thought to the ease with which their messages could get into the hands of unintended recipients, nor of the hurt they might cause certain people. Demeaning something with the phrase 'that's so gay' is common on both sides of the Atlantic, despite several campaigns to address it.

AN AGGRESSIVE ENVIRONMENT
AND DESENSITISED TO INSULTS

There is considerable discussion about whether or not young people are affected by watching violent films or playing violent games. It is thought that a few have difficulty discerning the boundary between real life and fantasy. There are also many psychological experiments in deindividuation,[6] and this phenomenon is often seen in behaviour like 'flaming' or arrangements for a mob to gather for a fight.

The killing of a boy in Victoria Station, Central London, was coordinated on Facebook, and the organiser is said to have asked people to bring knives as tensions between groups of boys in West London ran high. Boys swarmed into the station in broad daylight after school, and 15-year-old Sofyen Belamouadden lost his life in a crowded public space as teenagers kicked, stabbed and beat him.[7] One member of the gang, Samuel Roberts, 18, told the court he joined in the violence simply because 'everyone else was doing it.' The attack was planned the night before on mobile phones and Facebook.[8]

Frequently after such events, we hear that friends did not believe that the leader would actually do what he said he would because there was so much bragging and threatening language flying around; they simply discounted it as joking.

People find that social norms no longer hold sway when they are online or their identity is hidden. A pack mentality takes over. Under cover of a mask or an alias, how might we behave if egged on by the group from which we crave acceptance?

The famous Halloween experiment by Ed Diener in the 1970s explored three situational conditions in which children would steal candy or money – alone, when anonymous or in a group, when one child was made responsible for the others and blame could be shifted. A total of 1352 children entered the 27 selected houses across Seattle, some alone and some in groups, many emboldened by their Halloween costumes. In each house the host, after the experimental manipulation, left the room and watched the children, waiting to see how the anonymity would affect behaviour. The percentage that cheated rose from only 8 per cent among those who came alone and gave their name, to 80 per cent among those who were not identified and came in a group, with the blame shifted to the smallest child. Further, their results suggested there was a modelling effect because in groups where the first child cheated, the other children were also more likely to cheat.

This experiment is relevant in some ways to how groups of children and young people behave online – often anonymous, sometimes in a group and led on by a leader, they exhibit the classic 'deindividuation' behaviour when 'aspects of situations cause people's sense of themselves, including their ethical and moral codes, to recede and allow them to be easily influenced by the actions of others.'[9]

CLICKTIVISM: JOIN A GROUP WITH LITTLE COMMITMENT AND LOSE YOUR IDENTITY?

Online there is little commitment called for – you can join a group or a movement without delivering much on your part, save for a few derogatory rants. This means young people can find themselves strongly influenced by people they barely know and have not assessed face to face in the real world.

People gather with like-minded individuals or get sucked in if they are lonely. Now they find that they have a community, but it can be one that advocates self-harm, suicide or anorexia. It might be a community inciting hatred of one particular group of people. Google search engines display options in line with previous searches so it is possible to keep seeing more of the same like-minded material.

Websites also attract 'trolls' who roam around, simply wanting to wreck or hurt – their pleasure is in being destructive. They ignore all the rules of the discussion, drag down the debate and take pleasure in shocking their audience.

Jaron Lanier, in his book *You Are Not a Gadget*, describes a 'drive-by mentality' in which people create a pseudonym behind which they hide in order to promote a provocative, contentious or violent point of view. These people flock and cluster – often ruining the online community they infiltrate or attack. Lanier argues that this is a feature of the internet and could threaten to undermine the way humans communicate with one another. Although an architect of some aspects of our online world, he now questions the ways Web 2.0 and social media are used. Grossman of *Time* magazine sums up Lanier's message that Web 2.0 and social media 'sell us short as human beings, both in our relationships and in our sense of who we are.'[10]

For teenagers this is a real dilemma. At this age they strongly want to be individual, yet they are more influenced by the crowd than at any other time of their lives. They believe that they are more alive when online. Some do not go to sleep until the last message or tweet has stopped. The fear is that if they are not awake and monitoring the action, someone might be talking about them behind their back. Friends could be making arrangements to meet or go some place and they would be left out. Worse still, friends could be talking about them. So the internet crowd enjoys displays of wit at someone's expense and everyone joins in without thinking (or for fear they may be the next target). Friends or enemies, it seems, are sorted via a binary code with no shades in between. They are 'friend' or 'blocked'.

COERCION AND PRESSURE

The Cybersurvey revealed that large numbers of young people experienced messages 'that try to make me do something I did not want to do.' Among teenagers these messages were likely to include provoking others to post bullying messages about a chosen target. By being the leader of the pack and triggering their 'henchmen' to try and outdo one another in the hate speech or prejudice-driven bullying, bullies wield power in a public forum. They are stating that they have power, that they are the in-group and that they can command others to do their bidding. Respondents also describe indirect bullying behind their back. This can pressure teenagers to try to be accepted by the dominant group, even if it means doing something they did not want to do.

Cases of this sort can begin apparently innocently with a photo posted on Facebook and an 'invitation' to comment. A storm of denigration then follows. This leaves the poor victim in a publicly humiliating and hurtful situation. Even if this page is then taken down, the hurt is irreparable, and to the victim, it is the fact that it was deliberate and planned which gives it greater power to hurt, unlike a fight that suddenly erupts on the playground. It also hurts the perpetrators. They may be consumed with guilt about their former friend who is now a victim. They may fear it could be them next.

Some of the coercive messages are chain letters with death threats if the recipient does not pass the message on, while others may be asking for a nude photograph. Recipients of homophobic bullying in cyberspace were the recipients of more coercive messages than their peers.

So educators and parents find themselves in a new world in which young people are exposed to an endless 24/7 audience in front of which they may flaunt an identity their parents might find shocking. There is the anonymity and the loss of inhibition described above, as well as the threats and coercion or pressure exerted by groups or mobs of people. There is casual commitment to a cause, or clicktivism, where groups of people flock together sometimes briefly around a cause, or refuel one another's prejudices.

ACTIVISM

On the television in 2011 we saw revolutions and riots blamed on new technology as old-style politicians struggled to understand Twitter and Facebook or BBM (BlackBerry Messenger), and their roles in the Arab Spring or the English Riots. The irony was that children as young as ten now owned these 'dangerous' tools courtesy of their parents, and over the course of 2011 more young children became owners of mobiles than ever before.

BUT ARE OUR FEARS JUSTIFIED?

At the most serious extreme there is the influence of websites urging risky behaviour such as race hate, suicide or anorexia, and there is predatory grooming. A tragic spate of suicides linked to cyberbullying of young people has shocked and appalled everyone. Each tragedy is a call to act. Understandably there are charities that grab the headlines with these statistics in order to obtain funds and support for their work, but this increases the perception of danger because they are picked up by the media and sensationalised. The current narrative describes young people as 'feral,' roaming a world full of dangers. Is it any wonder that adults have become so paranoid about young people that David Finkelhor has coined a word 'Juvenoia' to describe our moral panic?

But these fears can be exaggerated. Finkelhor, of the Crimes Against Children Research Center at the University of New Hampshire in the USA, usefully points out that crimes against children have been steadily falling. Sexual solicitation and porn exposure fell in 2010, and the Center found no significant increase in harassment.[11]

Indeed, the majority of the children and young people in the Cybersurvey, conducted in the UK, did not experience any abusive or malicious incidents or messages. Many who did receive one or more of these messages declined to classify themselves as victims of cyberbullying. But although cyberbullying affects relatively low numbers, there is also no doubt that those who are cyberbullied can have a shocking, severe and distressing experience. If we are to act effectively, it calls for balance and evidence of what works, rather than moral panic.

While it is essential to acknowledge risks and prepare young people for life in a digital world, we might remember that as long ago as the 1940s and 1950s there was another sense of moral panic about mass media as young people went crazy for a new form of communication. Wertham, a psychiatric researcher, warned that this latest pastime was 'a distinct influencing factor in the case of every single delinquent or disturbed child he studied.'[12] Laws were hastily passed. Committees were formed. The new threat was the comic book. After the war, comics changed to meet a thirst for excitement and were now carrying crime and horror stories!

Sixty years later we see a similar panic as anxious parents learn words such as 'sexting', 'frape', 'munch' and 'poke' (see Appendix 1) – and fear their child will upload unsuitable photos of themselves that will circulate forever in cyberspace. But research shows that large numbers of young people are navigating this new environment with flair and good sense. There is a growing argument for a more balanced view. Indeed, Emma Bond suggests that mobiles might be the new bike shed, where teens go to share what they don't want adults to see.[13]

The key question is, how well are we doing teaching our children to be citizens of this digital world? E-safety has only been taught for a short time, and there is little that has been fully evaluated. Now may be the right time to reassess the messages we give young people. The Cybersurvey found that although 96 per cent of young people aged 10–16 had received e-safety education, fewer than half always followed the guidelines. By age 14–15 as many as one in five said they 'don't really' or 'never' did so, and only 29 per cent – less than a third – said they *always* followed e-safety advice. Furthermore, those who are regarded as most vulnerable to cyberbullying or other dangers seem to follow the guidelines least of all. While e-safety experts are well informed, teachers, parents and care workers often feel out of their depth faced with day-to-day situations. There is often a disconnect between those 'experts' whose career is in the digital or e-safety world and a class teacher facing 30 pupils day to day.

To sum up, while some young people are doing fine, there are some very legitimate concerns, and a need for more effective and targeted e-safety education. This book describes a three-tiered approach, using universal, targeted or intensive support. Panic will not help us; it is time to teach young people to drive or to cross the road in the digital highway.

Chapter
2

BULLYING AND CYBERBULLYING – WHAT DO WE MEAN?

'Every child is unique – in characteristics, interests, abilities and needs; and every child has the ability to enjoy his or her rights without discrimination of any kind.'[14] (Thomas Hammarberg, formerly Vice Chair of the UN Committee on the Rights of the Child)

This term 'bullying' has been used so broadly that it can easily be misunderstood. On the one hand it is too mild to describe some of the deeply hurtful, vicious and possibly criminal behaviour seen, while on the other it is overused in some mild situations that do not really merit the term. To understand cyberbullying, we first need to clarify bullying itself.

If not properly defined, any small slight, a short-term friends' falling out or even light teasing can be interpreted as bullying by parents and children. Teachers would be inundated with reports if every time a child felt someone had been slightly unkind he rushed to report it. Agreeing on this definition together can be one of the most important steps in raising awareness of what is meant by bullying and cyberbullying. It should be discussed and agreed in school. Child-friendly definitions should be developed with primary school children.

In schools and services for children and young people in the UK, since 2007 the government definition has been:

Behaviour by an individual or group, usually repeated over time, that intentionally hurts another individual or group either physically or emotionally.[15]

Researchers have identified elements that define bullying:

- an imbalance of power so that the victim/s cannot defend themselves
- an intention to hurt, humiliate or embarrass
- repetition, in a campaign to hurt.

New children enter the social world of schools every year and some new forms of bullying emerge. In a changing youth culture, helped by new technology, this is not surprising. The definition discussion will need to be endlessly repeated with new intakes, and new teaching staff will need induction into the school's policy and procedures.

A brief useful definition for use by teachers and practitioners is:

Bullying is the persistent intentional harming of another person within an unequal power relationship.[16]

For a more child-friendly definition we can explain it as:

Nasty behaviour, lots of times, on purpose, when someone can't defend themselves.

HOW DOES BULLYING DIFFER FROM BANTER?

- There is a deliberate intention to hurt or humiliate.
- There is an unequal power balance that makes it hard for victims to defend themselves.
- It is usually persistent or systematic.
- The joke is not funny to the intended victim.

DECIDING IF IT IS BULLYING OR NOT

A fight or argument between two people of equal power is *not* usually seen as bullying. Although many bullying episodes begin when friends fall out, we usually judge it to be bullying when one person or a group deliberately singles out others as a target and sets out to repeatedly humiliate or threaten them: a systematic abuse of power.

REPETITION

One word of caution: there are a few situations in which it is not helpful to be too rigid about the concept of repetition.[17] When bullying happens to a child with special needs, for example, it may be clearly seen as bullying even if there is only a single incident. This is because it might be very difficult, if not impossible, for this child to recognise bullying and defend himself or report it. In addition the bullying behaviour is targeting the child *because* of the child's difficulties. Bullying behaviour can exploit or manipulate the victim with special needs or disabilities in particular ways that must be stopped at once. In a series of consultations with young people with special needs and their parents, they returned to this issue time and time again. They did not want any repeat behaviour to be permitted if someone was bullied in a way that exploited their disability.[18]

Racist incidents and sexual bullying also often demand that we act at once, rather than wait for this to happen again in order to determine that it is bullying 'according to the definition'. Physical injury requires swift intervention and could be regarded as assault. Generally, however, we think of bullying as a deliberate 'campaign' to hurt someone.

WHAT IF THE BULLYING CHILD DID NOT MEAN IT THE WAY THE VICTIM TOOK IT?

Some situations occur where the victim is convinced that he has been bullied, but all too often the bullying child denies it. And the parents of the bully deny it most vociferously. This is when a definition, agreed with all pupils and the whole school community, helps to iron things out. If everyone has agreed this definition and parents have been notified when their child starts at school, then there are fewer opportunities to deny that bullying was intended if a campaign of cruelty has been inflicted. Messages and texts are all too easily interpreted as hurtful by the recipient when the sender did not mean it. No facial clues or context are available to mitigate the words on the screen. To the recipient it can seem pre-planned and spiteful on a bad day, even when meant as a joke. This 'grey area' takes up huge amounts of a teacher's time. School policy should minimise it by being absolutely clear what is meant by bullying and cyberbullying, and ensuring pupils and parents understand this, aiming for consistency across the school as far as possible.

There are some children who may not understand the way their behaviour will be interpreted by others. A child with special educational needs may require help to understand they have been hurtful or provocative. It is possible that ambiguous statements were not meant in a deliberate way, or, as we see often at primary school age, homophobic insults are used without the user knowing what they mean because this language is heard in the playground. This situation requires work to educate the accused child, and to ensure the class or group all understand that some behaviour is not acceptable, whether intentionally hurtful or not. Children need to know that some language is simply unacceptable. Non-malign bullying can be hurtful or socially unacceptable, even if unintended.

On the other hand, a young person may persistently deny it and have absolutely no intention of changing his ways. This type of case requires a long game. Group work, drama and role-play and discussions in circle time all play a role in bringing someone to acknowledge the hurt they have caused. But above all, separating them from their supporters is an essential step. Bullying is generally carried out in front of an audience – in cyberbullying there is a limitless audience. But bullies often have 'henchmen', reinforcers or an outer group of audience participants who shore up their confidence and act as obedient colluders. Craig and Pepler (1997) observed that peers were present in 85 per cent of bullying episodes that occurred on the school playground.[19] Now they can be anywhere and join in on their phones or online. These peers need to be made to understand how their behaviour is contributing to the bullying. (Many of the approaches described later in Chapter 10 can help.) When the bystanders understand the harm they do and no longer encourage the perpetrator, a powerful step is achieved in changing the behaviour of the bullying child. Cyberbullying is often audience-driven and the pain is made worse by the number of people who see it, snigger, talk behind someone's back and 'gang up' against the victim.

WHAT TYPES AND FORMS DOES BULLYING TAKE?

Verbal: threatening or intimidating behaviour, name-calling, put-downs and sexual, racial, sectarian remarks.

Physical: kicking, punching, hitting, spitting, biting or tripping someone up, damaging belongings or schoolwork.

Coercion: threats or forcing someone to do something they do not want to do, such as giving up money or stealing something. Messages that try to make the recipient do something they do not want to do are common.

Emotional: rejection and isolating tactics, staring or threatening looks, playing on fears or sensitivities (commonly used towards children on the autistic spectrum), remarks about physical appearance or taking friends away. Cyberbullying is often used because of jealousy or in retaliation for some incident that occurred in the offline world.

Indirect: lies and rumour spreading, talking behind a person's back, using chatrooms or web pages to spread or invite hatred.

Prejudice-driven: when bullying is driven by negative attitudes towards another group of people, or because the selected victim is 'different' in some way, the prejudice itself needs to be tackled. Prejudice-driven bullying can become more entrenched or severe over time[20] and it can eventually lead to hate crime. It can be related to negative views on:

- 'race', religion or culture
- special educational needs or disabilities
- appearance or health conditions
- sexuality and gender
- perceived sexual orientation
- any so-called perceived 'differences' including family poverty or working too hard.

Having defined the meaning of 'bullying,' the question follows, what is wrapped up in the term 'anti-bullying work'?

- inclusion
- participation
- equality
- rights
- citizenship.

Bullying management is about the essential tools we give children and young people to resolve conflict, to respect others and to forge a society they want to live in. Some of the most exciting sessions are when the facilitator has inspired young people to negotiate values, debate what they deem unacceptable behaviour and generally develop an agreement or a manifesto – setting out what they want in their class or group. It uses every skill available from mediation to diplomacy by way of creativity in art, drama, debate and behaviour management. Work of this kind can be the most uplifting experience for young people and adults alike, and can turn around a child's experience of school. It demonstrates democracy in action.

THE EXTENT OF BULLYING BEHAVIOUR

In TellUs, England's annual pupil survey last carried out in 2009, 48 per cent of school children said bullying had happened to them at some time. Over a quarter of pupils said they 'often' worried about bullying.[21] The report *How Fair is Britain?* estimates that one-third of children and young people experience cyberbullying.[22] The Cybersurveys found that although 38 per cent had experienced cyberbullying in one wave in 2009, in the combined data for 2009 and in the following two years, this dropped to around 19 per cent. This may be more to do with better question design than simply with better strategies to counter cyberbullying. We do know that just under half of respondents experienced one or more of the types of aggressive or hurtful behaviour online or on mobiles that the survey describes, but when asked if they were cyberbullied, they did not all choose to say they were victims of cyberbullying.

BULLYING BOTH IN THE REAL
AND CYBERWORLDS

Bullying often starts in schools and migrates online if not stopped. An example of how cases often involve both traditional and online bullying is that of Emily Moore. This case also demonstrates how bullying is not confined to one domain – either in or out of school. It knows no boundaries.

In 2009 Keeley Houghton, then 18 years old, became the first person in Britain to be jailed for bullying on an SNS. Emily Moore had been victimised by Keeley Houghton for four years, the court heard. She had previously suffered a physical assault in addition to damage to her home. Houghton had two previous convictions in relation to Moore. The first was in 2005 when she assaulted Moore who was walking home from school. Houghton was expelled but was convicted again two years later when she damaged Moore's home. Her latest conviction was for threatening to kill Moore on Facebook. This case illustrates how traditional bullying has developed into cyberbullying along one continuum of aggression. While not all cases take this form, there are many that exhibit both traditional and cyberbullying. Large numbers of cyberbullying targets know their aggressor.[23]

CYBERBULLYING

We cannot look at cyberbullying as an entirely separate activity – the intent is the same as in many of the situations described above – but new electronic tools now make it easier to harass a target anonymously, wherever and whenever. In addition, new ways of hurting or humiliating a target are made possible. To the anti-bullying prevention menu teachers already have, we need to add new digital literacy skills, understanding of the online world of children and young people and an understanding of the resources available to address cyberbullying.

THE EXTENT OF CYBERBULLYING

We know relatively little of the true extent of cyberbullying because the research is fairly recent (since 2002) and it is not yet comprehensive. For example, the questions used in some early work did not encompass all forms of cyberbullying, while figures obtained through teenage magazine surveys in the early stages may reflect a self-selected group of respondents. Another factor is age. Not all studies look at the same age groups. Furthermore, technology is ever changing, offering new opportunities for bullying which may not have been present even a year earlier. Studies do not define cyberbullying the same way and questions vary, with some using illustrative examples, or simply a general question. There are those that focus on the internet and email and omit mobiles and texting or messaging. Prevalence is also measured differently: do studies count single occurrences or multiple incidents? This has contributed to the alarm and panic felt by parents faced with dramatic media stories. It also makes it difficult for schools to know how their figures compare.

More longitudinal surveys are emerging such as the Rivers and Noret five-year study, which are to be welcomed.[24] The Cybersurvey, run over three years, provides some consistency. Even then, one or two questions have been added to keep up with technology and some samples may be younger than others.

DOES THE RESPONSE VARIATION DEPEND ON *WHAT* WE ASK?

There are very different responses when pupils are asked a general question 'Have you been cyberbullied?' in contrast to a list of questions about specific types of electronic aggression. The latter can produce answers from almost half the sample.

Large numbers of young people experience abusive or aggressive messages or incidents, but do not consider all of them as bullying. Perhaps they do not want to be seen as victims or are angry about it at the time, but move on with their lives. It could be that the aggression was not repeated or severe. Some people may not recognise online or mobile harassment as bullying – acknowledging that you are a victim can be humiliating in itself.

It is useful to have a broad picture of young people's experiences online and via mobile phones, even if they do not class them as bullying. I have called all those on the receiving end of any online or mobile hurtful behaviour 'recipients' to distinguish them from a smaller select group of self-identified cyberbullying victims who, after reading a definition, decided they were cyberbullied. The recipients tell us a great deal about how resilient they are, whether they reported it or got it stopped, and the types of behaviours that are widespread among their age group. Comparing their answers with those of the cyberbullied pupils creates a context. They can serve as an early warning system, and their experiences can help shape prevention and response strategies. True victims need more intensive support, but some targeted work and e-safety updates are indicated for the recipients.

In the Cybersurvey 2010, 49 per cent of respondents had experienced at least one of the forms of online aggression described and 32 per cent had experienced at least one on a mobile phone. In a subsequent question, respondents were given a definition of cyberbullying and asked to state explicitly whether they had been cyberbullied or not:

> Bullying is behaviour that intentionally hurts others, either physically or emotionally. It is usually repeated over time and can make us feel powerless. Cyberbullying is when mobiles or the internet are used as tools to bully. Have you been cyberbullied? (Yes/No)

Twenty per cent considered their experience to be cyberbullying; 18 per cent did so the following year. This is interesting because after the first wave in 2009 the question was improved and a definition given. From then on, the responses were very similar in different parts of the country. In ten schools in Oxfordshire the average was 20 per cent. In the first round of the Reach Project survey in 2011 it was 19 per cent. Figure 2.1 illustrates the results over three years.

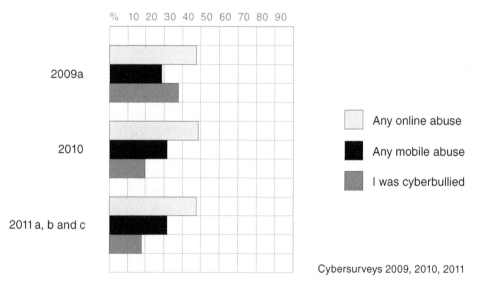

Figure 2.1 Cyberbullying: the extent of online and mobile abuse

This distinction between any experience of cybernastiness and true cyberbullying has been pointed out by others: for example, Hinduja and Patchin (2009) found that 43 per cent of respondents had experienced at least one form of abuse or harassment listed in their survey, in contrast to slightly more than 17 per cent who said they had actually been cyberbullied in their lifetime.[25]

Wolak *et al.* (2007)[26] have argued that, in the majority of cases where young people report being harassed online, terms such as 'bullying' or 'cyberbullying' may be inappropriate, particularly where there is little or no evidence that they are being bullied offline at the time. The intent on the part of the perpetrator and repeated attacks are needed to define it as bullying and the victim needs to perceive it this way.

danah boyd and Alice Marwick describe how girls tend to use the word 'drama' to describe their experience, rather than 'bullying'.[27] They point out that 'many teenagers who are bullied can't emotionally afford to identify as victims.' Instead they were using the term 'drama' to describe interpersonal conflict, as a protective mechanism. 'Admitting that they're being bullied, or worse, that they are bullies, slots them into a narrative that's disempowering and makes them feel weak and childish.'

It has also been argued that different forms of cyberbullying have varying impacts on the recipient. This could affect whether or not they report the incident as bullying: Smith *et al.* (2006)[28] and Ybarra and Mitchell (2004)[29] have shown that although the effect of cyberbullying is generally perceived as highly negative by students, some types of cyberbullying are viewed as more hurtful compared to traditional bullying, since they were interpreted as very intentional and planned.

In the Cybersurvey, boys seemed to under-report. They either accepted it as part of the rough and tumble of everyday life in which their friends swore and used aggressive language or names, or avoided describing themselves as victims because they didn't want to admit to being weak. As many as 33 per cent of males in the Cybersurvey 2010 who had experienced some form of cyberabuse chose to say they were 'not bothered' by it. They might be unlikely to report it if they wanted to be seen as tough enough to 'take it' and this could affect the incident rate reported. Most found this approach worked for them, but some held off reporting it until it had become unbearable or explained that they wanted to protect their parents from this pain. There was a risk that eventually they would find it all too much to deal with and a few would take impulsive steps that included revenge or suicide. This may partly explain the spate of suicides of young men who had been homophobically cyberbullied in the past two years.[30]

DOES THE RESPONSE VARIATION DEPEND ON *WHO* WE QUESTION?

Responses varied markedly if specific groups were questioned. For example, children seemed more likely than their peers to be victims of cyberbullying if they were already being 'badly bullied'. In a study for Dudley Metropolitan Borough Council, while 11 per cent of 2897 secondary school pupils reported being cyberbullied, this rose to as many as 31 per cent among those pupils already identified as 'badly bullied'.[31] It seems that students' roles in traditional bullying might predict the same role in electronic bullying. In addition, being a victim of bullying on the internet or via text messages has been found to be related to being a bully at school.[32]

The age group questioned will also influence results, because cyberbullying seems to peak at age 14. A sample that is younger will not be likely to produce the same levels. Girls experience some kinds of cyberbullying more than boys, so the gender mix of any given sample can affect the result, as could a set of questions skewed towards girl bullying.

WHAT ELSE COULD BE INFLUENCING THE RESULTS OF SURVEYS?

As cyberbullying has increasingly become defined and discussed, more recipients are likely to recognise that they are being bullied and come forward to report it. Cyberbullying may be increasing at the same time as research expands to examine it. What we do know for certain is that increasing numbers of children have mobile phones and access to the internet than ever before. Certainly cheap phones with cameras are a recent development in the last few years, allowing images to be made and sent in an instant. Smartphones, tablets and BlackBerries are owned by young people in ever greater numbers. Therefore, although there is a trend in the US showing cyberbullying increasing,[33] some of this increase might be due to greater recognition of cyberbullying alongside increased access to new technology. The Cybersurvey has not shown an increase in the last two years, but a very similar rate each year. Anecdotal evidence from schools and the increased number of schools asking for help with serious cases reveals more complex and difficult cases.

Another factor is the type of phone packages on offer for internet access from service providers. Young people are dependent on their parents to pay for their access, and in countries where it is still charged by the number of minutes spent online, they can be very concerned about racking up large debts for their parents. In the UK there are many cheap monthly packages allowing the user to be online all the time, only charging for downloads or excess above a limit. This and large numbers of minutes on offer for text and calls can make it easier to be 'always online' without worrying about the time spent. Service provider packages can therefore be affecting young people's behaviour online.

Finally, the time of year could influence the response. Surveys early in the first term of the academic year will be unlikely to reveal much about new pupils' experiences, as they will not have spent enough time in the school. As they are usually worried about being bullied, for example, in a new high school or secondary school, their views are important. I would suggest waiting two months or more so that they can contribute near the end of the first term or early in the second. Pupils often regard surveys in the summer term as a chore, like another exam. The survey works well if you pick a quieter week when you have not yet lost the pupils who are on study leave for public exams, or away doing work experience. National Anti-Bullying Week is the third week in November every year in the UK and in October in the US, and this can provide a convenient window in which to run a survey.

WHAT DO THESE LIMITATIONS SUGGEST?

With these limitations in mind it may not be useful to focus exclusively on whether rates of reported cyberbullying increase or fluctuate slightly, but also to consider the quality of support and education young people receive and above all, how they rate the effectiveness of this. Whether they follow what they have been taught is a key measure to watch. Another is whether they got help if they did report a problem. Too few who do come forward successfully got help – this is no incentive to come forward.

We know that where good support exists, more young people come forward to report what has happened to them because they know there is a good chance they will get help. Where there is poor support, reported incidents may be lower because young people don't believe it is worth reporting. They think nothing will be done and they might be exposed to new dangers. Schools should not be judged only on the rate of incidents, but on whether their pupils think the school is effective in dealing with all forms of bullying and cyberbullying.

As educators we need to identify social triggers for behaviour change to turn e-safety knowledge into action and to find ways to challenge feelings of inevitability and powerlessness described by young people faced with cyberbullying. Young people need methods of reporting cyberbullying effectively and service providers must play their part in protecting users from inappropriate behaviour online.

Furthermore, there is a challenge to privacy that needs addressing. Children and young people are giving out personal details and uploading photos without privacy protection, often thinking they are among friends. When friends fall out, this material is often used maliciously and can find its way into a public sphere.

Sites are also collecting personal details. In 2007 *The Guardian* newspaper reported on research by the University of Bath investigating how children's privacy was protected online. Out of 20 sites popular among children aged between 9 and 13, 85 per cent collected personal information on children, and on each site it was possible for a child to disclose personal information without consent from parents. Location services will enable the whereabouts of the child to be identified by a quick search.[34]

Other researchers had suggested that between 20 and 25 per cent of children and young people report that they had experienced some cyberbullying in response to a general question on the subject. However, when respondents were asked whether they had experienced specific forms of harassment, responses tended to be higher, as explained next in Chapter 3.

Chapter
3

NEW TOOLS FOR BULLIES

TYPES OF CYBERBULLYING

In 2009 Cowie and Colliety wrote, cyberbullying is 'a form of covert psychological bullying using electronic devices such as email, mobile phones, text messages, video clips, IM [instant messaging], photos and personal websites in order to engage in repeated hostile behaviour.'[35] At the time this was a robust definition.

In the short time that has elapsed since this definition was written, teenagers' use of email has dropped away and a marked rise in SNS has taken place, with all the messaging and photo or film sharing options that encourages. Mobile phones have features undreamed of in 2009, and their use among teenagers has soared. BlackBerries, smartphones, tablets and games consoles offer internet access that is mobile, private and no longer fixed to a computer. On the horizon is internet via the television and more. All this rapid change suggests that schools should develop a simple definition that might be valid longer if it focuses on a malicious intention to harm via any electronic device.

While new technology has revolutionised young people's social networks – being fun, cheap, convenient, instant and above all, desirable – there is much to learn about the less positive ways it might be used and how we might help children protect themselves.

WHAT TYPES OF CYBERBULLYING ARE SEEN?

There are easy ways to hurt and gain power or create 'in groups' and 'out groups'. This behaviour is more covert if you can be anonymous or avoid being face to face, and there is the relentless 24/7 aspect of cyberbullying.

In 2011 these are some of the common cyberbullying patterns. They will doubtless change very quickly and it will be those teachers who are in touch with their young people's behaviours who will know where to look next.[36]

USING A MOBILE

2009	2010	2011
29%	32%	32%

The percentages of respondents who had experienced one or more of the following via mobiles in each of the three waves:

- A humiliating photo of you sent round to deliberately humiliate you
- Insults because of your disability
- Insults calling you gay
- Unwanted sexual words and suggestions
- Racist words or comments
- Unpleasant name-calling
- People text you about where to meet then change the plans on purpose to exclude you
- Bullying carried on from your life in school
- Scary or threatening messages

(Rumour spreading was discussed in a separate question on indirect bullying.)[37]

Text message bullying: messages via text or IM that contain threats, harassment, insults or hurtful content, including photos. Texts can also be used to spread rumours, set up victims for humiliation and to share information about someone.

A new form of bullying has emerged that is typically text-based. The micro managing of social arrangements offers a new and cruel way to exclude someone deliberately. Imagine that plans are made to meet a group of friends at the weekend at a shopping mall – it is easily done by texting the group. But if one person is then deliberately dropped from the texts so that she does not know that the meeting point has changed, she turns up at the appointed place. She could be standing there in her latest outfit, painfully self-conscious. Now there are new options available to those who want to humiliate her. If this was pre-planned and not a genuine mistake, we might see the group leader tell a colluder to take photos of her standing all alone and post these with a tag 'Who'd want to be friends with her?' or 'Who wants to be seen with her?'

This type of scenario was described by young people at an early stage in the development of the Cybersurvey, and a question was included to explore this further. We asked young people about the use of texts to deliberately exclude someone from social arrangements. Twenty-eight per cent of recipients said they had experienced this in the Cybersurvey 2009, rising to 30 per cent in Cybersurvey 2010, a third of cyberbullying victims. Although boys do this, it is more common among girls. It is highly unlikely that someone would report this to a teacher as bullying; it is too rooted in social acceptance. Yet it can inflict misery because it seems so intentional and planned.

Picture/video clip bullying via mobile phone cameras: using photos taken on a phone to hurt or humiliate someone, with the images usually sent tagged, sent to several other people or posted into a public forum online. 'Happy slapping' involves filming and sharing physical attacks. Intimate photos from a relationship are often misused after friends fall out (often referred to in the media as 'sexting'). Images can be altered easily. Recruiters are increasingly likely to do an online search, and one of the reasons given for rejecting candidates is 'inappropriate images' online.[38]

Phone call bullying via mobile phone: silent calls or abusive messages are often used, with the caller disguising their number or using someone else's phone. The bullied person's phone may be stolen and used to harass others, who then think the phone owner is responsible.

Email or messenger bullying: bullying or threatening emails, with or without images, but often with an invented pseudonym or using someone else's name and email account to avoid discovery. BlackBerry Messenger is widely used by teenagers and is not traceable. Email use is diminishing among this age group, but chain letters are common.

Bullying through IM: unpleasant or threatening messages sent in real time, online conversations. Some games also permit messaging.

Using someone else's account or phone: disguising identity by using a computer at a friend's house, stealing a phone or simply using it for a few minutes to send a bullying message that may get someone else into trouble. When someone's Facebook account is entered and perhaps their status is cruelly changed to 'single', or messages are sent to all their friends by someone intent on being hurtful, this is known as being 'fraped' (meaning 'Facebook raped'), a case of the language showing just how disturbing this is for the young people.

Chatroom bullying: when children or young people are in a web-based chatroom they may feel they are among friends. It is especially hurtful and embarrassing to receive menacing or upsetting responses in this public forum. Those with weak friendships in the real world often spend a lot of time in chatrooms seeking friendship and intimacy that they lack.

Bullying via websites: includes defamatory blogs (see Appendix 1), websites set up to humiliate someone (may use images) and online personal polling sites. 'Burn' pages are set up on SNS – these are pages where people are invited to post hurtful abuse about someone and messages crowd in as people flock to do this. Recent examples in Portsmouth and Hampshire in the UK have been local and the victim knew the perpetrators. Police have been involved leading to the removal of some of these pages by Facebook.

SNS: the Essex Cybersurvey, carried out with 1452 respondents in the spring of 2010, found that 76 per cent of young people aged 10–16+ had a Facebook page or used another SNS. Facebook is meant to be for 13-year-olds upwards, yet this data, with its largest cohort being 12–13, reveals that age limits are not observed. These sites allow users to seek, admit and reject friends in the glare of public view. Blocking someone on an SNS is a common form of bullying. They are also frequently used for rumour spreading via friends or posting malicious comments.

Users invite 'friends' to post malicious remarks about others in a scene in which the sharp-witted cruel wordsmith comes out on top. 'Frapers' also post dirty, nasty, humiliating updates on their victim's Facebook status page and generally behave in a way that is considered a violation of the victim's Facebook page.

Via electronic games: hacking into someone's account or score to alter it or using a game box to send messages. Using handheld devices to access the internet is now commonplace, and children can send messages leaving no trail. We know that among boys who use portable games consoles, a quarter play with people they have never previously met.[39]

'Rude insults on Xbox live has happened to my friends.'

Twitter: fast becoming known as mean girls' gangland, Twitter is where those who are quick and skilled with put-downs and wisecracks can take pot shots at others who are less witty and quick with ripostes. Girls may post a humiliating photo of someone and tweet about it or comment on each other's Facebook photos. Twitter gives an added sense of being in or out of the 'club'.

Harvesting identity: sites and games are also collecting personal details. This could leave a child open to stalking or other forms of predatory harm.

Flaming: online fights with escalating angry and vulgar language. For example, Russell and Jay were trading insults and name-calling which was becoming more extreme, when anger flared and Jay threatened to make Russell's life hell in school. One message threatened to beat him up beyond the school gates. Russell knew where Jay lived. The whole thing got out of hand very quickly.

Harassment: continually sending threats and stalking; often a storm of repeated cruel or vicious messages. Harassment can include sexual harassment. For example, Aisha reported that Kelly had been harassing her – there were messages on her phone, her IM and SNS page. There was no part of her social life without these nasty messages from Kelly. She also said she was watching Aisha and sometimes the messages showed that Kelly knew where Aisha was. Kelly included other girls in her messages so that they could join in and they began sending messages to please Kelly. Some were anonymous. This grew to a deluge. No part of Kelly's life was free of this hate.

'Dissing' someone online: sending or posting gossip or rumours about someone in order to damage their reputation or disrupt their friendships or relationships. For example, Rachel was jealous of Carina because she had got together with Rachel's former boyfriend, Jay. Rachel sent messages to Jay and all his friends saying nasty things about Carina. She set up a web page and invited friends to post comments about Carina and uploaded an embarrassing photo of her saying she was a 'slag' and had slept around. As another example, Isabel was in a relationship with her boyfriend Tray. They shared intimate photos. Tray showed one to his friend Jaime. Although Tray and Jaime were close friends, Jaime fancied Isabel and asked her to leave Tray for him, but she rebuffed his approach. He then posted her intimate picture that

Tray had shown him and her contact details on *craigslist*, offering her for sex. In the crisis that followed, Isabel's parents called the police and she broke up with Tray because he had taken his friend's side. Isabel was left devastated and betrayed. All her contact details were changed. She felt scared and violated.

Impersonation: pretending to be someone else and sending or posting material in order to get that person into trouble, put them at risk or damage their relationships with others. For example, Theresa stole the login details of her friend Stacey's phone, and when she was at Stacey's house one day she grabbed the phone when she was alone and sent off some messages in Stacey's name that were offensive and hurtful to people in their class. Theresa wanted to keep Stacey to herself and she felt that if she could make the others move away from Theresa she would have her where she wanted her. But when Stacey finally found out, she wanted nothing to do with her. As another example, a teacher hacked the school system and obtained the login details of staff at his school and sent racist messages in their names to colleagues. It was only proven when one teacher could prove she had been abroad at the time and could not have used the school's internal system from there.

Outing: sharing someone's secrets, potentially embarrassing information about them or images online. For example, Peter is smaller than the others and is developing slowly. They insult him and say he is gay. One day, changing for sport, the group shunned him and he was left alone in the corner. Eventually one boy took pity on him and went over to talk. The ringleader took a photo of the two of them and pinged it around the group, labelling them a gay couple.

Manipulation: for example, Rio met Marsha in a chatroom, and they struck up an online chat. He persuaded her to use her webcam and she gradually posed in clothes or underwear she thought enticing. For a while it seemed fine. Then Rio threatened to break off the friendship if she did not go further. When Marsha became anxious and worried, Rio threatened to post images of her in an online forum if she did not send more. She felt trapped and realised he had had this in mind from the start.

Isolation: intentionally and cruelly excluding someone from an online group. For example, social arrangements for parties are made and everyone in the group is included. Suddenly one girl is cut out of the texting or Facebook group. Everyone else talks about the event. Then they 'unfriend' this person and cut her out of the texts.

Cyberstalking: for example, Pete and Natasha had an intense relationship that eventually broke up, but Pete could not accept that it was over. He tracked her location, turning up wherever she was. He sent her messages 24 hours a day using Skype, BlackBerry Messenger, text and SNS.

Fraping: for example, Avril and Gary were in a relationship and spent many happy hours together on Facebook. Their status as a couple was proclaimed on their pages beside photos and messages to and from friends. But this relationship descended into a vengeful battle in which each tried to damage the other via Facebook. Dumping Gary by simply changing her status online, Avril triggered a rage in Gary when he found out that led him to share personal photos, humiliatingly altered images of Avril, and to send all her friends some ugly messages about her.

Sexting: sending explicit or suggestive images via any new technology. For example, Misha thought nobody would ever ask her out. When Omar took an interest in her she was flattered and happy. But Omar sent her more and more explicit photos and she was shocked. When Omar realised she was upset, he laughed and he and his friends began sending more photos to Misha and said she was a prude.

A study for the South West Grid for Learning by Andy Phippen on sexting reminds us that, not surprisingly, young people will not readily tell an adult about a form of bullying that could be degrading and embarrassingly personal. This study also revealed a lack of concern for privacy and its effect on intimacy among young people. The study found 79 per cent of respondents saying they used phones or other digital technology to take images and videos, and 78 per cent said they distributed them. More than half the young people were aware of occasions when images or videos were distributed further than intended, but most did not think this was with intent to harm. Seventy per cent said they would turn to their friends if they were affected by issues related to sexting. Only around a quarter (24%) of young people would turn to a teacher for help.

The study also found that young people's attitude towards what might be considered an inappropriate image may differ somewhat from the adult population, with 40 per cent not seeing anything wrong with a topless image, and 15 per cent not taking issue with naked images.

The report concluded: 'It is immediately apparent that such practices are cause for concern. It shows a population who are unconcerned about intimacy or privacy yet are ill equipped to understand the implications of their actions.'[40]

Sexting is not always bullying, and most instances of it will understandably never come to the attention of a teacher or parent. But in some cases it is clearly an exploitative behaviour and there is harm intended. Vulnerable children, including those with special needs and those who are unhappy and lonely in their offline life, are more susceptible to exploitation of this sort.

Chapter

4

THE KINDS OF BULLYING YOUNG PEOPLE EXPERIENCE

Most of the messages received on mobiles were irritating, some were downright upsetting and a few were very serious. Young people soon develop their own coping mechanisms in relation to 'nuisance' messages. The Cybersurvey did not explicitly mention chain letters, but many children wrote about these in their own words in open questions. Ten-year-olds were understandably scared and upset by them, but older teenagers shrugged a lot of them off, unless they were among the vulnerable.

It was surprising that the ten-year-olds had not been taught in their e-safety lessons or by parents that they should ignore chain letters or laugh at them and not be afraid. This would be an easy message to get across and would reassure large numbers of young children who receive them on mobiles and online. Many contain death threats. More ten- and eleven-year-olds are likely to receive a chain letter than will ever experience predatory grooming.

In line with the changes in mobile phone technology of the past three years, in 2009 the experiences on mobiles and on the internet were looked at separately, but by 2011 the lines had become blurred as so many young people used their phones to access the internet. Questions were added in 2011 to include the use of Twitter and to find out how many had a smartphone or a tablet.

EXPERIENCES ON MOBILE PHONES

When we read of cases and the distress or long-term damage abuse on mobiles can cause, it is easy to forget that it does not happen to everyone. Based on data collected in 2010, encouragingly around two-thirds of young people had not experienced any abuse via their mobiles, but one third had been subjected to one or more of the forms of phone abuse or targeting described in the questionnaire. We call these people 'recipients'.

The experiences of these recipients included a variety of ingenious, manipulative or humiliating messages, sometimes with photos. Some messages demonstrated the total lack of inhibition shown by the sender shielded by this medium, no longer face to face in the traditional bullying style. Apart from directly nasty or aggressive messages, there were messages that were a form of indirect bullying. For example, a message could be from a so-called 'friend' to tell the victim about an online hate page about him or give clues about gossip going on behind his back. It can be hard to tell who is a genuine friend in these circumstances.

One reason why they may not report it is that these recipients identified in the Cybersurvey do not all regard what happened to them as cyberbullying. Among them are a smaller number of individuals who believe, after reading the definition of cyberbullying, that what had happened to them was definitely cyberbullying. Of all the respondents, 32 per cent were recipients of phone aggression and only 20 per cent of the total sample considered themselves victims of cyberbullying.

IT IS NOT ALWAYS CYBERBULLYING...

Making children or adults panic about every unpleasant message they might ever receive is no route to resilience. What this exploration showed was that some children and young people are resilient and cope well with one or two nasty messages, while true victims are in urgent need of better support. Children may regard a couple of messages as jokes or teasing gone wrong – they may not feel so vulnerable if they have good friends and a sharp wit or ability to make quick ripostes.

It doesn't help to insist that it is cyberbullying in all these situations, but instead work should focus on the way pupils in a class treat one another and to improve the emotional climate by working on what friendship means, or what kinds of behaviour are unacceptable. Strengths-based support could focus on all the ways pupils can be good friends and the qualities they bring to the group, rather than a relentless focus on problems that can 'label' a young person a victim even if they had not previously seen themselves this way.

...BUT IT COULD BE VERY SERIOUS

At the other end of the spectrum, some types of message are threatening or enticing people into risky behaviour but are not bullying. They might be a serious safeguarding concern. In those cases work to keep young people safe immediately, especially if they respond to messages asking to meet someone or to do something they do not want to do. If they are encouraged to visit sites encouraging suicide or anorexia, intervention should be intensive. This is where a school Serious Incident Protocol is needed (see Chapter 11). Every staff member should be alert and, with training, should be able to stay calm and act appropriately.

At the time of writing, CEOP (Child Exploitation and Online Protection Centre, the agency that fights child exploitation in the UK, see Appendix 1) has put out an appeal for potential victims regarding a case they are working on. It relates to a non-UK offender who hacks into the online accounts of children and young people, threatening and forcing them to perform sexual acts on webcam. CEOP believes this has been going on since 2008. At the end of 2011 they were seeking any as yet unidentified victims, and a helpline was provided by child safety charity the National Society for the Prevention of Cruelty to Children (NSPCC).

Generally, the offender's method has been to use an IM service and to pretend to be a friend of the targeted victim. During subsequent conversations, the offender directed victims to an internet link. When clicking on this link, victims were asked to provide their email account(s) and password(s), allowing the offender to take control of their login information. The offender was then able to take control of and hack into the victims' accounts, changing their passwords and security information.

The offender would then inform the victims that their account had been hacked and they no longer had control of it. The offender continued the threats, saying that personal information about them would be sent to friends and family on the internet, unless they continued to perform sexual acts via the webcam.

This is only one example of the serious cases CEOP investigate. Their work is vital. But while everyone needs to be vigilant, most of the cases a teacher will encounter every day are somewhat lower down the scale of severity, but distressing nevertheless.

The content of messages

In the following section young people who were interviewed for the Cybersurvey describe in their own words what happened to them. The level of abuse in the messages is sometimes shocking and very explicit. Some contain threats to beat up, rape or kill the victim. (All spellings are their own.)

Racist messages

'The person said I was a Nigga and she said that everyone was talking about me on Facebook.'

Swearing

'Some messages I had included CU Next Tuesday, the P word, the B word and the frequent F word.'

'People swear at me 'cos they think they're hard and cool.'

Personal insults about appearance

'[I got messages] about my looks. Appearance [weight]. I've had nasty comments about my family and friends by people who don't even know me and from my so-called friends.'

'Being called fat.'

'Being told I look like a pig.'

'They said I look like a sket and a whore, I suppose I do, I wouldn't know.'

'They laugh at my clothes but my mum is disabled and we can't afford new things.'

'Girls took a photo of me eating lunch and sent it round saying no wonder I was so fat, so I don't eat at school at all now.'

Homophobic insults

'Yes in year 6 people set up a page about me saying that I'm a gay b******* poor, and dadless, saying that it was my fault probably that my dad left.'

'People saying you gay lesbian.'

'They spread rumours I'm gay and then make a big thing of it in the changing rooms.'

'They beat me up, then when one boy came over to see if I was OK, they took a photo and pinged it around saying we are a couple.'

Disablist bullying

'People on msn kept saying my sister was a weird girl who had no friends because she has learning difficulties and a curvature to the spine.'

'No, but I have a friend who has had a few messages insulting him and his disability.'

Possibly predatory

'You look very attractive do you want to meet up? (I didn't know him and he was about 10 years older).'

'Make me go out with that person that I do not know.'

'Wants me to pose in front of the webcam.'

'I got this poem from someone I don't know saying he loves me and I must go on the webcam to show him how beautiful I am. I blocked him.'

Threats

Almost one-third of ten- to eleven-year-olds received scary or threatening messages:

'Scary chain mails saying if you don't send this to ten or more people then this story will happen to you.'

'Forward messages saying if you delete it you will see a dead girl/boy that night or your mum will die or something like that.'

'Saying I must send this to 10 people or a ghost will kill me at midnight.'

'Someone has sent another person i know a email saying they want me to die.'

'They said they'd beat me up after school and they did.'

'You should be dead punk.'

Unwanted messages from strangers

'Where people have hacked someone's account and were very abusive!!!!'

Messages of a sexual/sexist nature

'Threats in being raped.'

'I was put into a conversation with other people with a porn star and she wanted us to look at her naked pictures and have webcam "fun" with her. I was worried and scared and she said she was horny and naughty. I then discovered that this was true by her naughty and nude pictures.'

'Do you want to have sex with me?'

'I got a letter saying that someone will come and kill me or sexually assaulting me.'

'Someone got hold of a photo of me with my boyfriend that was private and shared it.'

'They said they would rape me.'

'Someone asked to come on webcam to strip but I blocked them and then deleted them and they couldn't speak to me again and I reported them and then they were banned off msn!!'

Retaliatory

'[I do it] When I have an argument on facebook or msn to my worst enemy who I hate sooo much.'

'Just when fallen out and we were having a fight on msn.'

Other

'A phone message to tell me about a hate website made about me by a girl in my high school!'

'They say all this hate stuff and swear about people on my estate.'

Links with bullying offline in school

More than a third of cyberbullying victims in the Cybersurvey told us that the mobile phone bullying they experienced was 'carried on from their lives in school'. Reducing bullying in school before it escalates must therefore be the first tier in the strategy to reduce cyberbullying.

This overlap between bullying in school and cyberbullying has led to calls for a greater focus on addressing behaviour in school with the hope of reducing cyberbullying as a result.[41] We know that the odds of being bullied outside school are greater for a child who is bullied in school. This has been described by Hayden as a 'multiplier effect.[42] School is one environment where attitudes and prejudice can be challenged and a more caring ethos established between young people. Ybarra and Mitchell show that 84 per cent of the young people who had harassed or embarrassed someone else online knew their target.[43]

Identifying aggressor/targets

It is within school that young people who are both perpetrators and victims – called aggressor/targets – can often be identified and their complex behaviour addressed. Ybarra and Mitchell found that over half of the aggressor/targets in their study had been the target of offline bullying.[44]

It is likely that this offline bullying took place either at school or on the journey to or from school. Once away from the bullies, they try to retaliate. Being able to hide their identity online they can stalk, intimidate or harass their target in ways they can never do offline. This may enable them to 'get back' at someone who bullies them in school in a reversal of power. But retaliation is a dangerous route that can escalate the bullying on both sides, leading to violence, or serious and risky situations. Lonely and isolated, with poor peer relations, these pupils may spend excessive time online. Although they may have good digital skills, their very loneliness and emotional vulnerability or depression could put them at risk when they seek intimacy in chatrooms and other online spaces. Two in five report problem behaviours (Austin and Joseph 1996).[45] Like traditional bully/victims who have been much documented, Ybarra and Mitchell say that 'aggressor/targets indicate the poorest psychosocial functioning and are likely to be in need of intervention and services'.[46] That is why they are considered vulnerable and require intensive support and e-safety advice.

Deliberately leaving someone out of social plans

The social arrangement exclusion tactic is often deployed. This is an inventive and cruel strategy used on mobile or cell phones. Children deliberately make and then change social arrangements by mobile phone/text to a group. Then, in a later round of texts they deliberately leave out one person, in order to humiliate or exclude that targeted person. This appears to be fairly common among all age groups but peaks at age 12–13 when almost one-third of recipients report being deliberately excluded in this way.

Indirect bullying

'I was bullied on MySpace by people who are still at my college now, they called me horrible names and really upset me and did it publicly so everyone on MySpace could see what they were writing. They also put pictures of me on MySpace and people commented on it and I also had a website made about me. I still don't talk to them now because of everything they did to me.'

Cyberbullying messages do not have to be personally received in order to hurt or create a climate of fear. Fifty-eight per cent of all respondents answered at least one of the questions on indirect bullying, 28 per cent of all respondents said others had deliberately sent round messages spreading rumours about them and as many as 46 per cent knew someone else to whom this had happened. Among the cybervictim group this was far higher, creating a general atmosphere of mistrust and fear. People then worried that they could be next in the firing line.

No one performs well in such an environment and this soon begins to show in absenteeism rates and drops in attainment. Pupils are distracted trying to keep track of what is being said by the powerbrokers. They furtively need to check their phones every few minutes in case someone is talking about them behind their back. Perhaps they have to make a witty, cutting remark in a quick text under their desk to show that they are against today's victim and on the side of the bullies because they are not secure. Pupils explain that this goes on even in class, and that BlackBerries are ideal because you can text without looking at the keyboard.

Indirect bullying is often seen as more hurtful than face-to-face bullying (an example could be being socially isolated or ostracised from a friendship group), and appears to be more damaging than straightforward physical or verbal bullying. Often overlooked as friendship feuds, especially among girls, researchers argue that schools should give this a higher profile. Tom Benton, in an analysis of reported bullying at English schools, writes:

> ...perhaps the most striking finding is that the type of bullying that appears to be the most damaging to the emotional wellbeing of children is 'being left out'. In other words, although both physical and verbal abuse can be very harmful to children, it is exclusion and being prevented in participating in the ordinary social activities of young people that is the most damaging of all.[47]

Benton argues that school approaches tend to focus more on explicit bullying and less on this more subtle form. He also suggests that parents may be less likely to report what might be considered 'low level' bullying.

John Khan, East Sussex County Council Anti-Bullying team leader, suggests that reasons for the damaging effects of indirect bullying may be:

* the importance that young people place on their friendship groups

* the frequency that young people experience indirect bullying (for example, on a regular basis) over other forms of bullying

* when a young person is socially rejected or ostracised this is often done by an entire 'friendship' group, class or year group, rather than by a single individual.[48]

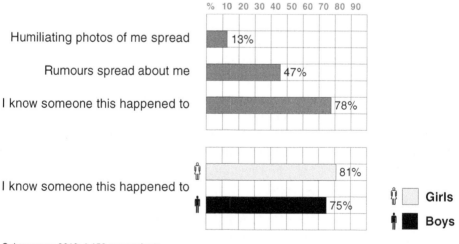

Cybersurvey 2010: 1,452 respondents
718 answered, of whom 256 said they had been cyberbullied
734 skipped the question as they had not experienced any of these

Figure 4.1 Indirect bullying

Comparing those who were cyberbullied with their peers

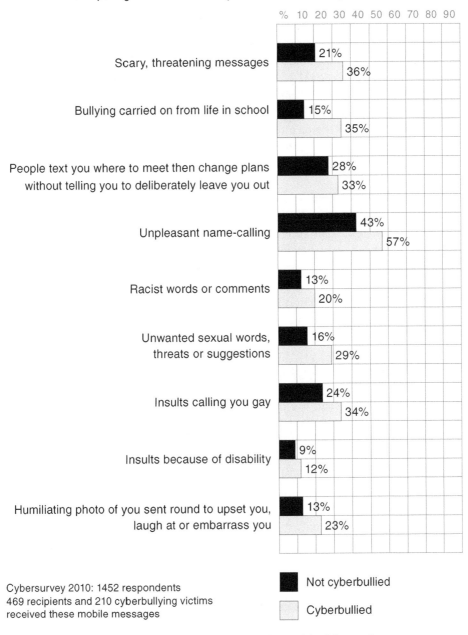

% 10 20 30 40 50 60 70 80 90

Scary, threatening messages
21%
36%

Bullying carried on from life in school
15%
35%

People text you where to meet then change plans without telling you to deliberately leave you out
28%
33%

Unpleasant name-calling
43%
57%

Racist words or comments
13%
20%

Unwanted sexual words, threats or suggestions
16%
29%

Insults calling you gay
24%
34%

Insults because of disability
9%
12%

Humiliating photo of you sent round to upset you, laugh at or embarrass you
13%
23%

Cybersurvey 2010: 1452 respondents
469 recipients and 210 cyberbullying victims
received these mobile messages

■ Not cyberbullied

□ Cyberbullied

Figure 4.2 On your mobile phone, have you ever had any of the following happen to you?

In the digital world, age-old name-calling remains common, even for those who do not think they are being cyberbullied. It is the daily fare of many – 43 per cent of recipients said they had been called names on their mobile, rising to 57 per cent of those who had been cyberbullied.

Homophobic insults are so often the tool of the cyberbully. Over a third of victims were subjected to insults calling them gay. Teachers often find it difficult to challenge this language, and it has now taken over playgrounds and school corridors. Where racist abuse is widely understood to be frowned upon, homophobic abuse has come to be used in all manner of pejorative meanings, sometimes combined with a racist intent. Like the easy rumour 'she's a slag,' spreading rumours about someone's perceived sexual orientation is simply done via mobiles or a click online, with devastating outcomes. Any damage to reputation will subtly remain, even if an apology is given or forced.

Bullying was often personal or retaliatory, and just over a third of victims said the bullying on their mobile had carried on from their lives in school. More than a third of victims suffered other people making social plans to exclude them behind their backs, using mobiles to do it.

Scary, threatening messages covered a wide range of possibilities, and more than a third said they had been on the receiving end of this type of message on their mobile. A child alone at night could receive a threat that left them awake and terrified in their bedroom, where suddenly they felt invaded.

Twenty-nine per cent of cyberbullying victims encountered unwanted sexual words, threats or suggestions, and 23 per cent had had a humiliating photo of themselves sent around deliberately to upset them, for others to laugh at or embarrass them. The cumulative effect of being subjected to a hailstorm of these acts is the fate of people singled out for what can only be described as a total 24/7 campaign.

To illustrate the concerted campaigns of harassment some children go through, the Cybersurvey 2011 explored the number of abusive messages individual recipients had received and found that 73 people had received ten or more of these, and 192 had received between three and five different types from our list. Twenty-one per cent of recipients had experienced five or more.

Thirty-two per cent of the total sample of recipients had experienced one or more forms of message described in the question. This included messages described by respondents in the open-ended question, in particular, among ten- to eleven-year-olds, chain messages containing threats. These young children are receiving cruel and distressing messages to a greater extent than adults appear to realise. One in four were recipients of at least one or more of the types of messages in the question, and one in five said they got 'scary threatening' messages. Sixty-eight per cent had not experienced any of these abusive phone messages.

Abuse on social networks or intranets

'Friends making accounts up and pretending to be someone to annoy you for a joke :).'

'Someone going onto my friend's account and writing horrible stuff about me, but I know she didn't say that.'

'Being bullied on the school mail by using bad words!'

'Someone got into my Facebook account and sent rude messages to my friends. Now they hate me. I don't know what to do.'

Comparing those who were cyberbullied with their peers

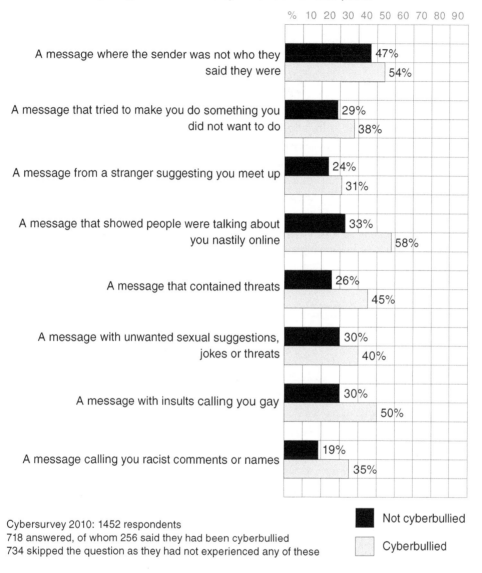

Cybersurvey 2010: 1452 respondents
718 answered, of whom 256 said they had been cyberbullied
734 skipped the question as they had not experienced any of these

■ Not cyberbullied

☐ Cyberbullied

Figure 4.3 Have you ever received any of the following online?

In Figure 4.3 recipients are compared with cyberbullying victims. Although all had received some of these messages, the cyberbullied young people were markedly more likely to have experienced each and every type of cyberbullying described. For the recipients, some targeted advice on e-safety would be helpful, but for the cyberbullying targets, intensive support and e-safety advice is required.

The most common incidents for the cyberbullying victims were as follows: 'a message that showed people were talking about you nastily online' (58%), 'a message from a sender who was not who they said they were' (54%) and 'a message with insults calling you gay' (50%). Threats were received by 45 per cent of victims while 40 per cent got unwanted sexual suggestions, jokes or threats. They were also more likely than their peers to be on the receiving end of racist comments and messages trying to coerce them into doing something against their will.

Cyberhomophobia

People who have been victimised in a way that attacks their very identity can be hyper-alert to other instances of homophobic bullying around them. They are watchful and nervous, waiting to see if the attacks are stopped. They notice far more than their peers, taking in the environment in which they must spend their time. When compared with their peers we can see how much more homophobically bullied students notice. Yet others are not unaware of it happening. A total of 875 young people out of 1969 said they had seen at least one form of cyberhomophobia happen to other people. But they are accustomed to it. In a recent visit to a secondary school, pupils said they regarded the pervasive homophobic language as 'only a joke'. Yet we know that there are pupils who find themselves in a threatening environment because this is not challenged. They fear it could happen to them.

Table 4.1 Homophobic bullying: have you ever seen this happen to others?

Have you seen this happen to others? 'Yes'	Homophobically bullied	Not homophobically bullied
Threatening messages because they are gay	28%	12%
Insulting homophobic texts, SMS and tweets	43%	25%
Web or Facebook page set up to hurt someone because they are gay	42%	26%
Rumours that someone is gay spread in cyberspace	39%	21%
Humiliating photos linked to homophobic insults	32%	15%
Using technology to isolate someone socially because they are gay (mobiles, SMS, BlackBerry Messenger, Facebook, etc.)	28%	11%

The experiences of those who have experienced cyberhomophobia compared to their peers

Chatrooms, texts and tweets are the most common medium for homophobic insults and bullying, with rumour spreading close behind. Almost a third of victims of homophobic cyberbullying had had humiliating photos used to hurt them with associated homophobic insults. Nine people said they had experienced web pages created by others to hurt them, and suffered some incidents linked to this two to five times a week, while 27 people said it had happened 'once or twice'. Eighteen individuals said that the cyberhomophobia was linked to their life in school once or twice. Seven said it was linked to life in school every day, and nine said this happened many times each day.

Table 4.2 Homophobic bullying: it happened to me

Personal experiences of cyberhomophobia: 'It happened to me'	Homophobically bullied	Not homophobically bullied
Insulting homophobic texts, SMS and tweets	21%	3%
Homophobic bullying in chatrooms	19%	3%
Homophobic bullying in SNS	18%	2%
Homophobic bullying in cyberspace linked to bullying in school	17%	1%
Web page set up to hurt someone on purpose	12%	3%
Rumours spread that someone is gay	16%	2%
Humiliating photos linked to gay insults	11%	1%
Using technology to socially isolate someone because they are thought to be gay	11%	2%

180 people were homophobically bullied among 1452

Chapter
5

MEETING THE NEEDS OF
BOTH BOYS AND GIRLS

Are there two different cyberworlds for boys and girls? Although this may seem a crude generalisation, some male/female patterns of usage and behaviour are emerging. These reveal differences in the ways young people use the internet, who experiences cyberbullying and the types of bullying they experience. There also appear to be differences in the way young people react if they are cyberbullied. Tracking these patterns over three years shows that some remain constant in every wave of the Cybersurvey.

In all three years, girls were more likely than boys to:

- report being cyberbullied
- report 'people talking about you nastily online'
- experience unpleasant name-calling on a mobile
- experience messages containing threats
- use chatrooms and have a Facebook or other SNS page
- receive e-safety advice from their parents
- become 'very upset and angry' if cyberbullied.

Boys, on the other hand, were more likely to:

- avoid saying they were actually cyberbullied, even when they experienced considerable abuse, name-calling and threats
- react to cyberbullying by saying they were 'not bothered' – this may be a tough stance or hard outer shell to conceal pain within
- say that they 'often' get around blocks set up by adults to prevent them accessing certain websites
- be homophobically cyberbullied.

While in all three years the Cybersurvey consistently found that being cyberbullied was more prevalent among girls, in 2011 this difference was greatest – almost twice the percentage of boys. In other years this difference was not quite as marked. (This could be because certain types of cyberbullying peak in the early or mid-teens. Therefore, the spread of the sample could influence the results.)

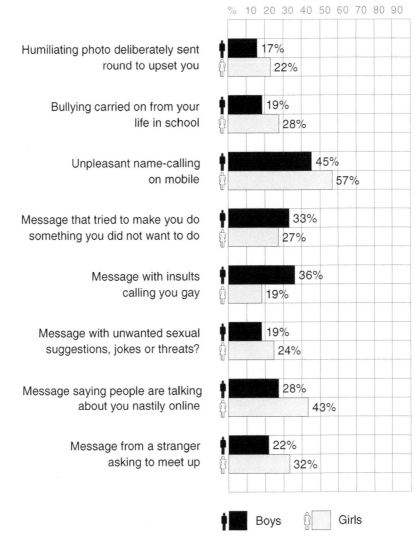

Cybersurvey 2010
718, those who experienced one or more out of 1,452 respondents

Figure 5.1 Examples of abusive messages received on mobiles and online

Research elsewhere confirms that girls are more likely to be cyberbullied. Research both in the USA and the UK has found that girls are more likely to be cyberbullied. For example, in the UK, Smith *et al.* found 'girls were significantly more likely to be cyberbullied, especially by text messages and phone calls, than boys.'[49] In 2006, studies by both MSN and Noret and Rivers found that girls were twice as likely to be cyberbullied as boys.[50] Noret and Rivers' work was based on regular large surveys over five years. They found that teenage girls were being targeted most often in a dramatic increase in cyberbullying by text message, email and video clips passed around on classmates' mobile phones. Girls were most involved in covert aggression. The UK charity Beatbullying found that girls were twice as likely as boys to experience persistent cyberbullying lasting months or even years.[51]

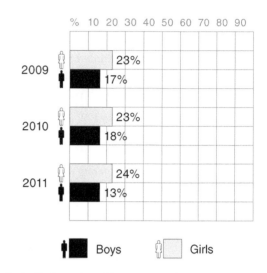

Cybersurvey 2011

Figure 5.2 Have you been cyberbullied? Girls and boys compared

Similarly, in the USA the Institute of Education Sciences noted that girls were more than twice as likely as boys to have been cyberbullied.[52] The Pew Internet and American Life Project, *Mean Teens: Forget Sticks and Stones, They've Got Mail*,[53] found that older girls and social networkers were the most likely targets of harassment online, while generally girls were more likely than boys to say that they had experienced cyberbullying. The Pew Project also found that the problem grew as girls reached mid-teens: older girls in particular were more likely to report being bullied than any other age and gender group:

> 38% of online girls report being bullied compared with 26% of online boys. Older girls in particular are more likely to report being bullied than any other age and gender group, with 41% of online girls ages 15 to 17 reporting these experiences.

SNS AMPLIFY WHAT GIRLS DO

SNS simply amplify the way girls commonly interact and make it easy to organise around a common interest – to humiliate or isolate someone else in front of an audience. Girls behave like this in the offline world, but new technology has brought this behaviour into glaring focus, where everyone can see it. Girls' friendships and feuds are well articulated by Val Besag in her book on the subject.[54] She describes how dealing with these female feuds is often extremely challenging for teachers because the girls can be subtle, treacherous and cruel. Male teachers can struggle to 'read' this behaviour that is sometimes all but unnoticeable to the casual eye. But now, new technology has made public what a 'queen bee' used to do only in front of her captive audience.

England's communications champion, Jean Gross, recently warned that the popularity of Facebook, Twitter and text messaging means many girls are now exposed to a 24-hour-a-day barrage of bullying. Jean Gross said social media and texting had given girls more ways of excluding each other. She suggested that girls should read and discuss Margaret Attwood's book *Cat's Eye*, or the Hollywood film *Mean Girls*, both of which deal with girls excluding each other.[55]

Constantly in touch

Instant messaging (IM) is also ideally suited to girls' needs to be constantly in touch, micro managing social plans in real time, exchanging messages over the internet with everyone they know, sharing photos and videos. The act of sharing seems to cement the friendship. The service allows users to communicate with a group or several people at once. BBM is the BlackBerry version that allows secret, cheap and instant communication.

The secret languages of childhood, so often invented in the past by siblings and playmates, have now given way to a new type of language using texting language and 'emoticons', faces that convey a mood or feeling, acronyms and letters being replaced by numbers. And girls are remarkably adept at using language to create an 'in' group, creating a cosy intimacy from which a target victim can all too easily be excluded.

IM: A HOTBED OF BULLYING

According to MSN's Cyberbullying Report (2006), IM is the most common form of cyberbullying as it can be used to make threats and spread rumours.[56] Girls in a study by Donna Kernaghan[57] said that:

> Instant Messenger was the place most girls experienced bullying on the internet. Instant Messenger can provide multiple ways to bully someone... The identity of the bully can be disguised by the screen name or even through pretending to be someone else. Results showed that 21.6% of girls had pretended to be someone else, while 32.7% said someone else had pretended to be them.

On some aspects of life in cyberspace and the use of new technology, the experiences are universal among teenagers. Teenagers refer to Twitter, which is a form of IM, as 'a mean girls' playground'.

A culture of crude language, threats and insults behind 'name-calling'

The Cybersurvey draws a picture of girls being subjected to rumour spreading and gossip, threat and indirect cyberbullying behind their backs. They encounter a range of sexual messages, threats and jokes as well as unwanted approaches and the misuse of humiliating photographs. This peaks at age 14–15 in all areas except a rural county in the east of England, where it peaks at 16+. But name-calling, just as in traditional bullying, still remains the most common form of cyberbullying. The term 'name-calling', however, is a weak description of what is actually taking place.

Every day young people use terms that would shock adults, because crude words have become commonplace. Young people who hear others being called a 'slag' and a 'slut' every day think a stronger insult has to be used if they wish to shock or hurt someone. This ramps things up. This hurtful language, often sexual or sexist, is widely used by both girls and boys. Both receive messages with unwanted sexual jokes, threats or suggestions in equal measure.

Jealousy or battles over boyfriends can unleash a torrent of abuse between girls. Boys tend to use threats and racist or homophobic insults. Recorded online or in a message, it gets seen by others and amplified. Adults may not have become so aware of the language and abuse that was swirling around in corridors and playing fields among teenagers, had it just remained verbal. But now there is a digital record that magnifies and retains the message.

Amid some media concern about young people's use of sexual threats and insults, a television programme set out to look at this. More than one in five of the teenagers questioned by the author for a BBC Panorama programme said they 'often' heard terms like 'slag', slut' and 'gay' used as insults, and two-thirds said that other people sometimes used more offensive words. Forty-three per cent said they personally used more offensive terms. Thirty-one per cent said they heard jokes about sexual assault or rape and 9 per cent had experienced this personally on SNS pages. Fifteen per cent said they had experienced unwanted sexual touching at school.[58] It is against this backdrop and emerging from this culture that sexual cyberbullying takes place. Perhaps this could point to one of the reasons so many people do not report cyberbullying when it is personal, intimate or sexual, and especially when it is homophobic: they do not want to show any adult the content of the dialogue.

Taking over your life

For girls in the Cybersurvey, the bullying in school could extend into all areas of their lives alarmingly quickly, as this girl aged 12–13, explained:

> 'I've had nasty voicemails left on my phone and now I'm scared to go to school or go out. I haven't been out to the park with my mates in a year. It started with people deliberately sending round rumours about me. I received nasty voicemails and unpleasant name-calling. I received messages from people who weren't who they said they were; it was racist names and comments and messages where I got called nasty names on Formspring and they set themselves as anonymous and then I got more nasty emails and stuff everyday.'

This young girl said that although she received e-safety information from her parents and the school, at the 'right' age, she only 'sometimes' followed these e-safety guidelines. She had a mobile, a computer she could use by herself at home, one she used a lot at a friend's house without an adult and a Facebook page and chatrooms she used regularly.

Are boys less willing to admit bullying?

While more girls say they are cyberbullied, this could be misleading. It seems they are more willing than boys to come forward and actually call it cyberbullying, but boys experience some of the types of abuse or victimisation to the same extent.

Boys describe their typical experiences:

'A kid being unfair to you calling you a retard.'

'On my Xbox people say there gonna hack me and swear at me.'

'Trying to make you jealous.'

'A kid saying I'm going beat you up then makes me get a bit nervous and then he goes and says he is joking.'

'They told me I should go die in a hole and slit my wrists.'

'Calling me a faggot, and threatening to beat me up.'

'Saying stuff about my dead relatives.'

'Calling me a gay bastard.'

'Chain letters saying my mum will die if I don't send it on to another 20 people.'

Those who did say they had been cyberbullied were asked how this made them feel. Boys tended to choose responses such as 'not bothered' or 'took it as a joke' whereas girls did not. This macho pose is clearly necessary for some and a defence mechanism that works socially.

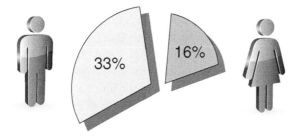

Figure 5.3 If you were cyberbullied, how did it make you feel? Not bothered

What is the true picture for boys?

In Figure 5.1 we see the many types of abusive or aggressive experience where girls experience this more than boys, with the exception of 'insults calling you gay.' But these are not the only questions asked. We could look at this data another way. Girls may simply be more willing to describe their experience as cyberbullying than boys. It could be seen as a macho defence mechanism to avoid victim status. There are strong hierarchies among groups of boys, and in their own eyes they may not want to see themselves as being 'weak' or disliked.

In the Cybersurvey, boys described a litany of aggressive or humiliating behaviour directed at them, but when asked 'Have you been cyberbullied?', many chose to say no. Perhaps they do not call these experiences bullying? It could be that they were not repeated or intense and they saw this behaviour as part of their everyday experience. Perhaps it was banter between friends. But they seemed reluctant to take on the role of 'victim'. If this is so, we need to acknowledge this in our anti-bullying work and avoid trying to make them tell someone that they have been a *victim* of bullying. Rather, we should empower them to take steps to keep safe and manage the situation as if it were simply a problem to solve, a problem that does not involve a loss of face for them.

We need to consider their responses throughout the survey and not only to the question, 'Have you been cyberbullied?' Looking across all three years we can see that the experiences boys described are not negligible, and for some their experiences were horrific, especially for those who were homophobically bullied. These victims suffered polyvictimisation – an intense and complex combination of attacks that can be experienced many times in a day, several times a week, often from a growing group of people and using mobiles, SNS, chatrooms and face-to-face bullying. These young people are the least likely to report it unless in an anonymous survey.

In the Cybersurvey, there are broader questions about any unpleasant online and mobile experiences before respondents are asked: 'Have you been cyberbullied?' When we switch our gaze from those who say they were actually cyberbullied and look at everyone who has had any unpleasant experiences on their mobile, we learn that there are several universal experiences that both sexes report. There are others where the differences are slight and a few that boys are more likely to experience.

Jokey insults and threats may be more commonplace in boys' everyday experience and they don't always class this as bullying. Adults may categorise this behaviour as bullying but it cannot be helpful to insist on this 'label' if a boy is reluctant to see himself in the role of victim with the loss of status this implies. His resilience may depend on maintaining his status on the fringe of a group. Besides, being seen as a 'grass' would make him a pariah; far better for him to pretend to 'take it as a joke'. But this does not mean he would not benefit from sensitive group work or other interventions that do not single out any one person. These messages from the survey can shape our bullying intervention work. Armed with these insights, adults may tread more carefully as we wade into these situations and try to resolve them. Too often they are made worse by clumsy intervention.

Across all three years, boys were slightly more likely than girls to:

- receive messages containing racist words and comments online and via mobiles
- experience insults calling them gay (whether true or not)
- experience insults because of disability.

Universal experiences reported almost equally by girls and boys:

- a message with unwanted sexual threats and suggestions via mobiles
- a message that tries to make them do something they did not want to do (online)
- a humiliating picture deliberately sent round to upset or hurt them (not a shared joke) (more girls in 2009 but equal in later years)
- scary, threatening messages on a mobile.

Girls were very slightly more likely to experience the following, but boys' experiences were not negligible:

- a message from a stranger asking to meet up
- a message containing threats
- a message online with unwanted sexual words and suggestions.[59]

SOME PATTERNS ARE CHANGING

Over the course of the three years we can see how sending unwanted sexual suggestions on a mobile has changed. In the first year more girls experienced this, in the second year we found no difference between boys and girls and by the third year more boys were reporting that they had received this type of message than girls (see Table 5.1). The percentages receiving messages 'trying to make you do something you did not want to do' also reflect social changes. In 2009 more boys reported this, then in 2010 more girls did so, but by 2011 the responses were similar.

The overlap between school bullying and cyberbullying is greater for girls

The bullying may be an extension of feuds or victimisation already going on at school. In both 2010 and 2011a, more than a third of cyberbullied girls said that this was carried on from their life in school.[60] By contrast, only 15 per cent and 19 per cent respectively of cyberbullied boys said the same. This suggests that boys are being cyberbullied by other people – perhaps those they met online through gaming or in chatrooms. They would be unlikely to report this to a teacher.

Boys are more likely to admit bullying others – when asked whether they had bullied others behind their back by rumour or posting messages on a web page, boys were almost twice as likely as girls to say they had done this type of indirect bullying to others.[61]

Table 5.1. Changing behaviour over time

	Boys 2009	Girls 2009	Boys 2010	Girls 2010	Boys 2011	Girls 2011
A message that tried to make you do something you did not want to do	33%	27%	29%	34%	29%	29%
A message from a stranger asking to meet up	22%	32%	24%	29%	22%	28%
A message containing threats	29%	30%	31%	35%	29%	34%
A message with unwanted sexual words and suggestions	26%	29%	33%	35%	29%	29%
Racist words and comments online	23%	21%	26%	24%	28%	23%
Scary threatening messages on a mobile	28%	28%	29%	28%	31%	29%
Racist words on a mobile	19%	13%	19%	14%	21%	12%
Unwanted sexual suggestions on a mobile	19%	24%	22%	22%	26%	24%
Insults calling you gay	36%	19%	34%	25%	37%	22%
Insults because of disability	10%	6%	12%	8%	12%	8%
A humiliating photo of you deliberately sent round to hurt you (not a joke)	17%	22%	19%	17%	17%	18%

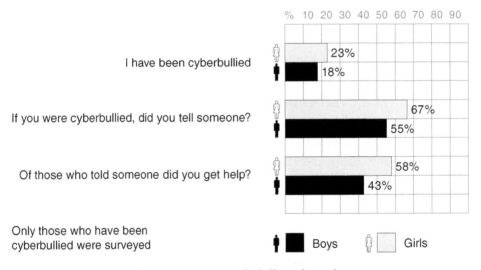

Figure 5.4 Reporting cyberbullying: by gender

How do boys and girls react to cyberbullying?

Girls were more likely to respond by telling someone. Girls who told someone were also more likely to get help. Of the boys who did report it, a smaller percentage was successful in getting help. This suggests that some boys will decide that it is not worth reporting cyberbullying if the success rate is low. When deciding to report bullying, young people weigh up the pros and cons. They might urge their mum not to go to the school and 'make a fuss' if she discovers what is going on. They consider their relationship with the other kids, what the disclosure might mean for them, what will be revealed and how others will see them. Unless pupils see other cases being resolved successfully, they may be reluctant to report it.

Skills are empowering. Boys tend to say they know what to do; in discussions they say they can keep themselves safe, just as this young man explained in a Year 9 workshop:

> 'I don't need e-safety lessons. I know how to stay safe. I've always known. I live on the internet. I am always shopping on Amazon or eBay. My Dad makes money on eBay.'

> 'How do you pay for it?'

> 'With my dad's credit card.'

> 'Can you tell us how you might check that a website is safe or genuine before you give the credit card details?'

A discussion followed in which we all explored the options. This group discussion filled in some of the missing information he needed without making out that he did not know it. His friend said he mainly used the net for gaming. I asked:

> 'How do you know whether the site is genuine or a copy – someone trying to rip you off? Say you get an email from a friend with a link to a game he says you should try…?'

From the conversation that followed it was easy to offer up some ideas by asking the group and talking about why it was unsafe to click on a link to a game in someone's email, but instead they should go to the URL of the game because fake sites are often set up to harvest personal details. Neither boy had known the information I offered, but both felt confident after the session and neither had been undermined. Several other pupils had joined the discussion and it was lively and relaxed.

These two boys said they felt able to teach e-safety to younger pupils and it seemed that with some training they would make excellent ambassadors to younger pupils or even to parents of younger children. But it would have been easy to bring them down by showing up their ignorance of certain security checks. While they were quite knowledgeable on some aspects of e-safety, they certainly had gaps in their knowledge. Instead, e-safety educators need to build on that sense of self-efficacy and autonomy and find out what they know. Boys often explain that they know how to look up how to stay safe online and use websites to inform themselves. They frequently said in the Cybersurvey that they had taught themselves about e-safety. This resource – knowledgeable students – should be deployed as much as possible! Activities could be focused on triggering them to find out more and sharing it with the class.

PUBLIC SOCIAL HUMILIATION: A NEW FORM OF BULLYING ENABLED BY TECHNOLOGY

In a workshop discussion with young people during the development of the survey questions, a new and cruel form of cyberbullying emerged. The ringleader makes use of group texts to set up social arrangements such as meeting at a shopping centre on Saturday. But, after several rounds of messages about when and where to meet, she deliberately sends another text to everyone except the target girl, with a change of plan. The lone girl would get dressed in her latest gear and eagerly wait at the agreed meeting place. The others, meanwhile, could be watching her from another level of the shopping centre or across the road. Abusive remarks were added to pictures uploaded onto Formspring, a social networking site that allows users to post questions anonymously, which makes it difficult for the victim to know who is responsible.

This is a deliberately set up public humiliation, all the more hurtful because it was pre-planned. It is then made more painful because the pictures are circulated at school. The young people felt it was 'really a girl thing' when discussed in the workshops. Girls insisted they recognised this experience. A question was created that reads: 'On mobiles: Have you ever experienced any of the following – People text you about where to meet, but then change the place on purpose without telling you – so that they can make fun of you or leave you out?' When the 2009 survey was being developed only girls tended to describe this behaviour. However, in response to the survey itself it was clear that boys experienced this form of bullying to the same extent as girls.

This question was suggested by the first group of young people as we developed the first draft of the survey. In every discussion group young people said they recognised this behaviour and thought it was important. So while other questions were dropped, this one survived. Without the lengthy development period and the discussions with young people in various locations, it is unlikely this question would have been included. This is an example of the value of consulting young people.

SUMMARY

When we compare the different ways that boys and girls answered the Cybersurvey, we find that certain messages remain consistent across all three years. It is possible to see these messages broadly falling into three categories. The first shows the questions on which girls are more likely than boys to say this has happened to them and the second where boys are more likely than girls to do so. Third, there are experiences and situations that both boys and girls report in almost equal measure. This is, of course, a generalisation and it cannot apply to everyone. But for the thinking educator, here is food for reflection. Are there lessons to learn which can help shape how you might prevent and respond to cyberbullying?

More girls than boys:

• say they are cyberbullied

• live in a world of gossip and rumour spreading

- are excluded from cliques or groups of girls
- are cyberbullied as an extension of bullying also happening at school
- tell someone if they are cyberbullied
- get help if they do tell someone.

In their mid-teens girls experience sexual bullying involving photos, insults, name-calling, threats, ratings and jealousy. This is in addition to the rumour spreading and name-calling they already describe at younger ages. Many types of cyberbullying peak among girls in their mid-teens.

Although boys are less inclined to say that they have been cyberbullied, they experience many of the same abusive or aggressive incidents or messages as girls. They may choose not to call this cyberbullying and in some cases do not want to see themselves as victims of cyberbullying. Boys seem to shrug off offensive language, insults and threats more easily than girls, but it may be a defence strategy to retain status among their peers and to avoid being seen as the 'weakling' or victim.

Boys are likely to experience more:

- cyberbullying that is not linked to their life in school
- homophobic bullying that is cruel and relentless
- racism
- disablist bullying.

Boys are more likely to have the ability to get round blocks set up to prevent access to certain websites. Boys are far more likely than girls to say 'I'm not bothered' (33 versus 16%) or 'I took it as a joke' if they are cyberbullied. Girls, on the other hand, tend to say they felt 'very upset and angry'. Boys talk of self-efficacy and autonomy when discussing e-safety and they want to be able to be self-reliant. They prefer to find out about e-safety from websites, friends, siblings or security software.

Universal experiences include:

- messages where you do not know the sender
- photos used to embarrass or humiliate you.

Translating these results into practice
Girls

- Address girls' relationships in group work through brief scenarios, drama, circle time, workshop discussions and strengths-based confidence building.
- Work to develop a strong group dynamic within the class – in which people support one another and exhibit caring behaviour.
- Minimise the power of individual girls who have built up power bases.
- Empower bystander girls to retreat from colluding with a bullying leader.

- Provide anonymised case histories for small groups to solve – who could the target of cyberbullying turn to? What are her options? Who could have helped her earlier? What could the bystanders have done? How many people knew about this cyberbullying?

- Address 'consumer' or fashion-based bullying through art – exploring image, identity and stereotypes.

- Be proactive where possible – if jealousy over boyfriends is apparent or a new pupil arrives.

- Ensure that pupils know that they can disclose cyberbullying that involves embarrassing content. Respond in a calm authoritative measured way.

Boys

- Improve routes to support for boys. Too few of those who do come forward actually get appropriate help.

- For those who want to access support independently, provide them with websites, helplines and other forms of advice.

- Publicly place advice on what to do on notice boards, intranets, mouse mats and school websites.

- Consider an email or online reporting system.

- When someone does report being cyberbullied, consider how you can address the behaviour without revealing that the victim has reported it.

- Help the target of cyberbullying retain a sense of self-efficacy and agency by asking their permission to take the next steps you propose.

- Check on what they do know about e-safety and how accurate this knowledge is by inviting pupils to share their knowledge with others – perhaps after a short training session.

- Ensure homophobia is not allowed under cover of 'we were only joking.'

Both boys and girls

- Work to obtain 'ownership' by all young people of the school/college Anti-Bullying Policy and Acceptable Use Policy (AUP) agreement.

- Use student councils to explore bullying within the school or college community.

- Carry out anonymous surveys to update your knowledge of current youth trends and the extent to which your approach is effective.

- Embed work on diversity and equality issues into the curriculum at all levels.

- Learning to understand about people who are different should begin at the earliest age.

- Sexist and homophobic language should be challenged just as racist language is currently.

- Warn all children and young people against taking chain letters seriously.

- Ensure that every pupil knows that the school has systems to help them should they need it. They should feel confident in reporting cyberbullying of any sort.

Staff training

Use anonymised case studies in staff training sessions to test out whether your school's Anti-Bullying Policy provides good procedural direction for teachers. Would they know what to do and what to record? Who leads on this? What gender-based behaviours have they noticed? Do they have ideas on what works? Are they aware of the differences in the way girls and boys react when cyberbullied? Ensure all staff know about local voluntary sector and local authority partners who can be called upon in complex cases. It is vital to have every staff member fully aware of all child protection procedures, as they could encounter a serious case at any time.

RESOURCES

Lesson plan: Cyberbullying and gender (Chapter 11).

Lesson plan: What do I do online? (Chapter 11).

Staff Training Needs Questionnaire (Chapter 11).

Chapter

6

MEETING THE NEEDS OF DIFFERENT AGE GROUPS

A PERIOD OF INTENSE CHANGE

The three years of the Cybersurvey cover a period of intense change in the technology and in the use children and young people make of it. In 2008 the number of mobiles overtook fixed line phones in the UK, heralding major changes in the following three years when even cheap mobiles given to children would come equipped with cameras as prices dropped and, a further major step-change, when mobiles could provide cheap access to the internet from the palm of your hand. These changes have affected younger and younger age groups as mobile and camera ownership has spread rapidly among children. By the time of the Cybersurvey 2010, 85 per cent of ten- to eleven-year-olds said they had a mobile. In 2011, 16 per cent of this age group had more than a basic mobile – they had a smartphone or a BlackBerry with access to the internet.

Seemingly overnight, parental filters came to mean less – children could access the internet on their phone or on their friends' phones. Advice about parental controls on a home computer in the living room became obsolete at a stroke. Only small children still used the family computer. By 2010, 12-year-olds using a hand-held device were lying in bed at night talking to friends on Facebook or playing games with people on the other side of the world until they were seriously sleep deprived.

In cyberbullying terms these two tools – mobiles that easily access the internet and digital cameras embedded in even cheap phones – have enabled and facilitated cyberbullying. It is easy to blame the tools and forget that the behaviour itself is human, but the behaviour is undoubtedly amplified by the reach and features of the technology, and our responses need to change to be relevant. The other great influence has undoubtedly been Facebook. In 2011 in the UK there were more 18-year-olds on Facebook than on the voters' roll.[62]

WHAT SHOULD SHAPE OUR DELIVERY OF E-SAFETY INFORMATION?

There are three major influences that should shape our strategies to educate students about staying safe. Not only do responses need to change with the evolving features of new technology, but, as we saw in Chapter 5, there are gender patterns that reveal different behaviours online and in cyberbullying. The third powerful factor to consider is age. It is this trio – changing technology, gender and age – that should shape our delivery of e-safety information and make it not only relevant to all these different audiences, but also more nuanced. The same trio could influence advice to parents to ensure they keep up with changing trends among children.

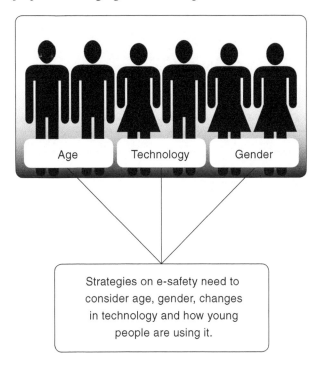

Figure 6.1 Age, gender and the influence of technology

Age groups tell a story

The Cybersurvey respondents are divided into four age groups for study. The youngest are aged 10–11 and the oldest 16+. This allows us to see how the delivery of e-safety education has increasingly reached almost all young people with younger age groups receiving more information than the 16+ group. Delivery in 2011 is wide reaching, but satisfaction and adherence to the guidelines dips dramatically at ages 14–15. Across all three rounds of the Cybersurvey, from 2009 to 2011, the mid-teens stand out. They were the least satisfied with the e-safety education they received. It seems that what they had been taught did not meet all their needs at this age, even allowing for natural scepticism. In 2010 and 2011, at ages 14–15, only 29 per cent of pupils thought the e-safety information they received was 'very good', down from half the respondents aged 10–11. This, and the way they ignore e-safety advice, makes the 14–15 age group challenging.

At the same time, the changing world of ten- to eleven-year-olds is not fully recognised. They are a fast changing group with ever more access to devices and the internet. E-safety advice in many primary schools will need to gear up and broaden out.

Twin peaks

The child with a smartphone has the whole cyberuniverse in his hand, complete with dynamic opportunities and the risks embodied in all that 'contact, conduct and commerce' outlined in the Byron report.[63] He can also access the internet at a friend's house, a club or library or on his own at home. The need to educate even younger children about e-safety across many devices in different situations has now grown markedly, in parallel with the very different challenges of educating mid-teens for the life they now live online. We might think of it as two peaks of concern – the ten-year-olds and the fourteen-year-olds – and the preparation needed before each peak arrives.

Table 6.1 Access changes rapidly

	10–11	14–15
Have a mobile	82%	97%
A computer they use on their own at home	81%	95%
A computer they often use at a friend's house without adults	30%	42%
A Facebook page	39%	92%
A chatroom they often use	21%	31%
A computer they can use on their own at a club, library or cafe	19%	35%
A Smartphone or BlackBerry	16%	24%
Twitter account	5%	16%

Source: Cybersurvey 2011

This is not to suggest we ignore the ages between these two peaks of concern – there is much to do to prepare them before they turn 14. Young teenagers have greatly increased access to computers and phones, as might be expected, but the vast majority still follow the e-safety guidelines at least sometimes, if not always. The increases in the percentage that are cyberbullied are small, although general nasty messages are on the rise.

But two developments are noteworthy: sexual bullying begins to affect a quarter of 12- to 13-year-olds and Facebook represents a sea change. It has become a rite of passage to have a Facebook page, and from the age of 12 children are eager to get onto it and are doing so despite the age restriction: 77 per cent of 12- to 13-year-olds have a page on an SNS. I have chosen to focus on the two 'peak of concern' age groups because ten-year-olds are clearly far more active in cyberspace than the e-safety advice we give would suggest, and the mid-teens are not being well served. Ideally e-safety education should, of course, address every age and stage.

FOUR KEY MESSAGES
- More than one-quarter of ten- to eleven-year-olds had experienced a nasty or unpleasant message on their mobile. Some of these are worrying.
- The age 13 watershed for belonging to SNS has been breached and become meaningless: 39 per cent of ten- to eleven-year-olds and 77 per cent of 12- to 13-year-olds have a Facebook or other SNS page.
- Cyberbullying peaks at age 14–15, and 92 per cent have a Facebook page.
- Adherence to and approval of e-safety advice is at its lowest at age 14–15.

GREATER E-SAFETY FOCUS IN PRIMARY SCHOOLS

The Cybersurvey results suggest that primary schools could address e-safety far earlier with younger children, offer practical demonstrations of skills – such as how to block unwanted messages and begin to develop strong self-efficacy at age eight upwards – so that at ages ten to eleven they are well prepared. By then, homophobic insults are already shockingly common and remain entrenched. More than a quarter of these still relatively young recipients have said they received messages 'with insults calling you gay'. Thirty-seven per cent had been subjected to 'someone deliberately spreading rumours about me'.

Pupils need help with managing nasty texts or voice threats on mobiles and the 'scary' messages that upset them. Twenty-two per cent of recipients said they had received another type of nasty message, that is, not one of the types listed in the question. These often proved to be chain letters with threats.

Parents of Years 5 and 6 require sources of constantly updated advice and signposting to help and discussions, as well as resources for young children. All parents should be able to recognise the report abuse button and understand how games consoles can introduce children to unknown players on the internet. They should also know how to set filters on mobile phones that access the internet.

ANTICIPATE TEENAGE BEHAVIOUR

In anticipation of adolescent behaviour and the peaks we see at later ages, intensive bullying prevention work should be in place in secondary schools before the age of 14 to pre-empt the cyberbullying this year brings.

Many schools cover e-safety and cyberbullying in Year 7 and feel this is adequate, with a once-a-year top up in the annual Anti-Bullying Week. Sadly, this will not prove effective unless it is embedded across all years and addresses the specific behaviours that are prevalent at each age. What these behaviours are should be monitored through anonymous surveys and circle time sessions to keep on top of changing youth culture. Young people should be enlisted to design age-appropriate resources, games and online pages in school intranets. As virtual learning expands, this allows creativity in delivering e-safety advice in new formats. Educators should take advantage of the excellent resources available online from Childnet and CEOP (see Appendix 7), for example. Perhaps young people could write a critical appraisal of a few?

The key may lie in being more responsive to the needs of the students. Very often it can take many weeks to get an e-safety strategy approved and implemented in a school, and this can make teachers reluctant to change it. It will remain in place for a couple of years. In this way e-safety advice remains fairly static while children and young people race past it. If they feel they know more than the teacher, they are likely to tune out. But not all the work required is directly linked to e-safety. Much of it could be addressed in personal, social, health and economic education (PSHE), citizenship or general anti-bullying work on equality.

By the age of 14–15 unwanted sexual messages containing jokes, threats or suggestions double. Messages where the sender was 'not who they said they were' increase by more than half as much again. Threats and rumours abound and strangers ask to meet up. Racism and homophobia do not diminish. This suggests that, as shown in a local authority study in the Midlands (see Chapter 7), prejudice is hard to shift and remains stubborn throughout primary and secondary years.[64]

WHAT ABOUT THE EARLY YEARS?

Before a child ever reaches the school gate, he may have played with his mother's phone, played on the computer, been into Club Penguin and played handheld games. He will watch his beloved toy characters on television and in games and recognise the icons relating to certain websites. I have seen one pre-schooler locate Club Penguin through icons on the desktop, copy his brother's password painstakingly letter by letter, and get into the Club to play. All this before being able to read!

The early years are, of course, very much mediated by parents, and children's first experiences of technology are usually at home. Parents' own attitudes and skills can influence how this develops.

Young children's use of technology is described in research by Atkinson and Staunton, jointly initiated by Plymouth City Council Early Years and Plymouth Safeguarding Children's Board in the UK.[65] Parents were surveyed about their children's use of technology and the study drew out parents' feelings about the impact of technology on their child's development, receipt of online safety advice from the early years setting their child attended and their own approaches to online safety.

Almost three-quarters of the children used the internet for an average of half an hour a day, and parents reported that the children knew what they wanted to do online – they would go to well-known sites for children linked with television such as the BBC's CBeebies or to play games on age-appropriate sites developed from children's television programmes such as Peppa Pig. Parents felt confident they had a good understanding of the internet and safety issues.

Within the venues the children attended, almost all made use of technology, with 37 per cent of venues allowing children online. This study describes an 'increasingly technology-rich environment' for small children who now have parents who are probably 'the first generation with online experiences throughout their own childhoods'.

The authors point out that the chosen parental approach to e-safety in these early years is most likely to be consolidated and remain as the dominant parenting methodology. They argue that 'reliance upon technical management is no substitute for effective behavioural guidance'. Furthermore, they are alert to issues such as new developments in technologies, and point out that even parents raised on the internet may fall behind their growing child's use of technology. I would add to this the changes in youth culture and how being online can alter behaviour.

IS SELF-EFFICACY THE GOAL?

If the desired outcome is self-efficacy, there is a lot of work to do. EU Kids Online research from Sonck *et al.* tells us that around one-third of 11- to 12-year-olds cannot bookmark a site and even more cannot block messages, while teachers' engagement with children's internet use is least among 9- to 10-year-olds.[66] The Schools Health Education Unit 2011 report found that as many as 33 per cent of girls aged 10–11 sometimes felt afraid of going to school because of bullying.[67] Sadly the rise in ownership of mobiles among this age group can allow bullies to reach their victims even at home, and the rapid increase in social networking between 2009 and 2010 in this age group has also played its part.

In Figures 6.2 and 6.3 the experiences of the two age groups are compared. The challenge is to prepare the ten-year-olds to know how to handle some of the messages described, to teach them not to send this type of threat or insult and to induct them into digital citizenship early.

By age 14–15 the messages received have become sexual and are more sinister and aggressive, and pupils are in some cases twice as likely to experience them.

What types of messages did recipients receive in the Cybersurvey during 2011?

On mobiles (see Figure 6.3), among one-quarter of ten- to eleven-year-olds who had experienced one or more nasty or unpleasant message on their mobile in 2011, 44 per cent experienced name-calling, the traditional bullying approach. A quarter had received homophobic insults and a message that said people were 'talking about me nastily online'. One in five received racist comments and 'scary threatening messages'. Fifteen per cent received a message with unwanted sexual words, threats or suggestions. Twenty-three per cent experienced texts about social arrangements or plans to meet that subsequently excluded them deliberately.

Online (see Figure 6.2), 40 per cent of all ten- to eleven-year-olds had one or more unpleasant experience. Of those, 38 per cent received messages where the sender was not who they said they were. Over a quarter got a message that 'tried to make me do something I did not want to do'. A quarter got a message that showed 'people were talking about me nastily online' and more than a quarter received 'a message with insults calling you gay'. Almost one in five received messages with racist comments or names and 16 per cent received a message with unwanted sexual suggestions, jokes or threats.

At this age, e-safety education barely covers these experiences but focuses more on stranger danger and the risks of giving out personal information. Large numbers of attractive resources are available online, but in some schools children cannot access the internet (because access is blocked) and explore these resources for themselves.

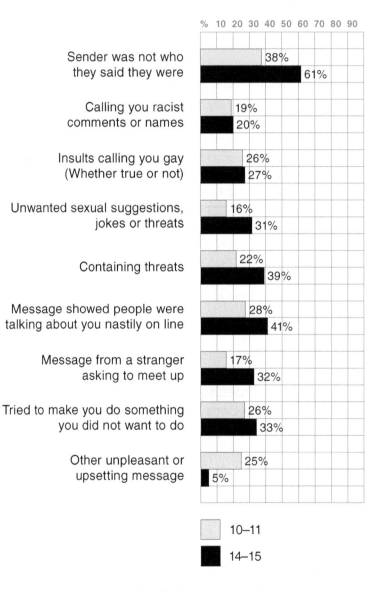

Figure 6.2 Examples of online messages and experiences

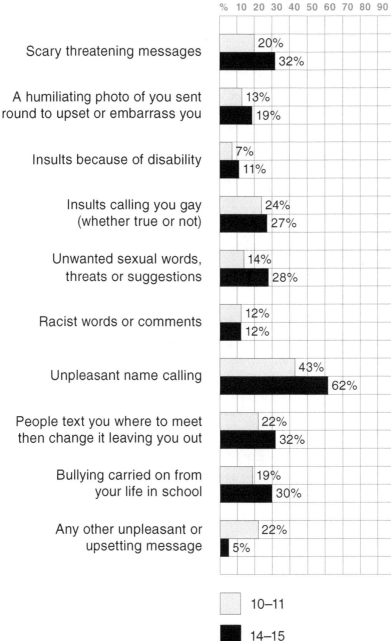

Figure 6.3 Examples of mobile message and experiences

Children say they might have a lesson about e-safety that covers a great deal, from mobiles to social networking. It teaches them some rules they should stick to (SMART rules). They often see film clips and have a talk by a guest. They say these lessons are good. But interpersonal issues and what to do about the pain of rejection or the fear from threats are seldom mentioned. Children are most upset by friendship issues and being left out or picked on. Very few are visiting unsuitable websites, influenced by older siblings or adults. They are candidates for the intensive support and e-safety described later in Chapter 7. Messages for children should include:

'It is safe to ignore chain letters, or tell an adult about it.'

'It is safe to show any threats or scary messages to an adult, but do not reply.'

'Some people are horrid, but don't be upset by them, together we can handle it.'

'You do not have to put up with it if people are rude.'

'It is never wrong to ask if you are worried about anything.'

'Like rules of the road there are rules of the digital highway and you will get all the help you need to deal with it safely as you begin this exciting journey. This also means you have to behave responsibly and I will show you how.'

Victimised for your appearance

The Schools Health Education Unit survey also found that up to 22 per cent of ten- to eleven-year-olds report being picked on for the way they looked.[68] This is the ideal age to address the whole picture of being victimised over appearance before it escalates in the teenage years. Use art, drama, circle time and fiction to approach this subject. Collages made from pictures torn from magazines can spark their interest.

Empower parents

Parents of ten-year-olds are increasingly talking to them about e-safety, as we see in the Cybersurvey. But evidence on the ground in schools showed that parents:

- often have no idea about the sites their children visit
- may not understand what a chatroom is or a Facebook wall
- allow ten-year-olds onto Facebook, sometimes even sharing their own page
- don't know enough about consoles
- don't know about 'report abuse' buttons
- often can't set privacy settings on Facebook
- are beginning to shop online with their child using a credit card
- are embarrassed if a 'sexy' picture is the problem, so their child does not say anything.

Schools could equip parents of primary age pupils with a greater range of useful advice and sources of information so that they can help their children.

Consolidate between the peaks of concern

The time between ages 11 and 14 must be a period of consolidation and development so that by the age of 14 they are better equipped to cope with the digital world in which they live. They are still willing to listen to and abide by e-safety guidelines, and cyberbullying is increasing but not as dramatically as we see at ages 14–15. Preparation now to pre-empt the problems we see at 14 could pay dividends.

The perfect storm

A perfect storm of factors at age 14–15 means that this peak should be anticipated and tackled in advance and with these young people. Now is when cyberbullying peaks, sexual bullying is common and young people say they are least likely to follow the e-safety guidelines they have been taught. At this age they are less likely to tell someone if they have been cyberbullied or had some other distressing experience, because these are often embarrassing, personal, relationship-driven or sexual. Teenagers understandably want to keep their social lives private. They also express the strongest wish for autonomy in handling e-safety issues and finding out about how to do things online as they wrote in open questions. 'I just know,' they said repeatedly. One stressed 'because I don't want to talk to perverts' as if this were self-evident.

Figure 6.4 Other sources of e-safety advice

At age 14–15 the percentage that always follow the guidelines drops dramatically to around one in four from well over half at age 10–11.

At the same age we see a rise in those who only sometimes follow the guidelines and we see that 14- to 15-year-olds are more than four times more likely than their younger peers to say that they don't really follow the guidelines.

Table 6.2 To report or not to report?

	10–11 years	12–13	14–15	16+	Total
Have you been cyberbullied?	16%	17%	21%	25%	18%
If yes did you tell anyone?	68%	71%	55%	63%	65%
If you told someone did you get help?	57%	65%	38%	50%	53%

Cybersurvey 2011: n=343, only those who have been cyberbullied

It is natural to report cyberbullying to a teacher or parents at the age of 10, but at age 14–15 this is least likely. One in five had been cyberbullied at this age. Of these, just over half (55%) told someone, but of those who told, only 38 per cent of 14- to 15-year-olds got help. They may have simply told a friend or sibling. It is for this age group that new approaches need to be tried. Instead of 'tell an adult' the advice needs to be more empowering. It could take the form of 'These are all the options open to you: let's explore together how to report abuse on a website; how to contact a service provider; better privacy settings and photo tagging.' Create scenarios and work with students to consider all the possible safe responses. This is the age at which we see a peak in cyberbullying and in sexual bullying. It is also the age at which they are least likely to follow e-safety guidelines. They need to be actively engaged and finding out for themselves. For this to work, they need guidance and practical demonstrations.

What do pupils think about results from the Cybersurvey?

Pupils from Years 9 and 10 participated in a workshop for the Reach Project[69] in a Bristol school in the UK. They were shown results from the Cybersurvey and were asked, 'Why do people stop following the advice as they get older? Is it still relevant, and if not why?' Their answers from some small group discussions included:

'Because they think it's no point. They think no one would bother to do that to them.'

'You don't get as much advice as you used to and the bullying's less obvious or everyone joins in. The advice is pratronising. You have a whole assembly about cyberbullying but only a couple of people would need the advice.'

'Because they become more mature and can think for themselves, know how to deal with the situation. Some people don't like being told what to do.'

'They're older. I don't think they're going to get cyberbullied when they're an adult.'

'Because they're older they feel they don't need to listen.'

'As people get older they get tied up in other things. Teenagers like rebelling.'

'Teenagers don't care what you tell them. Teenagers think they know more than adults. They have a sense of arrogance.'

In answer to the question, 'What would make e-safety education more useful to your age group?':

'Learn more about what websites are suitable. Learn how to report sites (report abuse).'

'Less patronising. Not repeating information and aim at our age group. The danger is not having them as a friend but meeting them in real life, so you should tell the danger is not online friends.'

'Learn more about it. Not everyone's aware of the risks.'

'Make it less boring and more interacting with the audience.'

'Roaming the internet.'

'People who get cyberbullied should avoid social networking sites. There will always be people who cyberbully so there's no point making a difference.'

In answer to the question 'What is needed?', from ten-year-olds we learn that they need more age-nuanced advice and fears about scary messages should be promptly addressed. They are already being asked to meet up with people they met online and need to know how to deal with this. They are scared by threats and chain letters. They need opportunities to develop know-how, skills and resilience. E-safety should be given before this age, and bullying should be discussed and explored.

From teenagers we learn that fixed lists of rules of 'what not to do' handed down from adults to children are not the answer. This is a very risk-focused approach. Restricting access with block, bans and filters is a common response in a risk-averse society, but is only likely to work with young children. Teenagers can get round blocks and filters if they want to, and adults may have a false sense of security if every technological block or filter is in place.

It is skills children need and the knowledge of where to get the help they might require from a trusted source whenever they need it. We need to teach the 'how?' and the 'why?' as well as 'what' it means to be a responsible digital citizen.

Tim Davies and colleagues argue for a more rights-based approach based on the United Nations Convention on the Rights of the Child in which protection and provision are balanced with the right to participation.[70] They suggest that this tripartite model can capture research insights into the relationship between opportunity and risk. While risks may give rise to a focus on protection, evidence suggests that protection is best realised by ensuring young people gain experience of the online world through positive engagement with it.

Many professionals are discouraged from exploring the internet with young people with bans operating in many schools, for example. Arguments abound in the USA over rushed legislation in the wake of tragedies and panics. The debate is about whether it is actually beneficial to ban teachers from using social networking; If teachers are banned from any sort of communication with students this bars them from giving personal support to students who may need it, or equally, constructive advice such as with a job application, for example.[71]

The opportunities and creativity that lie before these children are astounding. They are our partners in these early days of exploring all that technology offers and we should encourage them while keeping them safe, rather than limit their exploratory curiosity and creative imagination. They deserve an age-appropriate strategy that is well integrated into the life of the school and practice in the home. They have a right to be protected from unsuitable content, aggressive advertising and predatory behaviour.

SUMMARY

- There are two peak ages for attention, at ages 10–11 and 14–15.

- Anticipating the situations these pupils could experience, work should be done proactively at earlier ages.

- Parents of very young children should be supported to develop strong e-safety behaviours and good practice with online shopping.

- Those aged 14–15 see a peak of cyberbullying and a low in e-safety observance. They express a strong theme of autonomy and need to be educated on how and where to find out about safety for themselves and each other.

- Advice to 'tell someone' at 14–15 is not succeeding; other routes to get help need to be provided.

- Too many who do tell are not getting the help and protection they need.

Chapter
7

MEETING THE NEEDS OF THE MOST VULNERABLE STUDENTS

Nowhere is inequality seen more starkly than in the statistics on bullying. Being different is never a justification for bullying, but it is a fact that children who are perceived as 'different' can experience bullying disproportionately when compared to their peers. In this book I have suggested a three-tier e-safety programme, in which the most vulnerable students receive extra support and e-safety education at an intensive level. This goes beyond the universal delivery that works for the majority and some targeted work when people experience some cyberaggression. This chapter outlines who might be the most vulnerable people.

We can learn a great deal by exploring the responses of people who seem to be most severely bullied, in contrast to those who say they were only bullied a little. If there are victims in schools who perceive their bullying experience to have been very severe and long-term, we should know who they are and how we can prevent this.

We also want to enable them to report it and to get the help they need, but this is not always happening. The bullying they suffer is complex, multi-faceted and often takes place both in and out of school. Anyone bullied in school is becoming increasingly more likely to be cyberbullied too. Sameer Hinduja and Justin W. Patchin, of the Cyberbullying Research Center, showed that the majority of those who are *persistently* cyberbullied said this was an extension of ongoing offline bullying.[72] This can reduce them to a sense of helpless resignation to their 'fate' as they see it, bringing on negative feelings and distress (or aggressive behaviour), making them more likely to be persistently absent.

Bullying often originates in traditional settings like schools and then migrates online.[73] That is why this focus on reducing traditional bullying is always the first line of prevention for cyberbullying.

Some vulnerable groups are easily identified.

According to the National Pupil Database and Longitudinal Study of Young People in England (LSYPE)[74] a far greater proportion of persistent absentees are subjected to bullying than their non-PA peers, in particular social exclusion. Almost a sixth of persistent absentees are subjected to this type of bullying. This study found that the percentage of sessions missed through absence linked to bullying is 30.07. It also suggests that persistent absentees are more likely to be bullied, excluded from school and be involved in risky behaviours.

So one of the first places to look for potentially vulnerable pupils is among persistent absentees. If they miss so many sessions, it is likely they have missed the e-safety sessions too. Their risky behaviour and loneliness form a toxic mix that might send them online looking for friendship or intimacy. They require targeted e-safety advice and extra support.

To be proactive, it helps to know who the local vulnerable population groups are. These can vary according to catchment area, current influences from world news, neighbourhood issues, whipped-up fears in the media such as those around Gypsy Travellers, and also when there are personal family concerns for a pupil such as bereavement, imprisonment of a relative or family breakdown.

The UK charity Beatbullying found that traditionally vulnerable groups are at greater risk of persistent cyberbullying than their peers. This was true of children with special educational needs and children in receipt of free school meals.[75] Some minority ethnic groups suffer more racism in certain locations and this can vary according to local populations. It pays to have strong links with the local community organisations and voluntary sector so that you can be warned of any neighbourhood feuds or invite them into school to help address these matters.

A close look at a badly bullied group

In 2009 I was involved in a local authority survey exploring the lives of young people in the borough. A group of badly bullied pupils was identified from a survey of 4546 primary and secondary pupils in the Midlands.[76] Nineteen per cent of primary children and 10 per cent of secondary pupils were found to be 'bullied a lot' in contrast to others who were bullied 'a little' or 'not at all'. If we look closely at the responses of these badly bullied pupils (the badly bullied group) we can see how intense and prolonged their experience was.

Badly bullied people are less successful at getting it to stop

While those who are mildly bullied tend to get help more successfully and put the experience behind them, the badly bullied group are more likely to say the bullying got worse or stayed the same if they did tell someone. This might explain why very often they did not report it. Among those of secondary school age in this badly bullied group, only 28 per cent said the bullying stopped after they had reported it. For 13 per cent of them it actually got worse. This is more than three times the rate of their mildly bullied counterparts. Seventy-two per cent simply said it did not stop. This makes it hardly worthwhile reporting it – risking being seen as a 'grass', which is a sure route to ostracism. Not only do they not tell a teacher, one in five of the primary pupils and almost one in six of the secondary pupils in the badly bullied group did not tell anyone what was happening to them.

Badly bullied people experience more identity-based bullying

The badly bullied group in the secondary school experienced twice the level of racism, homophobia and 'being left out' compared to the levels reported by their classmates. They were also likely to encounter more than twice as much rumour spreading. They experienced more than three times the level of bullying because of disability or illness and more than three times the level of sexist bullying than other teenagers.

A permanent state of alertness or fear

Badly bullied young people are highly attuned to bullying that is happening to other pupils. They say they have seen this happen more than twice as often as other children do (37% versus 15%). This alertness may make them feel fearful and anxious or worried that what they see is not addressed. Alternatively it may suggest that they need help to become more resilient. Teachers and other support staff are often present when the bullying happens but do not intervene. Corridors and dinner halls, toilets and playgrounds become terrifying locations for hurtful ordeals. Phones can be used inside and outside the classroom to send an abusive text or IM. When a pupil knows it has happened to someone else it seems to increase their fear that it could happen to them next. They may respond with aggressive defences. They can be distracted from learning by the need to be constantly alert.

In Table 7.1 we can see the significance levels for those most vulnerable in the *Safe to Play* study (Midlands, UK).[77]

Table 7.1 Those who are bullied most

	Bullied a lot	Bullied a little	Not bullied	Significance level
Male	8% (102)	36% (486)	56% (761)	$p<0.001$***
Female	11% (155)	45% (615)	43% (577)	
Attends a PRU	39% (9)	30% (7)	26% (6)	$p<0.001$***
Doesn't attend a PRU	9% (247)	40.5% (1074)	49% (1309)	
Has a disability	22% (15)	38% (26)	38% (26)	$p<0.01$**
Doesn't have a disability	9% (244)	40% (1080)	49.5% (1322)	
Has a special educational need	26% (29)	41% (46)	33% (37)	$p<0.001$***
Doesn't have a special educational need	9% (230)	40% (1060)	50% 1311)	
Carer	18% (7)	56% (22)	26% (10)	$p<0.01$**
Not a carer	9% (252)	40% (1084)	50% (1338)	
In care	36% (5)	21% (3)	43% (6)	$p<0.01$**
Not in care	9% (254)	40.5% (1103)	49% (1342)	

n=3454

What is the pattern of prejudice in your school?

The badly bullied group illustrates who is most vulnerable across 26 schools, one college and eight youth groups. While the pattern in your school might differ from the one shown in Table 7.1, you will be able to tell from your own school surveys which groups are persistently bullied for prejudice-driven reasons. You may work in an area of sectarian divides, or among newly arrived populations. You may have a group of pupils who are in the care of the state.

There appear to be some prejudice-driven types of bullying that are constant and worrying. We would expect to see a reduction in prejudice or identity-based bullying as pupils grow up, mature and experience more education, but this does not seem to be the case, as shown in Table 7.2. Students with a disability or special needs, those who are in care and those who are themselves carers, suffered prejudice-driven bullying markedly throughout their school years.

Table 7.2 Percentage of vulnerable groups who are badly bullied

Primary	Secondary
30% of those with a disability	22%
28% of those with special educational needs	25%
28% of those who need help with English	12%
34% of those in care	36% (small numbers)
29% of carers	18%

We see that young people who are looked after in care are likely to go through the same level of victimisation in secondary school as in the first years of their school lives. This is true also for those with special educational needs. Young carers also emerged as a vulnerable group, and although this lessened somewhat in secondary years, it was still evident.

The young people on the receiving end of this hostility should be on the radar as potentially vulnerable. Those with poor peer relations in the real world are likely to seek intimacy online, and can fall victim to people with ill intent seeking out lonely and unhappy children.

One question to consider is, how good is the children's knowledge of how to keep safe in cyberspace? The Cybersurvey revealed that vulnerable young people might have received less e-safety information and that they are least likely to follow it. Because pupils in care undergo frequent school moves, they might have missed out on some crucial e-safety lessons. Gypsy or Roma Traveller pupils, for example, may experience the same patchy coverage. This could also be true for children from chaotic households or young carers whose attendance at school is poor.

These are some of the neediest children in our society and yet they are being exposed to venomous campaigns of abuse and harassment across their school career. Equally, bystanders are failing to learn to stand up for those who need help, and appear to accept the situation or join in. It is arguable that all pupils who witness this prolonged and unchallenged behaviour are affected by it.

The Midlands survey that I carried out also showed that those in the badly bullied group experienced almost twice the amount of racist bullying as their peers. Generally the pupils thought that those of different ethnic groups got on well or said they did not know whether they did. But the badly bullied group disagreed. They were twice as likely to say ethnic groups did 'not get on at all well'.[78]

Those who experienced racist bullying among the badly bullied pupils are as shown in Table 7.3.

Table 7.3 Racism experienced by badly bullied people

Primary pupils	Primary BB pupils	Secondary pupils	Secondary BB
12%	22%	11%	25%

BB = badly bullied

In a bullying environment, where prejudices are allowed to grow and stereotypes go unchallenged, the climate is poisoned. Cullingford, in his book about prejudice, points out that 'For some, each interaction has the potential for tension, so that the action taken by the other...is attributable to some characteristic from their ethnic origin or class.'[79]

Despite the importance to society of tackling community cohesion, teachers say that their own lack of training is the second most important barrier to educating against racism.[80]

Why it is urgent to address bullying of vulnerable people

If we know that bullying is 'physically harmful, psychologically damaging, socially isolating and associated with poor school adjustment,'[81] it seems extraordinary to subject those least able to withstand it to many years of ostracism and isolation. Louise Arseneault,[82] whose work has identified a long-term effect on children's mental health if bullied in the first years of school life, argues:

Empirical evidence suggests that bullying victimization can be an important risk factor for childhood and adolescent psychopathology. Research is needed to understand this type of victimization experience and how it contributes to the development of mental health problems. Intervention and prevention strategies warrant increased focus for reducing bullying behaviours in schools and in the community. Recent findings also highlight the need for mental health practitioners to consider the range of difficulties experienced by children who report being bullied. These children are at risk of experiencing other forms of victimization, dealing with other risk factors and developing mental health symptoms...

Multi-faceted and repeated – the intensity of severe bullying

This is no teasing or banter. It is not something a child can be told to ignore. In the badly bullied group in the Midlands, pupils were repeatedly bullied and also bullied in multiple ways, sometimes by several people. The term 're-victimisation' has been used to describe the 'persistence of victimisation across time', and 'poly-victimization implies a vulnerability to a range of different types of victimization.'[83] The badly bullied group experience both.

There is an additional 'multiplier effect' identified by Hayden (2008),[84] whereby children who are bullied a lot in school are much more likely than their peers to also be bullied out of school. This is a double blow because there is no escape from bullying when they get home. Ybarra *et al.* (2007) remind us of the overlap between bullying at school and cyberbullying[85] that we found within the badly bullied group and also in the Cybersurvey.

It is not surprising therefore that among the badly bullied pupils we find this intense poly-victimisation both in the real world and in cyberspace. This suggests that bullying in school needs to be urgently addressed at an early stage to prevent the development and multiplying of all the other bullying that emerges when it is tacitly accepted, that one individual is the target everyone bullies. It is vital to reassert the principle that every child has a right to be safe.

Forty-one per cent of the badly bullied secondary school group were bullied both in and out of school compared to 25 per cent of their peers. Thirty-one per cent said they experienced cyberbullying, which intensifies in the mid-teens. Sixty-two per cent experienced rumour spreading, 56 per cent said they were always deliberately left out and 90 per cent experienced name-calling. Forty-three per cent were bullied while walking to school and as many as 42 per cent were also bullied in the classroom with the teacher present.

Phones are used surreptitiously in class. One girl recently explained in a workshop why she preferred a BlackBerry to a smartphone – 'You can feel the keys with your fingers under the desk if you want to text someone during the lesson and we send off messages when someone is an idiot or if we're bored.' Her friend added, 'We make jokes about people on our BBs [BlackBerry] or attack girls who are slags.'

Another example of bullying in the classroom with the teacher present came from a boy diagnosed on the autistic spectrum. He explained how he could not bear the rustle of crisp packets or the grease of the crisps. His obsession was to keep his work clean. He washed his hands over and over again. Those who bullied him rustled their packets and spread crumbs of crisps on his work, leaving greasy spots and the smell on his books. They knew how to press his buttons, he said – they now had only to slightly rustle a packet to get him to kick off. They pretended to be taking things out of their bags in class and rustled crisp packets while doing so to taunt him. So he repeatedly got into trouble when he responded aggressively, and once violently threw a chair across the room and was threatened with expulsion, which then threatened his education. Then his tormentors sent him photos of crisp packets via a mobile phone. Teachers are often unaware of the undertow of misery in their class.

Kowalski and Fedina, in one of the first studies of cyberbullying and autism, show parents were often unaware of their child's involvement in cyberbullying. They highlighted the health impacts and a need for information on cyberbullying for these parents.[86]

Research your own vulnerable groups

I hope to have illustrated that it is urgent to intervene effectively to prevent bullying occurring to any child, but especially to those who are most vulnerable. To do so, you will need to have some idea of who these groups are, because while general proactive anti-bullying and e-safety work will be helpful for the majority of a school population, it will not be enough on its own to support the most vulnerable pupils. They require more targeted, and in some cases, intensive support.

Consider what you know about the more obviously vulnerable, such as those pupils discussed here, then address those who might be vulnerable for a local reason, and finally, think about those who may be going through some personal or family crisis, rendering them temporarily vulnerable. This can range from an ill sibling (I have seen a case where the sibling of a child in a hospice was cruelly bullied) to children where a parent is in the news for something – a high profile divorce or a crime (a child was bullied online and obscene material and dog faeces put through the letterbox at home when a parent was arrested). A further alert comes when a child is obese or anorexic: websites provide unsuitable advice to young people worried about their body shape urging them towards extreme diets. Also noticeably more likely to be involved in bullying are those whose parents are over-protective or controlling and those whose parents are neglectful, harsh or punitive.[87]

Children in care

Consider children in care: they suffer multiple impacts from bullying both in and out of school. Frequent moves can mean they are always the newcomer. This may mean there is no respite for a child who is targeted in this way. Those in care may be further bullied by different individuals in the home setting and in the neighbourhood of the care home. They are also likely to be in touch with friends from former placements and may do complex searches online looking for family or friendships. Liaison with the care home manager, and training foster carers in e-safety, is recommended alongside intensive in-school e-safety advice.

Learning difficulties and disabilities

Mishna (2003)[88] describes how those with learning difficulties suffer what she has termed a 'double jeopardy' when bullied, setting their social development back and exacerbating their relational difficulties in addition to suffering the pain of being bullied. Mencap, a UK charity fighting to support those with learning difficulties, found that eight out of ten children with a learning disability had been bullied.[89] This experience is shared by two-thirds of lesbian, gay, bisexual and transgender (LGBT) students in Britain, while only one in six secondary teachers believe their school is active in promoting respect for these students.[90] This suggests that teacher training is needed to help staff be aware of steps they can take, systems in the school and sources of advice and best practice.

Four-fifths of disabled young people report being bullied. Almost a quarter of young people questioned who practise any religion in England claim they are bullied because of their faith.[91] Meanwhile, racist bullying can destabilise neighbourhoods, lead to 'territorial' groups,[92] hate crime, gangs and weapon carrying in 'self defence'.[93] Reponses need partners in the field working with young people. Is everyone spreading the same messages about cyberbullying and e-safety? Is the youth service delivering this information? What can community safety teams tell you about the local youth climate?

When asked, 'What kind of message did you get?', young people responded:

'An insult at me because my sister is disabled.'

'A kid being unfair to you calling you a retard.'

'People on msn kept saying my sister was a weird girl who had no friends because she has learning difficulties and a curvature to the spine.'

'I have cerebral palsy so people sent messages say nasty things about my legs they called me a spastic.'[94]

Understand prejudice in order to tackle it

Prejudice is very difficult to change – it is often entrenched in families, and reinforced at home. Attitudes towards Traveller children and those in care most often originate from parents or the neighbourhood. Sometimes these attitudes are fuelled by the media after a spate of local articles about a dispute with a Traveller community.

After 9/11 Islamophobia was fuelled by the media and political leaders, while anti-semitism flares up regularly when Israel and Gaza are in the news. This means you may face some short-term peaks of prejudice. If you are aware of news of this type, group work and discussions can allow pupils to talk about their worries, challenge accepted thinking and formulate some principles. In this way you can pre-empt the ignorance that feeds prejudice. (There is an idea for a lesson on stereotypes in Chapter 11.)

THE CRUEL UNDERCURRENT OF HOMOPHOBIA

Homophobic bullying is widespread in English schools and evident from the age of around ten.[95] The UK campaigning charity Stonewall found that almost two-thirds of young lesbian, gay and bisexual (LGB) pupils at secondary school had experienced homophobic bullying.[96]

Face-to-face traditional homophobic bullying was severe before the arrival of cyberbullying, but this development offers new tools for bullies to pursue cyberhomophobia. Perpetrators can conceal their identity to pursue a victim into every corner of their life, 24 hours a day, and amplify the bullying in view of an audience. Thirty-seven per cent of young people who had experienced homophobic bullying via their mobile phone in a survey for the charity EACH said that it was bullying 'carried on from their life in school.'[97] The Cybersurvey also revealed that pupils encountered cyberhomophobia in chatrooms and SNS where they may have looked for new friendships in their loneliness and confusion.

The lure of cyberspace is that you can be another person, live another life or meet other people. The EU Kids Online study found that in the UK:

> Half (52%) 11–16 year old internet users say they find it easier to be myself on the internet, and 47% talk about different things. For a quarter of children (27%) more private things than they talk about when with other people face to face. This is especially the case for 13–14 year olds, who appear to find the internet a particularly good place to be themselves, perhaps to experiment with identity.[98]

From the safety of a bedroom or via a small handheld device, a screen is the gateway to escape from the struggles some children face daily, especially homophobic bullying. But excessive use and dependence can be risky. Sites that encourage suicide can masquerade as a genuine escape.

Language: joke or abuse?

Homophobic and sexual insults are so commonplace among English teenagers that they are having to ramp up the insults for shock value, so desensitised have some of them become to certain words. This creates an atmosphere of threat and aggression for those who do not share the 'joke' and misery for the targets. For example, in a survey for the BBC television programme Panorama, Youthworks found that one in five respondents had 'often' been called 'gay', more than one in five had 'often' been called a 'slut' and 18 per cent had 'often' been called a 'slag'. Additional people had experienced this 'sometimes'. One in ten said it was 'normal' to be called these words 'all the time,' while a third said it was normal to be called these words 'sometimes'. Sixteen per cent said they often use more offensive words. Thirty per cent thought it was 'mostly OK' that they or someone else were called gay.[99]

A narrow landscape or script for boys

Used to 'police' a narrow and limited script for boys, homophobic bullying allows boys to distance themselves from girls and anything 'girly' or perceived as weak, which specifically includes non-macho boys.[100] This attitude often includes denigrating girls. It also targets those who work hard or are seen as 'boffins'. Any boy who deviates from the narrow landscape of 'what a boy is' can expect to be bullied in this way regardless of his actual sexual orientation. While some popular boys laugh it off as the daily banter they encounter, for others the impact is devastating, as a spate of tragic suicides linked to cyberhomophobia have shown over the past two years.

Some of the names of these young people live on in the public eye as their legacy has been a flurry of legislative activity in the USA and there has even been a summit at the White House to discuss the issue. Pop star Lady Gaga has now set up a foundation 'Born This Way' to address the issue after one of her young fans killed himself at the age of 14. The UK has seen similar cases.

Severe impacts of homophobic bullying

The impacts of homophobic bullying and social isolation include increased truancy, leaving education early without qualifications and an increased risk of depression, self-harm and suicide.[101] Forty per cent of LGB men and women who had been bullied at school had made at least one attempt to self-harm, and more than 20 per cent had attempted suicide.[102]

The LSYPE data collected by the UK Department for Education have shown that victims of bullying are twice as likely to be what is termed 'NEET', meaning not in education, employment or training at the age of 16, when compared to pupils who were not bullied.[103] While this finding does not single out homophobic bullying, loss of attainment should be considered for homophobically bullied students who suffer persistent and repeated bullying in various forms. Being a victim for long periods can also lead the individual to take risky steps to stay safe including carrying a weapon, drinking or trying illegal substances to escape the pain of depression, while some join a gang for protection.[104]

Forced to come out

In order to report homophobic bullying, young victims are confronted, perhaps for the first time, with questions of identity and sexual orientation which they may not have had to address until now. They are often not emotionally ready to do so and may not be able to canvass these issues with parents. By reporting the bullying they may have to 'come out' at school. This major step can lead to further social isolation and shunning, and so many choose to stay silent.

Isolated and ostracised, is this worse than bullying?

Some researchers consider ostracism to be worse than bullying because it seems to deny the victim any acknowledgement of their presence.[105] Kipling Williams has commented in correspondence with the East Sussex Anti-Bullying Team that:

> Rather than making the victim the focus of unwanted and aversive attention (as is the case for bullying), ostracism makes the person feel like the object of inattention, that s/he does not exist and does not warrant the group's attention or interest. In other words, they aren't even worth bullying (which takes effort and indicates that the person does exist and warrants attention). So, both bullying and ostracism are aversive, but they are likely to have different psychological effects, short term and downstream.[106]

In one experiment comparing bullying to ostracising, Williams and colleagues found that, compared to bullied participants, ostracised participants felt 'less belonging, less control, lower self-esteem, and less sense of personal meaning. They were also sadder and angrier.'[107] This is confirmed by Benton, who found in data from 35,000 school children that being left out was the form of bullying that was most hurtful.[108] Williams also describes how those who are ostracised become more socially susceptible in a number of ways as they try to comply or ingratiate themselves with the in-group.[109] This behaviour rings alarm bells as victims are manipulated into acting in ways they would not otherwise do, in order to be accepted. The Cybersurvey found that over a third of homophobically bullied students said they received messages 'trying to make me do something I did not want to do.'

These findings have particular resonance in cyberbullying and cyberhomophobia where rumour spreading and social rejection are so easily used to manipulate a target into isolation. Coupled with ostracism at school, the target has truly been robbed of control and validation – indeed of meaningful existence.

Are teachers and lecturers aware?

A survey of members from the Association of Teachers and Lecturers (ATL) in England, Scotland and Northern Ireland established that more than 70 per cent of teachers and lecturers had encountered homophobic or sexually abusive language in their schools and colleges. Nearly two-thirds of teachers and lecturers had heard this language on a regular basis. Six out of ten teachers and lecturers had further experienced or witnessed the use of this language, mostly but not exclusively used by pupils against other pupils, as part of sexist and/or homophobic bullying.[110]

Does the e-safety information given meet their needs?

The Cybersurvey showed that homophobically cyberbullied students were less likely to follow the e-safety guidelines they had been taught and less likely to think it had been taught at the right time for them. They reported heavier use of chatrooms and social networking than their peers and might have been seeking to escape the misery of their social lives when they went online. They might not talk to their parents about what was happening to them. This is why they require intensive support and e-safety advice in the three-tiered programme this book proposes.

Hierarchies

Cullingford, in his book on prejudice,[111] explains that when children enter school they become aware of the hierarchies at work and multiple dilemmas face them such as who to attach themselves to and who to avoid. We need to challenge some of these rankings imaginatively. Primary pupils who bully can learn to become remarkable protectors of younger pupils and gain admiration and reward for this positive behaviour rather than for negative aggressive bullying. But do ensure they are still seen as a leader, a role they are reluctant to relinquish. Victims can have some strengths that we need to bring to the fore so that they are admired for something, such as designing an online reporting system for victims of bullying, or playing chess – often challenging the hegemony of football as the only route to hero status.

Anti-bullying practitioners know that the hierarchy among pupils dictates that if a pupil defends someone at the bottom of the heap, they can expect to find themselves there too unless they are very popular or good at sport. That is why it is important to choose peer supporters from all 'ranks' in the hierarchy if you run a peer support scheme.

Isolated young people with poor peer relationships are more likely to go online to seek intimacy and they also may take risks in SNS and chatrooms (see Figure 7.1) or agree to meet someone they have found on the internet. They could be more vulnerable to grooming. This is why it is urgent to disrupt the patterns of behaviour that leave them always vulnerable and isolated.

Livingstone and Brake (2009) point out that 'Specific attention is required for 'at risk' children, given growing indications that those low in self-esteem or lacking satisfying friendships or relations with parents are also those at risk through online social networking communication and further, that those at risk may also be those who then perpetrate harm towards others.'[112]

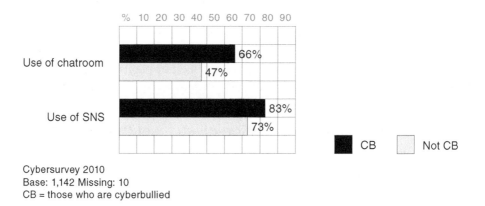

Cybersurvey 2010
Base: 1,142 Missing: 10
CB = those who are cyberbullied

Figure 7.1 Cybervictims' use of chatrooms and SNS

Badly bullied status is not necessarily permanent

While this chapter has been about identifying who might be vulnerable, it helps to remember that pupils' status may not be permanent. For example, there are pupils who move in and out of the vulnerable group, such as those who suffer a family breakdown and are bullied for a while when they are angry and depressed, but later recover and become reintegrated socially. Children may be experiencing significant levels of distress from family problems which should not be underestimated. The evidence from Buchanan et al. (2001)[113] shows that children going through court welfare cases demonstrate considerably more distress at the time of the proceedings than can be expected in the general population (more than twice the abnormal and borderline levels), and that children, especially boys, show even more distress when assessed a year later. The percentage of boys with emotional and behavioural distress had increased to 62 per cent a year later from 52 per cent at the start of proceedings – this level after 12 months is more than three times the level that can be expected in the general population.

The research by Buchanan *et al.* also showed, not surprisingly, that there was a relationship between high levels of stress in the parent and children's distress. When domestic violence was an issue, the children involved had a score more than three times higher than the general population. The scores for children in this study of court welfare cases mirrored levels of distress seen in children in care proceedings. At any one time there are likely to be a few pupils going through some family crisis. They can appear as aggressors or victims. This can lead to disruptive behaviour or withdrawal and depression. They can be both target and perpetrator at such a time.

Those who attend a Pupil Referral Unit (PRU) are four times more likely to be in the badly bullied group. Although most often thought to be difficult and often in the PRU because of their own behaviour, it is easy to overlook the fact that they may have been badly bullied themselves. But the support within the unit may help them change through acknowledging the pain they have experienced.

For those who lack resilience or supportive families and friends, cyberbullying can be life changing. It can come at just the worst time in their lives as they face a sudden crisis. Those who are vulnerable might temporarily include young people who are depressed or anxious, distressed about family problems or anyone recently bereaved. Children move in and out of a vulnerable state, so it is not helpful to label them as such and 'lock' them into being seen this way. But it is helpful to use our awareness of who could be vulnerable to focus on helping them acquire resilience and social acceptance.

Young people not in regular schools can have a very different online life

In so-called blended environments, which offer education and social care, staff are often aware that particular pupils are involved in more risky activities online. In a recent study of young people in a PRU, Stephen Carrick-Davies[114] found that 81 per cent of the staff in this institution said 'Yes' to the question 'In your experience are the young people you work with involved in risky behaviours online or via their mobile?'

These young people have a range of vulnerabilities including anxiety and depression that have implications for their online vulnerability. They can download material or an App independently of any adult through their phone, and roam far and wide online.

Carrick Davies points out that the students in the PRU are marked out by their difficulties. There is an absence of supportive adults, more unsupervised time, fewer directed activities and they are potentially missing e-safety classes. They crave a group identity but are often seen as outsiders. They are very likely to experience abusive environments, anger and violence with greater exposure to drugs and alcohol as well as early sexual experiences and possibly gang culture. This is why I have shown pupils from a PRU as being in the vulnerable group that requires intensive e-safety education and support. It is also likely that the types of message and incidents they encounter are more aggressive and sexualised than those described by the majority of young people. 'Fraping' leads to much status changing on Facebook, and password pinching is common, as has been reported in care home settings.

Shifts mean constant changes of staff reinforcing the reluctance of young people to form trusting relationships – this is also true in care home settings. Pupils in a PRU may have had many moves, and been in many schools. They are in some ways even more dependent upon their social media and mobiles, yet the staff in these settings may lack constant training, and some do not even use social media. Only 34 per cent of staff said they were 'very well' equipped to deal with cases of online or mobile abuse while 54 per cent said they were 'somewhat' equipped and 12 per cent felt they were 'not' equipped.[115]

Remote control

In the world of gangs, where the group can replace family, phones are sometimes given as an initial gift and later used for control and abuse. Former girlfriends have been monitored via their status on Facebook, and stalking or other controlling behaviour is then possible. The Carnegie Mellon study points out that 80 per cent of Facebook users have actually never read the Privacy Policy. Forty per cent are aware of the Privacy Policy on sharing with third parties. Most choose not to change their settings. This leaves them open to people watching what they do via Facebook.[116]

Bully/victims – the most vulnerable of all?

Bully/victims are young people who are at the same time both target and aggressor. These young people are harder to help and their complex behaviour may require professional help.[117] They may also be at greater risk of psychiatric disturbances and even criminal activity. Two in five of them (44%) report problem behaviours.[118] Mishna *et al.* suggest there are more bully victims in cyberbullying than in traditional bullying, and that they are more likely to be girls.[119]

Bully/victims may find it difficult to control their emotions, reacting angrily when targeted and in this way providing the bullying child with the reaction they seek. This can escalate the incident. They frequently retaliate and cyberspace offers the ideal environment in which to do so. It is here that they may be able to fight back on their terms; when face to face, they are too weak, isolated or powerless.

Bully/victims show social and emotional problems that are frequently found in victims of bullying, such as anxiety, depression, peer rejection and a lack of close friendships. They can also display the cognitive and behavioural difficulties often apparent in children who bully, including a greater acceptance of rule-breaking behaviour, hyperactivity and a tendency towards reactive aggression.[120]

Ybarra and Mitchell use the description 'aggressor/targets' to describe online bully/victims and to differentiate them from traditional bullying bully/victims. They found that these young people were intense internet users who are say they are expert or almost expert in navigating cyberspace. Over half were also the target of offline bullying (56%). They found young people exclusively involved in harassment online and some for whom it was an 'extension of the schoolyard with victimisation continuing after the bell and into the night.' Cyberbullying offered a means to 'assert dominance over others as a compensation for being bullied in person.' Bully/victims were online for lengthy intense periods, often six days a week.[121]

Furthermore, bully/victims were found to be highly strung. A British study measured the arousal levels of 13- and 14-year-old students. Bully/victims were found to have higher levels of arousal than all other groups, including passive victims. Over 23 per cent of bully/victims had arousal levels in the clinically high range.[122]

Although there is some debate about findings that bully/victims may be dangerous, it is worth noting that in the USA, bully/victims have been found more likely than pure bullies (those who bully but are not victims as well) to carry weapons.[123] They may also be more likely to believe that 'it's OK to bring a gun to school.'[124] And, according to one study of US middle school students, bully/victims were 'more likely to commit major acts of violence against other kids.'[125]

AREAS OF CONCERN

Sites that draw you in and 'mess with your mind' are addictive and powerfully seductive. They can be visited as part of a group identity encouraging bulimia, extreme slimming or even suicide. Depressed or disturbed young people tend to turn to these sites and are tragically swayed by them.

SURVEYING THE PUPILS IN AN INCLUSIVE WAY

- Surveying pupils regularly should help identify those worst affected.
- Adapt surveys to be inclusive and find ways to support those with special educational needs so that their voice can be heard.
- Surveys can be illustrated with simple graphics – the UK charity Mencap offers a guide to using graphics for those with learning difficulties, called *Am I Making Myself Clear?* It can be found on their website and is helpful in designing uncluttered communications for those with learning difficulties (see Chapter 11).
- The NSPCC provides an image vocabulary for children, 'How It Is', that covers feelings, rights and safety, among other subjects (see Chapter 11).
- A voice recording of the questions can be made to help those with poor sight or reading difficulties.
- Cards with the possible answers can be made, such as green for 'yes' and red for 'no'.
- Peer supporters can be trained to help administer the survey, providing help to anyone who needs it.
- Inventive use of computer software can enable disabled children to participate using touch screens and voiced questions.

SURVEYS AVAILABLE

- Your school or local area may have a standard survey that is regularly used.
- Free surveys for primary and secondary schools and further education colleges are offered to members of the Bullying Intervention Group (BIG) (see Appendix 7).
- The Cybersurvey, an online tool to measure cyberbullying and e-safety, is carried out by Youthworks Consulting.[126]
- Workshops can be used to explore the meaning of the findings and to ask what lies behind the figures and what pupils think should be done (see Chapter 9 for an example of this).

Are schools being proactive as the Equality Act 2010 requires?

An analysis of school anti-bullying policies collected in 2008 found considerable variation in adequacy and coverage. Prejudice, or identity-based bullying, was not well covered. Only 15 per cent of policies specifically referred to bullying due to disability, and as few as 7 per cent accommodated bullying based on religious beliefs. Only 25 per cent of the sample schools' policies mentioned homophobic bullying, while specific mention of racial bullying or harassment was found in 64 per cent of policies and sexual bullying in 48 per cent.[127] After this analysis was undertaken, the government guidance *Safe to Learn* was widely embedded, and schools began to ensure they addressed all these types of bullying. But since 2010, when this guidance was scrapped, anecdotal evidence suggests this is falling away. Check your school policy and approach – does it comply with the law?

The vulnerable pupils discussed here form a small percentage of the school population, but they do require intensive levels of support. Proactive steps may reduce the complexity of their needs. That is why a three-tiered programme is suggested: universal, targeted and intensive. If a student is identified early and supported at the 'targeted' level, she may never require the intensive support. Students with special needs should be provided with intensive support and adapted e-safety education.

Chapter

8

E-SAFETY
Presenting a New Three-Tier Strategy

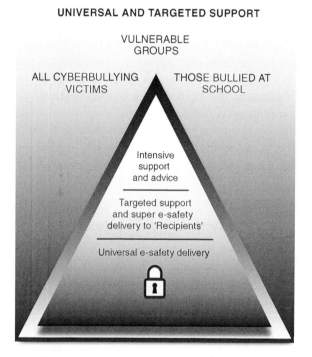

Figure 8.1 Three-tier e-safety strategy

USE A THREE-TIER E-SAFETY STRATEGY

An e-safety education and support programme could be thought of as a three-tier plan:

- a universal delivery of e-safety messages: this will suit the majority
- a more targeted delivery is needed for people who are receiving abusive or aggressive nasty messages via mobiles or online
- an intensive programme of support and education is recommended for the vulnerable groups, cyberbullying victims and those persistently bullied in school.

(Chapter 7 describes who is more likely to be vulnerable.)

This chapter argues that e-safety advice needs to enter a new phase in which a three-tiered, more finely tuned approach is developed. This would provide universal delivery, alongside targeted and intensive levels for certain young people who need more help. In the first phase of e-safety delivery, the goal was to develop e-safety tools, train e-safety champions and deliver e-safety messages to the school population. Now that delivery is fairly widespread, and almost all schools are doing some work on e-safety, it seems a good time for reflection. The Cybersurvey provides a springboard by looking at what pupils think of current e-safety advice and asks if they actually follow it. It tries to identify some of those who do not do so.

If this is to be a moment to stop and think where we are with e-safety education, the findings from the Cybersurvey suggest we should also question whether the messages themselves are the right ones, how the delivery approach could/should improve and whether e-safety education should be properly evaluated.

According to the Cybersurvey 2011, delivery of e-safety advice in English schools has rapidly expanded and is now reaching nearly all children and young people. It was less wide reaching when current 16-year-olds were younger. By their mid-teens, 94 per cent of today's teenagers have learned about e-safety in school, up from 87 per cent of 14- to 15-year-olds in the Cybersurvey 2009.

We can also see the improved reach of e-safety messages among younger pupils. More than twice as many of the 16+ age group say they were not taught about e-safety at school – 11 per cent compared to only 4 per cent of the ten- to eleven-year-old cohort.

Parents giving advice

When current 16-year-olds (in 2011) were younger, parents were less confident about teaching their children to be safe online – for example, fewer than half of the 16+ age group in the Cybersurvey 2011 say they learned about e-safety from their parents, whereas two-thirds of today's ten-year-olds have already been taught about e-safety by their parents.

When today's 16-year-olds were 12, parents often felt uncertain about some of their children's online activities and did not feel capable of giving e-safety advice. Some still feel this way. This is borne out by a poll of parents of 8- to 14-year-olds for the Anti-Bullying Alliance[128] in 2009, which showed that 89 per cent of parents believed cyberbullying was just as serious as other types of bullying, but the majority (54%) had not talked to their child about how they could protect themselves, or deal with cyberbullying, and 45 per cent didn't know about the 'report abuse' option on SNS.

Parents were understandably slower to address cyberbullying and e-safety in rural areas that were slow to get high speed broadband or WiFi coverage. Despite this hesitancy, parents are second only to schools as the most common sources of e-safety advice for young people, and schools have a role to play in supporting them to help their children.

Other sources of e-safety advice

Children and young people did not rely solely on school or parents, although these were overwhelmingly the main sources of advice for them. They learned from siblings, grandparents and other members of the family, friends, online sources of information, the media, government information, organisations for children such as ChildLine and the Guides, and computer clubs.

FOLLOWING E-SAFETY ADVICE

By 2011, delivery of e-safety information was successfully reaching almost all pupils according to the Cybersurvey, and young people generally said they received this information at the right age. Of those who were taught about e-safety, 88 per cent also said it was 'quite good' or 'very good'. But after all these positive results, it was disappointing to see that only 43 per cent always followed the safety advice they had learned, with some barely ever following it. A large group (49%) said vaguely that they 'sometimes' followed it – this is rather like saying you sometimes follow the rules of the road.

Safety consists of a coherent, consistent approach rather than an occasional ad hoc effort. On the cyberhighway 'mistakes' could have major repercussions, such as the misuse of a parent's credit card, or importing a virus into a computer. A rare but serious incident could have repercussions for years.

Those who don't follow the safety guidelines are more likely to receive unpleasant messages. We cannot say this is causal – it may be that they don't follow the guidelines for many reasons, or they are targeted in ways unconnected with their online safety practice. They may simply be risk-takers. But there is a clear relationship between being a recipient of any kind of nasty or abusive messages and not following the e-safety advice.

People who have never received these messages (non-recipients) are more likely to follow the e-safety guidelines. By contrast, recipients of nasty or aggressive messages are twice as likely to say they do not follow the guidelines: 'never' or 'not really' (16%). Fewer recipients say they 'always' follow the guidelines: 37 versus 51 per cent.

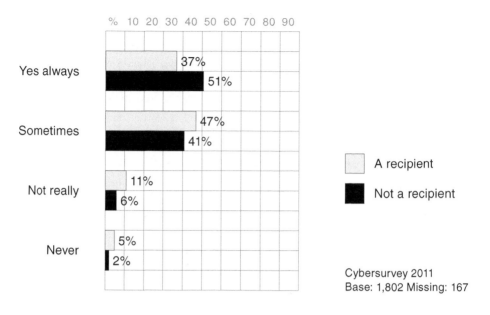

Figure 8.2 Recipients of nasty messages: do they follow safety guidelines?

Larking about with friends and doing risky things

Young people often use computers at friends' homes or in internet cafes or other public spaces, and may be swayed by peer pressure to behave in certain ways, especially when making rude comments or looking at 'sexy' images.

Ybarra *et al.* found that the role of friends in online behaviour was important. More than 40 per cent of online risky behaviour reported in the USA second Youth Internet Safety Survey (YISS-2) happened while young people were online with friends. Around two in five young people were with others when they harassed others online. The study's authors suggest that we should help young people to find strategies to stay safe when having fun with friends.[129]

Ybarra *et al.* also found that it was the global pattern of behaviour online rather than a single specific behaviour that increased risk. For young people engaged in four of the risky online behaviours selected for study, the odds were high – they were 11 times more likely to experience interpersonal victimisation than those not involved in any.

The researchers argue that we should look at the whole picture of all the risky online activities a young person engages in, with a cut-off point at four, for a useful indicator of the risks they might face. 'Online behaviours seem related to online interpersonal victimisation over and above personal psychosocial and behavioural problems,' they point out. They do not underestimate the influence of offline problems on a child, such as physical or sexual abuse, high levels of conflict among parents or even offline bullying, which are associated with higher odds for interpersonal victimisation. Some activities engaged in by young people are especially dangerous and so rare that they should act as markers for intervention (talking to unknown people about sex online is one of these, engaged in by only 5% of young people).

Are the messages the right ones?

Ybarra *et al.* also point out that some behaviour has become normative and our e-safety messages should be adapted accordingly. For example, in the YISS, more than one in two young people had posted personal information online. Sharing personal information was not found to be related to online interpersonal victimisation when other risky behaviour was considered.

The pattern of life led by teenagers on Facebook is a public one of self-advertisement. This makes the old advice of 'Do not post or share your personal details at all' seem out of touch with what young people actually do. If we give messages that teenagers ignore in order to conduct their social and personal lives, will they be more likely to ignore other messages we provide? Sharing personal information is essential if we are shopping online, interacting with people for advice and support, booking a cinema or airline ticket or downloading music. Indeed, when registering on an SNS we are asked to give these details including a date of birth, which many people falsify. It is impossible to operate online without sharing personal information, but it may be better to decide what you are willing to share and protect the other information fiercely.

In addition, life for young people online is all about meeting people, and they blithely ignore our advice not to talk to strangers they have only met online. Many children do not regard these people as strangers. Ybarra *et al.* suggest that the advice 'Don't talk to strangers online' could be modified to a harm reduction approach like this:

> I know many people your age are meeting people online. You probably know how easy it is to hide your identity. Be careful and know that you can discontinue a relationship any time by changing your login name or blocking someone.[130]

I am reminded of the ban on scissors. You may be wondering what scissors could possibly have to do with e-safety. Let's call it the scissors principle. Years ago I wrote creativity books for parents of young children. I learned that it is the mothers who banned their toddlers from using a pair of scissors who later found that their fascinated child grabbed hold of a shining silver pair at someone else's house and cut himself badly because he had not first learned how to cut safely with a child's plastic pair at home with his mother. The stranger ban is like this. We all meet people online in forums, through professional networks and on sites with people of similar interests. Imagine if we were banned from interacting with anyone online – we would surely break the ban. Children need to know the safe ways of interacting with other people online gradually and at the appropriate age, just as they need to learn safe cutting with plastic scissors before they go on to use sharp scissors. The SMART rules that work so well at age 10 can be adapted for anyone over 12 to suit their age and stage. But they are unlikely to work with a 14-year-old unless considerably adapted.

Young people may need to seek help online from a trusted service or charity. This is generally thought of as safe, and lists of approved sites with help services should be provided to young people, although this might, of course, involve talking to a 'stranger' online, another situation in which e-safety messages could appear to conflict with sensible behaviour. Children may seek advice about admissions to a course of study or a particular health problem – while they should be encouraged to use appropriate sites, they do need to be warned about sites that advocate suicide or promote anorexia, for example. The skill we should be aiming for is the ability to distinguish which sites are safe.

Age and adherence to e-safety advice

There were marked differences among the age groups in the Cybersurvey: those aged 14–15 were least likely to follow the advice and also the most likely to experience cyberbullying. They were adventurous, romantic and daring, spending time on Facebook and mobiles, conducting their entire social lives or an entire relationship through these media. Some reported starting a relationship online, conducting it and eventually being dumped online or by text message. Jealous gossip and rumour, ratings and sexual photos all formed part of the fabric of their lives, and they were less shocked by these images than adults. They also tended to be of an age when they thought adults knew less about their online world than they did and they commonly talked about wanting to find out for themselves, or take responsibility for their own safety. This is the age when sexual bullying is most prevalent, along with high rates of all types of cyberabuse, so it is time to re-think our advice to this age group.

Only 26 per cent of those aged 14–15 'always' followed the e-safety guidelines they had been taught, a dramatic drop from 54 per cent at age 10–11. There is a peak at this age among those who say they didn't really follow the guidelines while those who never did so remain a small minority. Between the ages of 12 and 14, young people tended to move to 'only sometimes' following the guidelines. They argued that what they had been taught was not always relevant to their activities online. They also talked about feeling immune as young people have always done in relation to risk: 'I don't believe anything will ever happen to me and it hasn't.' Or they explained that many people ignored advice 'Because they think it's no point, they think no one would bother to do that to them.' In part this is true because more than half the young respondents did not report any unpleasant experiences either online or via their mobiles. This suggests that scare tactics will not work in e-safety delivery to this age group.

But not everyone is so resilient, and some young people are cruelly targeted. Vulnerable young people are more likely to feel that the e-safety information was not given at the right time, but either too late or too early. Compared to their peers who were not bullied, cyberbullied respondents are twice as likely to say they got advice too late, and homophobically bullied respondents almost twice as likely to say it was too early.

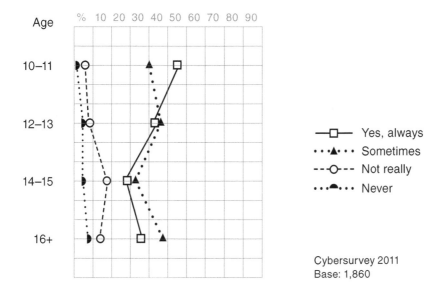

Figure 8.3 Those who have been taught about e-safety, by age: do you follow safety guidelines?

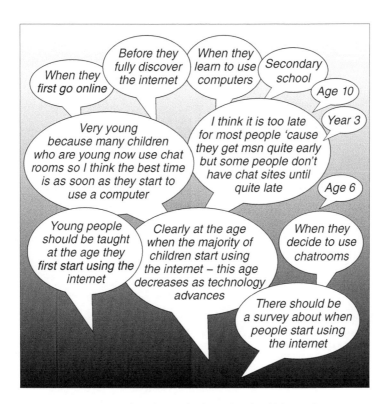

Figure 8.4 When do you think e-safety should be taught?

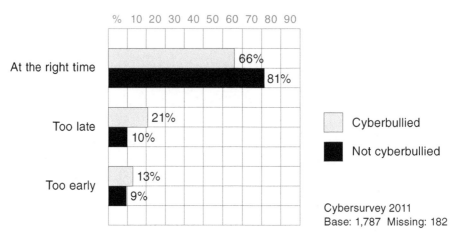

Figure 8.5 *Those who were cyberbullied compared to peers: were you taught about e-safety at the right time?*

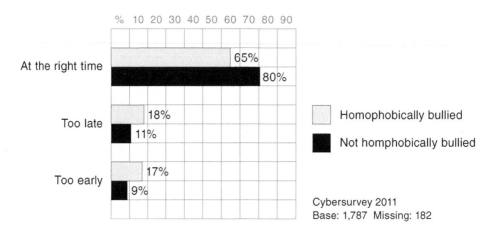

Figure 8.6 *Those who were cyberbullied homophobically: were you taught about e-safety at the right time?*

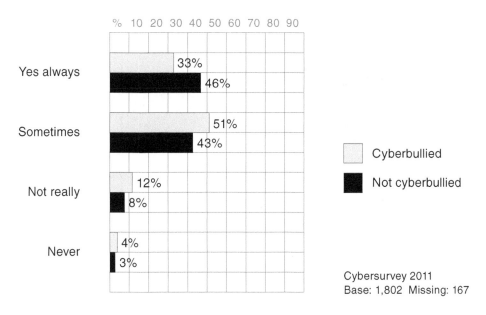

Figure 8.7 Cyberbullied respondents: do you follow the guidelines?

Pupils who reported being cyberbullied and those who experienced cyberhomophobia didn't follow e-safety advice as thoroughly as those who were not bullied. This, coupled with their greater use of chatrooms and SNS pages, and their ability to get round blocks, could be putting them at greater risk of being cyberbullied.

Children and young people with special needs or disabilities are another group who did not benefit enough from e-safety advice. They were twice as likely to say they didn't follow the guidelines (21 versus 11%), and as many as 18 per cent said they 'often' tried to get round blocks, in contrast to 11 per cent of their peers. This rebellious activity could represent people with emotional and behavioural difficulties who are assessed as having special needs.

On the other hand, perhaps the guidelines did not seem relevant or clear to some of the vulnerable young people? Some expressed a fatalistic resignation that nothing could be done to protect them from the abuse they suffered. E-safety lessons therefore need to tackle interpersonal abuse, which is a far more common experience for young people than stranger danger.

Clearly there are groups of young people for whom universal e-safety advice is not enough. They need targeted support and special resources to explain it. Interestingly, 22 per cent of pupils with special educational needs received e-safety advice from their siblings, who might be a useful conduit through which to deliver specially targeted support to children with difficulties.

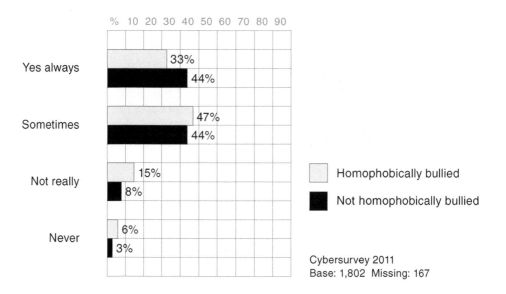

Figure 8.8 Homophobically cyberbullied respondents: do you follow the guidelines?

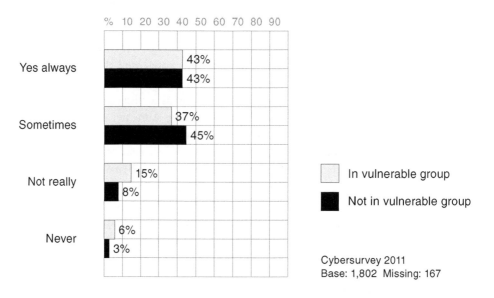

Figure 8.9 Those with special needs: do you follow the guidelines?

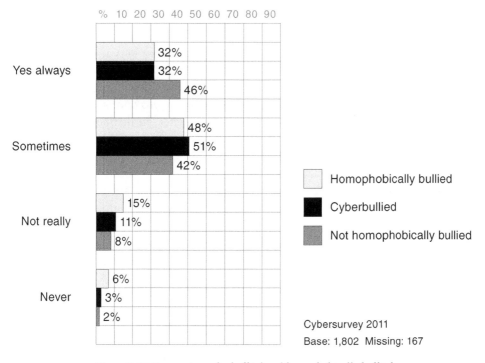

Figure 8.10 Comparing cyberbullied and homophobically bullied respondents: do you follow the guidelines?

WHAT NEEDS TO HAPPEN?

To reiterate: this book proposes that e-safety education needs to enter a new phase. While universal delivery of e-safety advice has almost been achieved, the next challenge is to convert this into behaviour change. To do this, e-safety messages must be more relevant and age-appropriate to young people. They must also reach vulnerable children and young people in a more targeted proactive way before problems occur.

The three-tier approach would provide a universal tier 1 delivery to reach most students. Tier 2 is a targeted proactive approach, supporting certain vulnerable people before any problems occur. Tier 3 would provide intensive e-safety education alongside support for the most needy and those who have already had a bad experience online.

Resources are needed for both age and stage. For example, if they have learning difficulties, teenagers will not want childish materials produced for younger children, but simplified messages suitable to their age and stage of development, so universal delivery is not enough. In some respects the advice given has neither kept pace with changing technology, such as smartphones, nor with changing youth culture, such as the migration to Facebook. Many schools do not allow a teacher to log on to Facebook on the school system in order to demonstrate how to set privacy settings. And teachers regularly complain that the filtering system in their schools is set too high, preventing them from teaching e-safety effectively.

In other respects, some sessions ignore some of the principles of good teaching when delivered in one intense visit by an outside trainer – many students simply cannot absorb it all in one session. They need to build on skills learned and progress in a staged sequence with recaps and checks to see that they have understood before moving on.

E-safety should be embedded across the curriculum as an integral part of the school programme – if it is all concentrated in single sessions once a term, it is all too easy for those who are often absent to miss out altogether. Furthermore, resources are needed that use different communication methods so that those who have difficulty with reading, for example, are offered other communication styles, social stories, graphics and step-by-step practical tools.

Some are vulnerable at certain times, and can also move in and out of a situation. They may therefore need a targeted or even intensive level of support and advice at certain times. (See Chapter 7 for a description of who is vulnerable and how to identify them.)

Because those who are bullied within school are also more likely to be bullied out of school, the first line of action should be to target them and ensure they get good e-safety and cyberbullying prevention advice. Other students will be vulnerable for a range of reasons, but anyone who is already a known victim of cyberbullying or cyberhomophobia should receive intensive support because, for example, they are more likely to visit suicide websites. Also in need of intensive support are students with personal or family problems who are isolated or depressed, and newcomers who are in the care system may urgently require e-safety advice and emotional support. Although the numbers requiring intensive support will be small, the need is great.

ASK THE PUPILS

The results of the Cybersurvey were given to pupils to discuss in workshops. Illuminating discussions followed. Young people debated how they would like to receive information on e-safety and the reasons why they thought young people were not following the safety rules.

To add another layer of understanding, video footage of Year 7 pupils was viewed. In this informal set of interviews made by their e-safety educator, pupils explained what they understood from a lesson they had just emerged from, and what they planned to do next. It was apparent that a large number of the pupils in this class had not fully understood the implications of the well-known film clip they had viewed, and few of them said they intended to go and check the privacy settings on their Facebook page or clean their 'friends' list as a result. Although pupils enjoyed the lesson, some were confused about what steps to take. This experience set me thinking about how the information might be absorbed better.

Evaluations are a vital component of an education module that is as new and untested as e-safety, yet there appear to be very few evaluations being used. It is very different evaluating whether or not the pupils enjoyed the lesson, or thought the quality of the film was good, rather than how much of the intended information they understood, but this is badly needed if these lessons are to be more effective. If too much information has to be delivered in one lesson on too many different aspects of the internet and mobile phones, people cannot take it all in.

Sometimes the information is given in assembly. This then needs to be followed up with small units in class settings in age-appropriate ways.

VIEWS OF YEAR 9 AND 10 PUPILS ON HOW E-SAFETY SHOULD BE DELIVERED AND BY WHOM[131]

- Chunked into short parts. Then you're more engaged and take more information in.
- Chunked sessions with friends talking to a young adult who has Facebook/Twitter. Fun but shocking.
- Chunked into short bits because it's a lot to take in. Modernising it.
- Short bits on the computer, experience.
- Make a quiz.
- By different charities.
- Trusted websites.
- By young adults.

New delivery

There was a strong theme of autonomy in the open responses, suggesting that young people like to be independent online and to find things out for themselves. The pupils were asked 'If you have been taught about e-safety, who taught you?' Some examples are shown in Figure 8.3.

The aim should be to increase autonomy and self-efficacy by signposting pupils to sources of help, providing exploratory time or setting homework in which they can find out and report back to a group. School websites or intranets should be used to set out sources of help that are regularly updated. A web tool could be created for reporting cyberbullying to peer supporters or a text message service for use by pupils and staff. A demonstration could be devised for younger pupils or a video clip that illustrates how to set privacy settings, for example.

Figure 8.11 Other sources of e-safety

PUPILS' VIEWS ON E-SAFETY LESSONS[132]

What should be included that is currently left out?

- Facebook – only add friends you know, learn how to set privacy settings, use trusted websites.
- Include more information about what happens when you actually meet one person, or the dangers of people receiving information that you post on Facebook or Twitter if they are your friend.
- Use more modern ways such as Facebook/Twitter, how it can affect people, what could happen to you if you did it, what exactly is cyberbullying.
- What report buttons look like and where to find them.
- What to do if you want to block someone.

PARENTS

There is convincing evidence that parents are not always aware of cyberbullying or the nasty experiences their children encounter. A study conducted by i-SAFE America (2005–06) found that parents overestimate how much they know of their child's online life. On the one hand, 93 per cent of parents thought they had a good idea of what their child was doing online, while on the other hand, 41 per cent of young people in grades 5–12 said they did not share with parents what they did or where they went online.[133]

Cyberbullying can be sexually explicit or hurtful to the family if racist, for example. These are the very situations that young people feel they cannot share with parents.

They might want to protect parents from ugly slurs, and may be reluctant for parents to see the content of such messages. If it is part of a personal relationship, they may feel it is private or revealing and could be humiliating. Parents may have warned them about this friendship already, making it harder to admit that their parents have turned out to be right. If the bullying is homophobic, new tensions may arise which a young person may not be ready to address with parents. In some cultures girls are not allowed to have relationships with boys for fear of shaming their family. If the cyberbullying suggests such a relationship has been going on, the girl may feel she cannot seek help from her family and may stay silent. In all such cases young people need other sources of help that will be non-judgemental, but to which they can safely turn, and teachers need to be skilled in sensitive responses when young people come forward.

The Cybersurvey showed that parents were more likely to talk to their daughters about e-safety than their sons, while those in rural areas were slower to begin talking to children aged 10–11 about e-safety than parents in urban areas. It might be useful to remind parents that they need to be as effective with both daughters and sons, and they need to start talking about e-safety earlier with their young children.

What do parents need from teachers?

Parents need advice that includes the knowledge that teenagers have always had some areas of their life they keep private – and this is even more likely online. Nevertheless, parents can and should be a major source of emotional support for their children and should provide calm practical advice without waiting for an incident to be disclosed. But they should not snoop!

An e-safety educator explained recently that she checks on her own child's SNS page and reads the child's personal diaries so knows what is going on. Of course it would be easy for her child to open another SNS page with a different name for her private talks and personal relationships away from her mother's prying eyes. This could happen the first time she had a boyfriend. But could this snooping drive a teenager to secrecy or deviousness? What does it teach her about taking responsibility for her own safety and behaviour? The same educator said she had the family computer in the living room and she often passed by when her child was online so she felt she had nothing to worry about. Although this advice on keeping computers in the living room works well for young children, it has been superseded by the arrival of smartphones. Besides, a child can go online at a friend's house. It is all too easy for parents to sit back and feel that they have it all under control. They should be encouraged to see their role differently. While it is a good idea to have filters and privacy settings in place, it is not only about trying to keep control; rather it is more about an ongoing dialogue and partnership with a child that matures as the child gets older, helping the child to learn safe behaviours and questioning what is read, searching appropriately and getting help if needed.

Parents need to know about report abuse buttons and how to get material removed from a website or how to block a sender. They have to become familiar with the websites and tools used by their children. Privacy settings on Facebook, for example, change frequently, and it is helpful to know about these changes so that they can help their child. Update parents, keep them informed with the latest advice and practical steps they can take, and signpost them to where they can get help. Consider an e-safety centre on the school's website that parents and pupils can access anytime. This could be updated regularly or a parents' news update sent out by email to parents.

Schools report that getting parents to come to e-safety sessions is difficult. Some approach this with more success by including a session on e-safety within another event when the parents are already in school. In one example, primary school parents were offered sessions on a bank of computers led by trained secondary pupils who taught these parents some basics about the most common online activities of their 11-year-olds. Young people will take more seriously any advice given by a well-informed parent, and will be relieved in most cases to find that they can rely on their parent for help if needed.

The work of EU Kids Online found that it was a myth that all young people knew more than the adults around them. On average, one-third of 9- to 16-year-olds (36%) said that the statement, 'I know more about the internet than my parents,' was 'very true' of them, one-third (31%) said it is 'a bit true' and one-third (33%) said it is 'not true' of them. Younger children clearly looked to their parents for advice and support: 'It seems that, although sizeable numbers of 9–10-year-olds use the internet, they have little confidence that they know much about it compared with their parents – 63% say this statement is "not true" for them.'[134]

CAN E-SAFETY BE LEFT TO THE INFORMATION TECHNOLOGY DEPARTMENT?

Dealing with cyberbullying is the responsibility of every member of a school community – just as face-to-face bullying needs buy-in from every section of the school community, the school ethos and the management of behaviour online cannot be left to one department. It is likely that the information and communications technology (ICT) department will administer the AUP, but all sections of the school should be actively involved in support.

Pupils will be using the internet and mobile phones for every aspect of their lives, including learning, so the school's policy will only be effective if every staff member and every pupil work together to make it a reality.

Duty of care requires that schools take care their children and staff. It is not likely that ICT staff will be aware of all pupils' abilities – class tutors and subject teachers know who is less likely to understand the universal advice or who may be especially vulnerable because they are often bullied in school, or indeed those who have other problems and relationship difficulties. These pupils need more than the universal delivery in a big group. Teachers may need to make a small club or other group that is fun to attend and invite such pupils to explore e-safety there with support. Alternatively, a learning support worker or teaching assistant may point out that a certain pupil is having difficulty understanding what they should do. If some students have communications difficulties, there are a number of resources developed to help them communicate (see Chapter 11).

WHAT DOES A GOOD SCHOOL OR COLLEGE APPROACH LOOK LIKE?

Schools rely on technology for blocking and filtering, monitoring and recording. But although these are useful sophisticated tools and limit the risks pupils will encounter, there is a growing awareness that technology is not the answer on its own. Indeed, too much reliance on technology may appear to lessen the need for face-to-face education.

There is also a growing band of young people who can get round blocks or reset filters. In 2011, one-quarter of cyberbullied young people said they sometimes got round blocks (25%), and 18 per cent of them often did so, but others did not have to work it out because they simply knew someone, a friend or sibling, who could do this.

There is considerable debate about the effectiveness of blocking access to unsuitable websites – the debate appears to be polarised as either pro-blocks or pro-e-safety education. However, as we shall see below, these are not necessarily the key concerns. The challenge is rather how to motivate young people to act on what they have learned, and to behave safely and responsibly online in what becomes a normative manner.

In the Cybersurvey 2009, 57 per cent of young people said they never tried to get round blocks set up by adults to stop them using certain websites. Nevertheless, 11 per cent 'often' did so and more than one quarter said they 'sometimes' tried this. This means that 36 per cent tried to get round blocks at least occasionally, and 6 per cent had either a friend or sibling who could get past them.

It seems that those who are determined to get past blocks appear to work on trying to do so for themselves, or find out from an older friend or sibling how to do this. But has the situation changed in the two years of the Cybersurvey? In 2011 the number of young people who said they never tried to get round blocks rose to 62 per cent, but by age 14–15 as many as 42 per cent sometimes or often got round blocks. So at best it is a mixed picture.

DIGITAL CITIZENS

Instead of a banning or control approach, the goal of e-safety education should be a blueprint for digital citizenship. This concept includes not only how to protect one's own safety, but how to behave towards others online. This responsible behaviour addresses issues such as plagiarism, illegal downloads and hate crime. It is about teaching critical thinking and how to make ethical choices about what we do or create online. The impact of our behaviour on others is a social literacy concern rather than a digital literacy one. There is so much more to embed than digital skills alone.

Rather than a top-down prescriptive design, in which adults deliver a set of rules to young people, the concept of a digital citizen incorporates the idea of the informed individual taking responsibility. I like to think of it in terms of empowering the young person to become a fully-fledged socially-aware digital citizen. It is our job to deliver the tools and to debate the ethical questions with them.

The principles of youth participation are badly needed in e-safety education, where a more top-down approach has been widely used until now. Holmer Lake Primary school in Telford in the UK developed a programme with children between the ages of seven and ten called 'I stay safe' that is an example of young children being enabled to take responsibility and to inspire others. After careful planning and discussion of the issue, they made radio jingles as part of a comprehensive cyberbullying and e-safety campaign. These were broadcast by a local radio station. They also created little folded paper 'anti-bullying chatterboxes' for Key Stages 1 and 2 that were circulated with lesson plans to all primary schools in Telford and Wrekin, reaching around 11,800 pupils with the support of the Local Safeguarding Children Board.

The starting point should not be a focus on adult fears about risks on the internet, which are driven by media scares and result in what David Finkelhor has described as 'Juvenoia', a paranoia about young people.[135] It might be more productive to begin with a vision of what young people need as e-competent, socially-aware citizens.

The model of empowerment

Young people will be:

- enthusiastic and aware of the opportunities offered by ICT
- confident users of technology
- able to show they have the skills and knowledge needed to use technology safely
- able to distinguish what search results to consider/avoid.

Skills, responsibility and knowledge

Young people will:

- be aware that some skills increase exposure to risk
- learn and share practical skills to stay safe
- communicate safely
- conduct themselves as responsible, ethical, digital citizens
- operate in a caring climate
- recognise that you cannot trust everything you read online.

Navigating risky situations

Young people will understand that they should:

- as a recipient, keep evidence, know how to block, 'unfriend' or report abuse
- as a participant, not join in abuse, pass on chain letters or humiliating photos, or post self-generated images that are inappropriate (drunken state, nudity, sexual images)
- know how to report abuse or request removal of offensive material
- be aware of helplines and services
- understand the terms of service on websites they regularly use
- be alert to fake gaming sites.

Understanding advertising

Young people should be able to:

- spot spam
- avoid risky offers
- deal with junk
- protect privacy (aware of tracking and cookies, identity theft, etc.).

Sharing safely

Young people should ask themselves:

- Should it be private?
- Does the material (copyright) belong to someone else? (Plagiarism)
- Should I have paid for this? (Illegal downloads, software, music)
- Privacy settings – when did I last check them?
- Are these my real friends? (Friends list on SNS).

Shopping safely

Young people should check they are:

- using reputable sites (a URL, not a link in an email)
- comparing prices and services
- taking care of credit card details (often their parents'), PayPal or bank verification

- retaining reference order numbers
- enjoying entertainment but are aware of games ratings, film classifications
- using an email address dedicated to shopping only, thus protecting their actual email.

SCHOOLS CANNOT DO THIS ALONE

The Family Online Safety Institute (FOSI)[136] has designed a framework that articulates the role of various stakeholders in delivering e-safety. They identify six layers of society that must act to keep children and teenagers safe online. These include government, fully resourced law enforcement, a self-regulating internet industry, tech-savvy teachers and empowered parents, as well as resilient young people who make good choices. While many of these areas show tremendous progress, in the UK initiatives are not coherent or collaborative enough across the whole sector. In the jargon of public services, this is usually described as 'joined up'. For example, some major e-safety initiatives or campaigns are launched at one level without information and training on the ground for the very people who are delivering anti-bullying programmes, or those who deliver programmes to reduce violence against women and girls. These natural allies need to be fully engaged. Teachers facing day-to-day problems often say they do not know what to do when faced with a case, showing that they need ongoing professional development training. Guidance for schools on dealing with cyberbullying was withdrawn in 2010, however, upon a change of government in the UK.

Further stakeholders can be found in the voluntary sector. There are third sector partners who specialise in specific forms of bullying such as cyberbullying, racist or homophobic bullying, and they can help with specialist resources, training and informative websites. Other charities work on behalf of people with learning difficulties or disabilities. They have developed communication tools and specialist knowledge that should not be overlooked (see Appendix 3).

What are the risks young people might meet on the highway?

The original categories of risk – contact, content and conduct – are still entirely applicable, and e-safety educators should continue to ensure they cover these. But each pupil has a different pattern of internet use, and new technology is changing how they access the internet. With the intention of giving young people a participating role en route to ownership, the lesson plan 'What do I do online?' was developed (see Chapter 11). This was based on a youth participation model, to trigger them to identify the risks they face and to find out how to protect themselves from harm in these situations.

Content	Inappropriate or upsetting content	Contact	Child in care contacting relatives without support
	Be influenced by suicide, self harm or anorexia sites		Grooming or enticement to act in a sexual way
Conduct	Anti-social or hurtful behaviour Cyberbullying, rumour spreading Incitement to hatred		Child goes to meet someone met only online Coercion
	Self generated inappropriate images posted online or used in webcams	Security	Viruses, spyware and spam
Commerce	Adware and pressure selling, Junk Mail		Identity theft
	Creating Debt on parents' credit cards		GPS location makes position known

Figure 8.12 Conduct, contact, commerce: common risks for children in cyberspace

Train teachers

Sadly too few graduates of computer-related degrees go into teaching. In 2011 *The Guardian* newspaper's Digital Literacy campaign highlighted that of 28,000 teachers who qualified in 2010, just three had a computer-related degree.[137] Such graduates tend to go into other fields. The Postgraduate Certificate in Education (PGCE) in IT has only been around for a decade and has not carried high status. It is not good enough to focus on teaching a few skills such as word processing and spreadsheets alongside a list of rules to avoid risk when pupils already often know more than their teacher. For e-safety to be credible, teachers either have to know more than their pupils or they have to explore and find out together in a scientific spirit of enquiry. Too many teachers instead make self-deprecating remarks such as 'I'm not really of the computer generation' or 'I'm not technical' when starting a session with students. It is hard to have faith in what you are told when the person delivering it is unsure.

IDEAS FOR BEING PROACTIVE, EDUCATING ADULTS AND YOUNG PEOPLE ALIKE

- Set up clubs. School computer clubs can be a creative core for the work of the school. They can also be a listening ear about problems pupils are facing online.
- Run a weekly quiz or question of the week.
- Use internal television screens to broadcast e-safety information.
- Put material in staffrooms, foyers, corridors and classrooms.
- Use innovative software to encourage pupils to create Apps or programmes for the school reporting system or artwork for campaigns or screensavers. See 'Apps for good' (http://appsforgood.org/about). (Software such as 'Scratch' allows pupils to create games or animations that can be used as advertising campaigns for e-safety and anti-bullying messages. Prezi. com allows students or teachers to develop exciting presentations or creative thinking sessions. SmartDraw allows pupils to create graphic representations of survey data or how to report cyberbullying.)
- Develop tools for the use of students with special needs and vulnerable groups, as described in Chapter 7. Deliver the messages repeatedly in short single-issue units.

See the Ofsted framework for school inspection in Appendix 3.

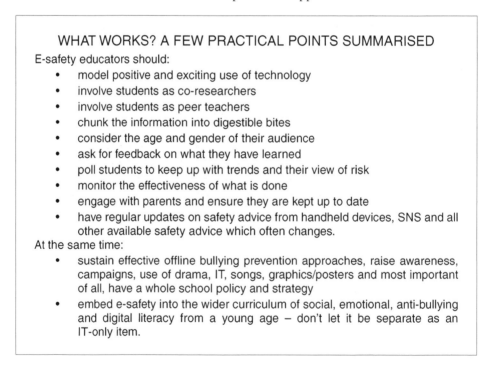

WHAT WORKS? A FEW PRACTICAL POINTS SUMMARISED

E-safety educators should:
- model positive and exciting use of technology
- involve students as co-researchers
- involve students as peer teachers
- chunk the information into digestible bites
- consider the age and gender of their audience
- ask for feedback on what they have learned
- poll students to keep up with trends and their view of risk
- monitor the effectiveness of what is done
- engage with parents and ensure they are kept up to date
- have regular updates on safety advice from handheld devices, SNS and all other available safety advice which often changes.

At the same time:
- sustain effective offline bullying prevention approaches, raise awareness, campaigns, use of drama, IT, songs, graphics/posters and most important of all, have a whole school policy and strategy
- embed e-safety into the wider curriculum of social, emotional, anti-bullying and digital literacy from a young age – don't let it be separate as an IT-only item.

What is in place in a session to support someone who may be upset?

When we deliver sessions on what can happen online or on mobile phones, there is bound to be at least one pupil who is deeply upset by hearing about it, either because it brings back the pain of what has happened or is still happening, or because the pupil knows it happens and fears he will be next. Indeed it could be that in other areas of his life he encounters problems, and this discussion is too painful for him in some way.

These sessions should have in place some clearly signposted support. Prepare to be told sometimes shocking information and to have to act. If visiting a school or youth service and the trainer is to leave straight after the session, it is vital to plan with the teachers, youth workers or other staff who will provide this support. Always be sure that safeguarding procedures are in place alongside child protection policy and procedures. Domestic violence or the use of porn by a relative is often revealed when it is least expected.

The right tone

Striking the right note and tone is a challenge when talking to teenagers about what is essentially their social world, often shut off from adults. Too adult and you are seen as remote, with no idea of what their lives are like. Too chummy and you are seen as 'sad' – trying too hard to be young. Perhaps knowledgeable and friendly is the tone we seek. Even better is the use of peer education.

Generally the message should be about acquiring competence and encouraging autonomy – avoid the big stick or threat approach. The lessons learned over many years from other advice to teenagers, particularly health advice, should be applied. Although adults know that smoking kills, outside every building is a cluster of smokers puffing away, beginning to take pride in their 'pariah' status. For teenagers, being seen as the 'bad guys' is even more attractive than it is for adults. Bullies in particular want to show their 'henchmen' that they are 'daring' and afraid of nothing. It is better to plan how to reach them, thinking about their motivation. For example, you might encourage them to think about their reputation and how they want to control that online, instead of saying, 'Don't do this because it is risky.'

How do you know they have understood and retained the message?

Safer schools police officers have been used in many schools in England, and these officers were often tasked with delivering e-safety to pupils. One such officer began to interview Year 7 pupils after his presentation. They were asked what they were now going to do as a result of what they had learned.

Looking at the video clips afterwards in training, we could see how some pupils had misunderstood commonly used videos from an England-wide programme, while others had no idea of actions they would take to keep safe. One girl said, 'If I go online some bad man will come to my house.' She was referring to a film that showed how a young girl was 'advertising' herself via her Facebook page with no privacy settings and lots of photos on show. The film showed an adult man walking past the house and stopping to view a large billboard of this girl's page at the gate. After a while he knocks on the door and asks to come in to symbolise how this girl was asking anyone to view her Facebook page. Not all the children picked up on the metaphor that what you put on your page without the privacy set correctly was *equivalent* to putting a billboard on your front lawn. The message that the trainer hoped these 13- to 14-year-olds would take away was to alter their privacy settings.

Several children retained only one message from the session and this was not always linked to the actions they should be taking, but instead was more likely to be something from a story used in a film clip.

Who should deliver the e-safety messages?

There is evidence that the same e-safety messages delivered by an adult are not as effective as when they are delivered by a group of young people led by an adult. Coventry Primary Care Trust in the UK carried out a programme in which young people helped a school nurse to develop resources for schools. The project sought to establish whether there were any differences in the effectiveness when it was delivered by the school nurse leading the project, or by a group of older pupils who had been involved in the development of the presentation. The project was carefully evaluated and it seems that cyberbullying messages and advice were received best when delivered with and by young people.

- Participants were encouraged to develop skills that would help them make informed choices.

- Existing strategies were complemented to tackle cyberbullying by working alongside children.

- A forum for debate was created and raised awareness of specific issues around cyberbullying through drama.

- A play script and DVD were developed to be used in schools.

- T-shirts and banners were produced.

Training sessions were delivered to teaching professionals and the production was delivered to three primary schools. Effective communication of key messages was delivered through drama and particularly peer-led theatre.

The children learned how easy it is to become a cyberbully without realising it and this provoked interesting discussion and debate. The children requested more support with hands-on IT skills to help them block, report and set privacy settings. This is being addressed in the schools involved in the programme. A copy of the DVD, play script, evaluation forms and lesson plans have been made available to every school in Coventry.

Despite the success of these young people there is clearly a role for caring, supportive adults, especially the young people who lack a supportive adult.[138] Some of the workers in social care or PRUS or youth justice settings may not feel skilled enough to challenge the risky behaviour they believe the young people are engaging in. Training for these adults as well as foster carers should be part of the e-safety programme.

Inform parents so that they can help their children

It seems that parents are becoming more involved in giving their children e-safety advice – the percentage who have done so has risen over three years in which the Cybersurvey has asked about this, and parents are beginning to deliver it earlier to younger children. Parents wait longer to address this with their children in some rural areas, whereas in more urban areas they appear to begin at a younger age (ten). This could be influenced by a slower spread of broadband and WiFi to these areas.

However, the Cybersurvey also found that those who were homophobically bullied were less likely than their peers to have been given e-safety advice by their parents. So not only were they less likely to tell their parents about how they were being victimised because of all that might entail, but they also reported receiving less support about staying safe generally. When we consider that those who are having difficult peer relationships in the offline world are the very people who seek intimacy in chatrooms and SNS, we can see how urgent it is that these vulnerable young people receive better and more relevant support.

Involve students as co-researchers

Using students as peer researchers to explore what they think are the current risks can be useful. They could identify where these risks emerge from, such as new devices or new behaviours, and explore how they might avoid harm. They could also help discuss survey results.

Reach is a Lottery-funded programme in the UK that aims to explore with young people the issues and concerns around homophobic bullying and cyberbullying. It is run by the charity EACH in the West of England in partnership with UK Youth, a nationwide youth programme. In addition to a survey and intensive information-gathering events, it offers young people courses to develop their skills such as photography in order to contribute to the materials being created. The project will go on to develop resources for schools, and will use data from the quantitative Cybersurvey to inform their debates in an iterative cycle. This includes a leaflet with feedback of survey results for young people and an executive summary for teachers, as well as lesson activities to research their views.

How do I chunk all the information when it is so interlinked?

With pupils who are owners of BlackBerry devices or smartphones it is not simple to separate talks on safety online and on mobiles because through their mobiles they are online all their waking hours.

Many younger children are now accessing the internet via games consoles. This makes it hard to discern boundaries to be drawn around information to help break it down into deliverable chunks.

A few years or even months ago it might have been tempting to draw the line between the internet and mobile phones. This line no longer exists. Along with the boundary between what is private and what is public, it too has become blurred. It might be better to use graphics to go where the young people would like to take the discussion. Students could lead and create a diagram together of all the linked devices, Apps and gateways they use. Then the pathways of this map could be explored in a series of sessions.

If young people are involved in developing an AUP, there is more chance they will 'police' or enforce it among themselves. They will use language other students can relate to and it will not represent something being done *to* them but rather something developed *with* them. Students who struggle with behaviour or who struggle with literacy may see the AUP as one more thing they can fail at, and delivered from above it can be legitimately ignored by those who do not want to know. But if the exploration and development process is creative and inclusive, it serves to engage them and draw them in. They will be more likely to follow the guidelines they have been involved in developing.

SUMMARY
School e-safety programme elements

- Declare a common goal or vision.
- Define cyberbullying clearly, and explain the concept of e-safety.
- Have practical effective policies and procedures and review them regularly.
- Continually educate and train staff, pupils and parents (start at a young age).
- Promote and advertise easy systems for reporting cyberbullying.
- Check IT uses up-to-date security systems, filtering and real time monitoring.
- Implement an AUP for staff and students.
- Devise a recording and evaluation system that is quick and straightforward to use.
- Reflect and review the whole strategy at regular intervals.
- Ensure all stakeholders are engaged, including parents.

- Ensure there is a Serious Incident Protocol (see Chapter 11) and child protection procedure in place.

- Be aware of the extra needs of vulnerable groups.

- Fine tuning: e-safety messages must be reviewed and updated since smartphone and BlackBerry ownership by young people has soared.

- Scare tactics will not work in e-safety delivery – move from a risk focus to a skills and youth participation model.

- Interpersonal victimisation needs to be a larger component of e-safety education than stranger danger, which is rare.

- Respect young people's desire for autonomy and build self-efficacy, focusing on the concept of digital citizenship and interpersonal relationships.

- Educate parents.

- Adjust the e-safety messages: sharing personal information has not been found to be so risky and is a necessity for those who shop, download and share files and operate online.

- Tailor safety messages to what pupils actually do online – by exploring this with pupils.

- Distinguish between age groups and address cyberbullying before each of the peak ages arrive at 10–11 and 14–15.

- Be aware of gender patterns and interests and tailor e-safety accordingly.

- Enable peer education and provide training for peer educators.

RESOURCES

Meeting the needs of the most vulnerable students (Chapter 7).

Workshops on Cybersurvey data (Chapter 9).

Example of an Acceptable Use Policy (AUP) (Chapter 11).

Lesson plan: What do I do online? (Chapter 11).

Short activities (Chapter 11).

The law relating to cyberbullying and traditional bullying (Appendix 2).

Chapter

9

CYBERBULLYING
Prevention and Response

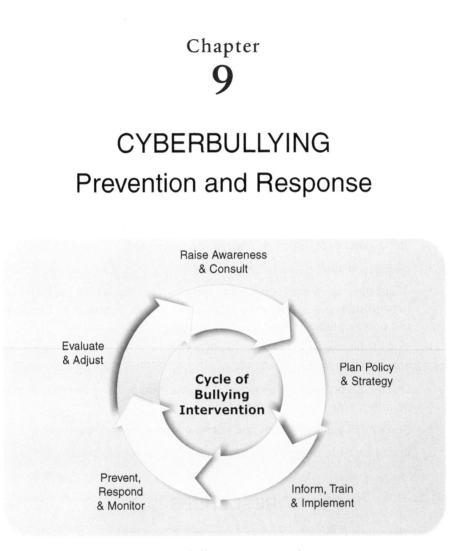

Figure 9.1 Cyberbullying: prevention and response

A FIVE-STAGE PROGRAMME

Effective bullying prevention is a five-stage programme, to be endlessly repeated with tweaks and improvements through constant evaluation and monitoring of its effectiveness. To prevent cyberbullying, these steps are similar, but the process is entwined with e-safety delivery.

The whole programme should be flexible enough to respond to new developments in technology and to absorb the impact of critical views from students, parents or staff. It should be a dialogue between partners rather than a top-down approach the school decides upon and imposes.

Stage 1: Raise awareness and consult

Awareness of the issue of cyberbullying and the need for acceptable use of the internet and mobiles across the whole school community is raised. Pupils, parents and staff should be consulted or surveyed to construct a picture of the position in the school, as well as finding out the extent of staff knowledge, their training needs and priorities. A nominated governor with this remit should be identified. This would be a good time to develop an advisory group that is fully representative, from senior management team to student delegates – a lone enthusiastic teacher initiating this programme will be less effective than a whole school 'buy in', and time spent engaging leaders at this stage will be very helpful in the future.

Stage 2: Plan policy and strategy

Has the school's Anti-Bullying Policy been updated or reviewed recently? How well does it address cyberbullying? Is the AUP adequate and up to date, bearing in mind new developments in technology? Is there a procedure to follow in the case of a serious incident? The designated person for child protection should be talked to about the school's safeguarding systems. Talk to the head of ICT and the network manager about the types of incident they are currently seeing within the school's system. Beginning with a statement of the school's vision, design a coherent approach for the whole school using the information gathered at Stage 1, and ensure it complies with current legislation. (See Appendix 2 for an explanation of the law and guidance, and Figure 9.2 for a diagrammatic illustration of how policies overlap and interact.)

Stage 3: Inform, train and implement

Parents, staff and pupils of the new approach should be informed, and staff and peer supporters/mediators trained. The policy should be communicated across the school. Universal e-safety sessions for pupils should be run, and parents of young children invited to sessions. In a primary school, the new policy should be available in a child-friendly version. The policy should be on the school website along with easy ways to report bullying or cyberbullying.

Stage 4: Prevent, respond and monitor

Prevention describes all the proactive work of the school and covers the implementation of the overall strategy as well as a variety of specific activities that embed the work across the curriculum. These include workshops, assemblies, poster campaigns, drama, PSHE lessons, e-safety sessions, assignments and young people's contributions. The curriculum has many appropriate links from History, English, IT and PSHE to bullying, equality, citizenship and copyright. Art and drama can be used to develop scenarios, to create and perform plays and to make films to convey the message while posters, screensavers, graphic art and internal television screen messages can support the work. Competitions can be run in which pupils are invited to design a new web page for the school, or a messaging service, a poster, a mobile phone App or another contribution to reduce cyberbullying. A lunchtime computer club could be set up. Positive behaviour should be celebrated, and awards created.

The Equality Act 2010 requires proactive steps to be taken to prevent discrimination and this stage offers opportunities to develop all equality and diversity work. Once the programme is embedded and running, incidents will be reported – if pupils trust that something will be done, they are more likely to come forward and report cyberbullying, especially after the awareness raising that has been carried out. This may make the incident rate appear to go up at first, but it is normal. All incidents should be recorded so that effective monitoring can be undertaken. A step-by-step response to incidents, the Serious Incident Protocol, is described in Chapter 11. It is especially important that people who do come forward to report cyberbullying are kept safe and dealt with sensitively. If students discover that it is futile to report cyberbullying, either because they get little help or because it makes matters worse, they will not feel it is worth it. The entire programme can fail at this point if pupils view it just as 'window dressing'. Cynicism sets in and the programme is quickly trashed in the corridors and playgrounds.

Stage 5: Evaluate and adjust

The final stage of the cycle is regular evaluation. Pupil surveys should be repeated, with an added question: 'Does the school deal effectively with cyberbullying?' Check how many pupils say they have experienced cyberbullying but not reported it. Were they able to sort it out themselves using information they had been taught? Or did they do nothing? If they did report it, how good was the help they received?

There is other evidence within school that might be a useful indicator. Has persistent absenteeism changed at all? Are cases being resolved effectively or re-appearing? (Check the incident records.) Are cases appearing mostly in one class? Should more effort be focused there? Check how many people are actively following the e-safety guidelines they have been taught. Now is the time to re-think or reassess your strategy and to make the adjustments necessary.

A living, responsive strategy

The goal is the creation of a safe, peaceful school climate. Weapon carrying and other violence should be addressed as part of a whole continuum, along with all prejudice. This vision was perfectly expressed by the Whole Student Development Policy of Connecticut in the USA: 'The District shall provide an educational experience that develops students' social, emotional, creative, and physical skills and talents. The experience shall be designed to develop and reinforce students' knowledge and skills to become creative, capable, compassionate, and responsible members of society.'[139]

STAFF TRAINING

Teachers sometimes question why they need this training. Apart from the fact that cyberbullying is relatively new and was certainly not a major issue when most teachers were young, the research on teacher interventions in bullying generally shows that responses need to improve when a student reports being bullied. Outcomes are frequently ineffective and in some cases the bullying even gets worse. Smith and Shu found that in only around a quarter of cases did it actually stop.[140]

In a study of badly bullied students in the Midlands in the UK, only 28 per cent said the bullying stopped when they reported it, and for 13 per cent it got worse.[141] Cyberbullying cases are often more complex to resolve, taking up extensive teachers' time – it is estimated that the cost of dealing with cyberbullying in UK schools per year is almost £18 million.[142] For this investment of time and money, the outcomes should be more effective!

Another reason for training is the changing landscape of government policy and legislation alongside inspection requirements, with everyone requiring regular updates. Finally, the school may change its strategy, its approaches may evolve and so it is vital that all members of staff share in this process and deliver a consistent whole school approach.

To plan training for staff, support staff and school nurses should also be considered – they are trusted individuals and a student may confide in any one of them. They also tend to notice things around the school. They need to be equipped and informed and they especially need to know what steps to take if a serious case comes to light.

The Staff Training Needs Questionnaire in Chapter 11 highlights the training needs of your team and shows which areas they feel confident about and what should be included in the training agenda. When planning training, it is invaluable to measure staff confidence both before the training session and afterwards. This will help identify what they want and issues to cover or recap on in the future.

Most teachers can expect to have to deal with cyberbullying cases reported to them – the UK charity Beatbullying questioned teachers in 2011 and found that over three-quarters had dealt with such cases and on average, these teachers had each dealt with 13 cases. The majority of cases were reported by the victim or parents, but more than a third were reported by other staff.[143] Do all staff members know the routes to report a case? How quick and easy is it to use your school reporting system?

Schools often ask what should be included in a staff training day. Begin with basics and ensure everyone knows about the school's Anti-Bullying Policy and its AUP for ICT. Then draw attention to any recent changes in law or government guidance with a brief outline. If you have your own survey data from your school, now is a good time to explore a few key messages from it to set future priorities. If this is not available, use other survey data from your local area or recent national data to talk about young people's experiences. You may have case notes from peer mentors or incident records to draw from. Once the picture has been outlined, turn to prevention and response, exploring ways in which the school can work coherently to reduce all forms of bullying and how to respond when incidents occur.

A prevention strategy

In the first stage of your prevention strategy there are some basic questions to ask about needs within the school, described below.

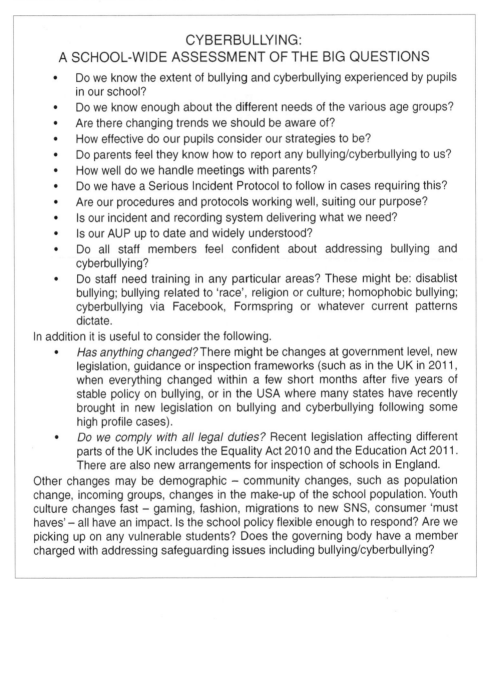

CYBERBULLYING:
A SCHOOL-WIDE ASSESSMENT OF THE BIG QUESTIONS

- Do we know the extent of bullying and cyberbullying experienced by pupils in our school?
- Do we know enough about the different needs of the various age groups?
- Are there changing trends we should be aware of?
- How effective do our pupils consider our strategies to be?
- Do parents feel they know how to report any bullying/cyberbullying to us?
- How well do we handle meetings with parents?
- Do we have a Serious Incident Protocol to follow in cases requiring this?
- Are our procedures and protocols working well, suiting our purpose?
- Is our incident and recording system delivering what we need?
- Is our AUP up to date and widely understood?
- Do all staff members feel confident about addressing bullying and cyberbullying?
- Do staff need training in any particular areas? These might be: disablist bullying; bullying related to 'race', religion or culture; homophobic bullying; cyberbullying via Facebook, Formspring or whatever current patterns dictate.

In addition it is useful to consider the following.

- *Has anything changed?* There might be changes at government level, new legislation, guidance or inspection frameworks (such as in the UK in 2011, when everything changed within a few short months after five years of stable policy on bullying, or in the USA where many states have recently brought in new legislation on bullying and cyberbullying following some high profile cases).
- *Do we comply with all legal duties?* Recent legislation affecting different parts of the UK includes the Equality Act 2010 and the Education Act 2011. There are also new arrangements for inspection of schools in England.

Other changes may be demographic – community changes, such as population change, incoming groups, changes in the make-up of the school population. Youth culture changes fast – gaming, fashion, migrations to new SNS, consumer 'must haves' – all have an impact. Is the school policy flexible enough to respond? Are we picking up on any vulnerable students? Does the governing body have a member charged with addressing safeguarding issues including bullying/cyberbullying?

ACCEPTABLE USE AND ANTI-BULLYING POLICIES

Figure 9.2 shows the overlap and interaction between policies. Policies are not stand-alone documents operating in isolation – the way they work together should be interlinked and coherent. They are often written by different people and it is seldom that a school has reviewed all their behaviour and ICT policies together, along with what they communicate to students and parents. Once every couple of years it would be helpful to look at how all your relevant policies interact and to make sure that everything is covered in at least one of them.

	A-B Policy Pupil Version	Anti-bullying Policy	ICT Acceptable Use Policy	Teachers' Internal Advice	Parents' Information
What is bullying? Provide a definition everyone can use	✓	✓		✓	✓
All types of bullying described, protected characteristics and cyber	✓	✓		✓	✓
What is the school's vision and overall stance?	✓	✓	✓	✓	✓
How to prevent?		✓		✓	
How to report?	✓	✓	✓	✓	✓
How to preserve evidence/keep diary of events	✓	✓	✓	✓+	✓
How the school will respond when an incident occurs?	We take it seriously	✓	✓	✓++	We take it seriously
Signpost to helplines/websites and further advice	✓	✓		✓++	✓
What school will do: sanctions, support and re-educate		✓	✓	✓++	✓−
Rules for using school IT safely and respectfully, plus plagiarism			✓	✓	✓
Advice re: safeguarding pupils online and using handheld devices				✓	
Advice re: protecting themselves online/phones and school data				✓	
Recording and monitoring		✓	✓	✓++	We will monitor
Reflect, review and consult		✓	✓	✓	We will review
Serious Incident Proceedures and working with police/other agencies.			✓	✓++	
Other languages offered if required					✓
Language that is child-friendly	✓				

The internal advice for teachers should go into greater detail indicated by the sign +.
Less detail is shown by the sign −.
'Protected characteristics' refers to the Equality Act 2010 and describes those who are protected under the Act.
Schools must promote positive images of all protected groups and ensure they do not face discrimination.

Figure 9.2 How do policies overlap?

Bystanders

Bullying does not take place in a vacuum. Bullies have supporters who are 'henchmen', and a wider group of 'colluders' who actively support their actions by laughing or jeering or passing on images or rumours in front of an audience, who view the material. Without all these people the bully might be disempowered.

Help all bystanders recognise the role they play in bullying: do they decide to ignore the feelings and distress of the victim? Help them to acknowledge their own role in the bullying episode. Are bystanders drawn into becoming colluders or henchmen supporting the bully? If so, how can they avoid taking this role?

A coherent programme of prevention has a wide and deep foundation that supports the structure and intensive work required when serious incidents occur. These are some of the layers of prevention to have in place.

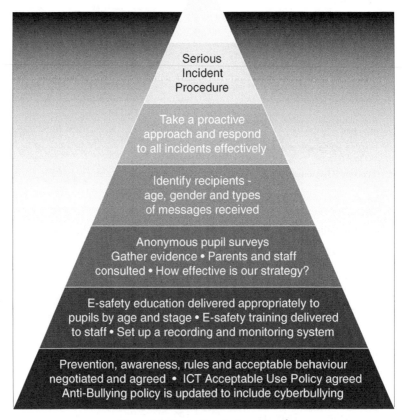

Figure 9.3 Prevention strategy triangle

WORK WITH THE WIDER GROUP OR WHOLE CLASS DYNAMIC
- How could we understand each other more and react less?
- Provide opportunities for reflection and compassion.
- Recognise emotions – use emotions charts, scales and posters.
- Reward empathy and supportive behaviour with group rewards/outings.
- What is a good school climate in pupils' view? (What would an ideal school be like?)
- How good was our class this week (or today)?
- What could we do differently? What did we learn about ourselves?

MONITORING AND EVALUATING
Why collect children's views?

Youth participation is now a well-established principle that has developed since the United Nations Convention on the Rights of the Child 1989 was ratified. Following this revolutionary convention, a number of legislative steps and frameworks of good practice now routinely include the voice of the user, and the participation of children and young people has become regarded as necessary evidence in inspections. Children increasingly have the right to have their views heard.

However, youth participation can be an opportunity for far more than just collecting data for evaluation, inspection or monitoring. It can be innovative and creative, enabling children of all ages and abilities to fulfil their roles as citizens. They can reflect on the results and come up with solutions. Active participation is a powerful democratic tool through which to communicate with young citizens and to build trust. Put simply: people know they are valued if the participation is genuine.

Further benefits of youth participation are:

- evidence-based changes to services are more likely to succeed

- inclusive approaches fully involve children with special educational needs or disabilities[144]

- staff and pupils involved in anti-bullying and e-safety work are informed and rewarded if their efforts are successful

- reviews are undertaken if the strategy is not successful

- the data can be used in school self-evaluation and inspection

- it models the democratic process

- planners in senior management and governors have accurate information.

Survey data should be considered together with incident records to get a detailed picture of what is happening in a school. There are also other sources of information, such as absenteeism or truanting figures, requests to leave the school or to be home schooled due to bullying. Taken together, they can provide a great deal of interesting data. Additionally, attainment should go up if pupils feel safe and secure.

Parent satisfaction can be monitored with parent surveys, and staff training needs can be met by asking staff what they feel they require and designing a training session for them.

Such survey data should be reviewed annually. In East Sussex, for example, the annual pupil survey showed slight year-on-year drops in the number of people bullied. This ran parallel with a highly trained team delivering training and support to schools. Leicestershire County produced a similar pattern of slowly reducing figures, year on year.

A huge or sudden change in the percentage of pupils who are bullied should not be expected, but rather a slow diminution of incidents after a possible initial rise when the programme first begins. People tend to come forward when awareness is raised and there can be more reporting of incidents after a visit by a guest who talks about cyberbullying or if students trust that something will be done if they do come forward.

On the other hand, a major change can be expected in the answers to questions about the effectiveness of the school's approach to dealing with cyberbullying. Those who were cyberbullied should be asked if they reported it and if so, if they were given help. This is a question that can be a good indicator and is more reliable than incident figures. A popular question is: Does your school deal effectively with cyberbullying?

Incident recording

Some schools prefer to do this using one of the software packages they already have in place for behaviour, such as SIMS. Others design specific incident forms. Unless the system is simple and quick for staff members, however, it will not be used. A trail of emails, actions or correspondence should be kept so that if one member of staff is away ill, others can continue with a particular case. The school might be required to show this evidence for some reason one day, or may need it if consulting a service such as educational psychology or child protection. In the worst scenario it is needed if the case were to escalate and become serious and meetings with parents are held.

Racist incidents should be identified and if the school is within the local authority the number of incidents should be reported annually to the council.

WHAT MAKES A GOOD SURVEY?

- Write the questions in child-friendly but clear language.
- Ask no leading or ambiguous questions.
- Keep it short.
- Use communications tools for those with special needs or record questions on tape for those who have sight problems. iPads offer a text to speech facilty.
- Use simple scales and tick boxes but leave some areas open for respondents to comment.
- Run some focus groups with students to explore the issues that should be covered within the survey.
- Write and test the questions.
- Analyse a few to see if there is any area that could be improved or clarified.

Exploring e-safety education

You will want to know if pupils have received e-safety education and what the source of this was. They might have had it from several sources such as school and parents and siblings. A question about the quality of this e-safety education will tell you what they thought of it. This will lead on to asking whether or not they actually follow the advice. If not, perhaps consider asking why not, and how they think the advice could be improved.

About cyberbullying

Ask about the device, the type of bullying and how often they experienced cyberbullying – it could be once a week or many times a day. Ask about how they reacted and if they reported it to someone they trust. If they did report it, what was the outcome?

Always ask if the victim thinks it was related to their disability or illness/special need or appearance, 'race', religion or culture. It may be they see a link to other aspects of their identity such as gender or sexual orientation or perhaps to a family member.

Some questions should be left open so that pupils can describe types of bullying not listed – that way you can keep up to date with trends.

What can make data unreliable?

A self-selected sample may mean only interested people respond which can skew results – for example, a girls magazine could run a story and ask people to fill in a survey. Readers who were interested or had experienced the issue would be more likely to do so than those who had not.

Badly constructed questions, such as biased, leading or ambiguous questions can make data unreliable, as well as where language is not understood by young people or when the format is not user-friendly or suitable for people with learning difficulties.

The time of year when a survey is carried out is important – are many absent on work experience? Are pupils newly arrived in September? Is the survey anonymous? Is there a gender bias?

Finally, there must be a clear definition of bullying.

RESPONDING WHEN INCIDENTS OCCUR
Understanding reactions

Much anti-bullying work consists of teaching young people interpersonal skills to reintegrate them socially within their year group. Addressing cyberbullying is not an isolated ICT role or a detective investigation – it should be: embedded into the anti-bullying and relationship skills work of a school.

Unless the case is extremely serious, goals should be: to make the student safe and reintegrate them socially, while addressing the perpetrator's behaviour and teaching the whole group that this is unacceptable. Good practice promotes resilience and self-efficacy rather than dependency or helplessness.

Sanctions often satisfy the victim's parents, but are unlikely to address prejudice-driven behaviour on their own. Challenging these views, which are quite often reinforced at home, requires more subtle careful ongoing work. Some cases can be learning experiences that lead to improved practice. That is one of many reasons why record keeping is so important.

If there are threats of violence or any child protection concerns, report this at once to the appropriate authorities via a Serious Incident Protocol (see Chapter 11). It is assumed that the situations discussed below are not of this serious level – teachers spend a great deal of time dealing with cases involving friendship feuds, jealousy and social isolation or exclusion.

Successful responses begin with understanding the reactions of the person in front of you. Some of the most common are explained here.

Toughing it out

Many teenagers, as danah boyd and Alice Marwick point out, '…can't emotionally afford to identify as victims, and young people who bully others rarely see themselves as perpetrators. For a teenager to recognize herself or himself in the adult language of bullying carries social and psychological costs.'[145] boyd and Marwick explain that in the USA many girls will instead describe their cyberbullying problem as 'a drama'. In the UK, I found that teenagers prefer to insist they are 'not bothered'. This widely used expression featured as a catchphrase in the Catherine Tate television comedy show, and it is the ultimate illustration that the user 'couldn't care less'. In other words, they are denying the bully the satisfaction of having upset them. But it does not mean that they are not hurt by the events, or that they don't want it stopped.

In the first Cybersurvey, those who said they had been cyberbullied were asked how this made them feel. A quarter said they 'took it as a joke'. Yet they had chosen to classify their experience as cyberbullying after a clear definition of cyberbullying was given. More than one in five said they were 'not bothered', with boys twice as likely as girls to say either that they 'took it as a joke' or were 'not bothered'.

In a later wave of the Cybersurvey, homophobic bullying was explored. Those who suffered homophobic bullying were more likely than their peers to insist they were 'not bothered' (14% compared to 10%), perhaps because it seemed more manly to do so.

This bravado is important to the individual, as it indicates their choice of how to present themselves; it should not be punctured by intimating that they are weak or helpless.

RESPONDING TO AND PREVENTING CYBERBULLYING

- Initially, ask neutrally what has been going on.
- Explain that you take it seriously.
- Ensure you take steps to keep this person safe immediately if this is required.
- Ask for any evidence, or give advice on how to obtain or keep the evidence, and arrange to speak again within a short time when you have reviewed this.
- Discuss together what the student wants to happen.
- Check school incident records to find out if any similar incident has been reported before between these people, and if any action is underway.
- Follow the procedures and protocols in your school setting.
- Report abuse on a site or service and try to have humiliating images removed.
- If the perpetrator is identifiable, consider a discussion with them. This is a delicate decision as some targets of bullying fear retaliation. If it is a friendship feud, tread carefully as they could be best friends in a day or two.
- An immediate school-wide activity addressing cyberbullying can sometimes be more successful at stopping cyberbullying than a confrontation with the perpetrator/s. Within this activity you can state that you are aware of several examples of cyberbullying going on in the school, year or class, and they are entirely unacceptable. This way you will not have to say you have had an incident reported by the victim.
- If the cyberbullying continues, collect the evidence and confront the sender. However, if many people are bullying someone, it is easier to announce that you know about this. Do not give the source – it could have been anyone involved who leaked this information. React fast – consider calling in your safer schools officer if you have one. Confront pupils with the evidence and insist all are equally guilty for passing on these abusive messages or images. Apply sanctions.
- Record and monitor the behaviour. Check that it has stopped.

Circles of support

Both bullies and victims report being very helpless or isolated at times, so it can help to identify who is there to support them. With the young person, draw a diagram of the support he has. This can be a spidergram or spokes, as in the example shown in Figure 9.4. Help victims and bullies to realise they are supported and there are people they can turn to if they need to. They can take away a diagram and complete it in private and keep it for themselves; it can be reassuring.

Figure 9.4 Circle of support

Different reactions

You may also have to deal with someone who is reacting in one of the following ways.

Anger: shouting, kicking and hitting, impulsive behaviour without thinking – the person overcome by anger simply reacts to the emotional and physical feelings. In an aggressive competitive environment children can believe that demonstrating their anger will make people scared of them or look up to them so they choose to show anger to 'look big'. If parents always behave this way, it can seem normal.

Others cannot control their anger. On receiving an abusive message on his phone, for example, Andy says he lashes out at his family, although they do not know why. Anger itself is understandable and often justified – Andy has been betrayed by his friend who has circulated a humiliating picture of him with sarcastic comments, and he feels furious. 'I want to smash things up,' he says. But the challenge is how to help children and young people handle that anger in an acceptable way. First they need help to recognise the sensations they commonly get just before the anger gets out of control. In this way they might learn to take steps to control it before it swamps them. Very often it helps to simply have someone listen effectively – the complaint 'nobody listens' is frequently heard from angry teenagers.

The young people in the examples below have been learning to control their anger and to think carefully about their next moves:

'Last year I got upset when it happened, but this year if I get annoyed I do heavy breathing and calm down and also I write it down and give it to a teacher or member of staff.'

'They showed me a picture of a fork in the road. If you go one way, you fall into the hole, if you choose the other path, things work out differently. But you have to stop and make a choice. Slowly I am learning to take time to choose what I do instead of kicking off.'

'They taught me to say how I feel – I give a number between one and ten. Then my teacher knows if I am about to explode. She helps me, like she can send me out of the classroom to do something for her.'

Aggression: thirst for revenge (and justice) – 'I'll smash his head in' or 'I will get my friends together to attack him on Facebook, it's what he deserves!' This reaction is common in parents and pupils alike after a bullying incident. It can help to let someone vent their feelings in a meeting with staff or peer supporters and then, gradually, when they feel validated and listened to, it might be opportune to try and move forward with a plan to address the problem.

If a child is bullied, aggressive parents tend to come in and shout at school secretaries, challenge headteachers' approaches or threaten to complain to a 'higher authority'. Some parents have gone to the press, and in one case even got a local television station to follow the story for some time because their child was bullied and it did not stop. Other parents have gone online to create a hate page.

Young people can take risky actions in their rage and hurt. Some report that they begin to carry a weapon 'for self-defence'. The internet makes retaliation easy – a pack of friends can be summoned and attacks on and offline can be planned, as we learned when a boy was stabbed in a busy London railway station in a mob attack orchestrated on an SNS.

This anger must be defused. Quite apart from the risks to young people and the damage to the reputation of the school, it interferes with any smooth running of the anti-bullying strategy and most importantly it is not helpful for the child who is the victim of bullying. Staff must stay calm and model the behaviour they want. In cases where teachers shout at a pupil for repeatedly bullying others, it is not unusual to see this young person shouting back, swearing and making everyone's lives miserable.

Passive: resigned – this person is thinking, 'My feelings don't matter or are always trampled on, so what's new? Maybe I deserve this?' Or 'It is always like this, I had better get used to it.' This behaviour is common in girls who have been brought up to allow others to be in control and to put their own needs last.

'I was brought up to turn the other cheek, my parents were very religious. I said nothing when this girl bullied me.'

'They called me a whore, apparently I look like one.'

Passive/aggressive: this person seems compliant but is secretly planning to trip up or 'get' the person who bullied them. A passive/aggressive person masks their anger. They may also turn anger inwards – 'I hate myself', 'It's because I am so hateful.' They could self-harm or over-eat. They may try and use someone else's phone to send a nasty message in the other person's name to get them into trouble.

Indirect aggression: can be an expression of powerlessness. If someone feels angry or upset but cannot express this directly, she may be overcome by her strong feelings and run out of the room. Teenagers withdraw to their rooms; adults often use the silent treatment. But some people, frequently girls, resort to indirect bullying such as rumour spreading, and new technology is the perfect tool for this. It can be immensely destructive and hurtful with serious consequences. If a girl thinks someone has 'stolen' her boyfriend, she may spread rumours about the other girl online. These usually imply the other girl is a 'slut', a 'sket', or has been sleeping around or been unfaithful. In this way she hopes to regain some power.

Asked 'Has anyone deliberately sent round rumours about you?' 19 per cent of girls said this had happened to them compared to 13 per cent of boys in the Cybersurvey 2009. This behaviour peaks at age 14–15 across all waves of the Cybersurvey.

Compared to their peers, cyberbullied respondents are three times more likely to have had humiliating photos deliberately sent round to upset them, and two-thirds experienced someone spreading malicious rumours about them. In their turn, in the Reach 2011 Cybersurvey, 13 per cent had done this to others compared to 9 per cent of peers who were not victims.

Assertive: an assertive person makes their needs clear in a calm but strong way and tries to put a stop to it. Steps taken are practical and thought out, rather than impulsive. Assertive behaviour does not hurt others. This is the most effective response but it takes strength and often training to be able to behave this way. However, if through anti-bullying work children were helped to resolve conflict and taught to be assertive rather than aggressive, the work would provide them with skills for life. Teachers often have to behave assertively when dealing with conflict.

SOME ASPECTS OF ASSERTIVE BEHAVIOUR TO SHARE WITH CHILDREN AND YOUNG PEOPLE

Take charge of your own life – no longer accept being controlled by others or the victim of fate.

- Make a plan of action.
- Collect your evidence.
- Contact the service provider/school and report the abusive behaviour.
- Use 'I' instead of 'You'. Explain how you feel, starting with 'I feel…' rather than saying 'You always make me feel…': 'I felt extremely upset when I saw that picture online. I believed that it was personal. It seemed totally wrong to me.'
- Avoid blaming or judging – simply give your views and express how you feel: 'I cannot accept this.' 'I want something done about it.' 'It has to be taken down at once.'
- Stop apologising or feeling inappropriate guilt. If it is your fault, say sorry, but if not, don't keep apologising for who you are or your actions. Don't feel guilty about things you could not have done anything about. Do not say, 'I'm sorry but could I just say…'
- Make good eye contact and relax your body language – no threatening stance! If your shoulders are tense and your head down, you give the

> impression of being a victim; if your hands are on your hips, you look angry. Avoid pointing a finger and wagging it at the person – it can be infuriating and can crank up the tension.
> - Keep your facial expressions calm and consistent. Many women and girls apologetically smile when they are saying something important, which diminishes its impact. Think about what you are saying and reflect the importance of these feelings.
> - Position – stand or sit at the same level as the other person.
> - Voice – don't shout; keep your voice strong and low pitched.
> - Accept criticism – if fair, this is an opportunity to learn, grow and improve. If not, say you will think about it and 'park' it out of the way for now. Don't defensively shout back!
> - Say no – learn how to say 'no' when that's what you want.
> - Express your anger or distress assertively. Do not pretend that you are not really upset or angry. Use your strong feelings to power your assertive response but do not let them overwhelm you. Be prepared for the other person to feel threatened or upset upon hearing how you feel. Think about how you might handle this.
>
> Some scenarios could be written and acted out in class – role-play is an easy way to convey these messages.

Conflict resolution

Formal conflict resolution programmes have been found to work in cases where the parties are suitable for a mediated approach. This work teaches life skills, it can deliver a lasting sustained outcome and is often seen as 'fair' by young people and parents. It does, however, require trained teachers or support staff. Richard Cohen, author of *Students Resolving Conflict: Peer Mediation in Schools*,[146] argues that it teaches skills that need to be repeatedly practised and that these skills can then be applied in real life:

> Peer mediation uses an essentially extra-curricular distraction – interpersonal conflict – as a teaching tool. While mediators model pro-social methods of resolving conflicts, student parties practice resolving their differences using criteria of fairness and mutual benefit rather than brute strength and intimidation. Confronting their adversaries in a non-punitive forum like mediation encourages students to accept responsibility for their actions.

This method is enabling and moves away form the learned helplessness that Troy, age ten, exhibits: 'When I am bullied I just tell the teacher,' he said. What happens then? 'Nothing, it just goes on happening.' Oh, so what do you do then? 'I just go and tell the teacher.' This cycle was well entrenched. To the teacher, Troy was becoming a nuisance, and the teacher was discounting his endless reports. Troy was learning nothing about how to handle difficult social situations and his repeated visits to the teacher made his classmates think of him as a tell-tale and weak. More of them joined in making fun of him. He was becoming resigned to this pattern but simply put the onus on the teacher to act even when she plainly did not. In a reflex action, without thinking, he simply went to the teacher every time it happened, but never saw himself as an active agent.

At no stage was there any attempt to discuss what all the parties might do or to get anyone to take any responsibility for their behaviour. Cohen writes that in contrast to many school structures and systems, peer mediation expects the best from students:

> ...the mediation process provides a forum in which young people can rise to their highest potential. In this setting, students regularly impress educators with their creative thinking, their willingness to forgive, and their propensity to act upon motives other than self-interest. This is as true for parties as it is for mediators. Mediation challenges students to be the best that they can be, and they usually respond to the challenge.

Not all cases are suitable for the peer mediation conflict resolution approach, but the principle of involving students and having them take responsibility for behaviour can be used in many ways.

Below is an outline of a session that is useful if the bullying is not yet entrenched. It is vital not to mention a specific case, nor indicate that the victim has reported it. I have shown some typical responses young children have offered. Discussions like these put the children into an active role where they have to think about behaviour and come up with solutions. It is the opposite of a top-down approach, but the sessions must be well led and planned.

EXPLORING AGGRESSIVE FEELINGS WITH CHILDREN

In a workshop with eight- to ten-year-olds the children explained their thirst for revenge when bullied. 'First you punish the bully and then when he does it again you punish him worse.' After listening respectfully, I asked whether they thought these actions would make the bullying stop. 'No, but I might feel better,' said a boy who went on to explain that bullies 'just bully someone else or fight back, or they do it but don't get caught.' This opened up the discussion so that we could explore as a group how we all feel like fighting back at first, but actually there are other better ways of dealing with it.

By the end of the session we had a list of possible actions you could take if bullied. But at no time did we deny that the feelings of aggression were valid feelings – the group understood them and several people needed to voice these feelings – but on reflection, other behaviours were thought to be more successful. Prompting was required and a clear plan of prompts was structured in advance.

All that was needed was a safe space to reflect and a few questions to start us thinking about this as a group. Although these discussions can be more sophisticated with older pupils, the principle is the same – allow people to vent their desire for revenge and then explore what might actually work. This type of discussion, without identifying either a victim or a perpetrator, is often enough to encourage the bullying child to stop once they hear the views of the class. The aim should be to illustrate that bullying behaviour does not increase popularity. Try to influence the supporters and colluders in the bullying.

Workshop: how to stop bullying

Aims

- Explore what could help bullying to stop.
- Illustrate that bullying does not increase popularity.
- Allow bystanders to use their knowledge to formulate a plan.
- Enable the victim/s to hear that they are supported by others.
- Enable bullying pupils to hear how others feel about their behaviour.

Agree ground rules

- Nobody is to be mentioned by name.
- People agree to speak one at a time and to respectfully listen to one another.

Table 9.1 How to stop bullying

Questions	Typical responses
What do you think we should do if someone bullies another child?	'Punish them' 'Say they can't come to school'
Does this usually work?	'No, they do it again but you must punish them again and then punish them more' 'Give them a yellow card first and then a red card'
Do you think this works well?	'No, but I feel better' 'They just bully someone else or fight back, or they do it, but don't get caught' 'They threaten you 'cos you told' 'They make fun of you with their friends and laugh at pictures of you on their phones' 'They send you threats on your phone'
If it does not work so well, what else could we do?	'Work out why they are doing it' 'Tell them I'd be their friend if they stopped' 'Maybe they've got problems' 'Teach them to behave better' 'Tell everyone to leave them alone' 'Make them see how they hurt people' 'Read stories about bullying in class' 'Make them see how their cyberbullying looks to an outsider' 'Show a DVD to the class' 'Keep a record of what is happening, then call their parents' 'Take their phone away'

cont.

Table 9.1 How to stop bullying *cont.*

Questions	Typical responses
Can we agree on what we think works well? What are the most important of these?	'List all practical suggestions such as peer supporters or cybermentors, sanctions and learning opportunities; include restorative approaches'
Who can offer this help? Elicit suggestions such as: What should teachers do? What should pupils do?	'Teachers can give a prize for being kind' 'We've got peer supporters, they can help' 'You could tell someone if your friend is being bullied'
Do you think we should put your suggestions into a list or a drawing? Should we all tweet an idea to the headteacher?	'I want to make a poster' 'Yes, can we do it on the computer?'

Traditionally schools turn to sanctions. This can make the parents of a victim feel better in just the same ways the children described in the group discussion above, and schools argue that it sends a message to others about bullying. But, while this may deter some students from behaving aggressively to others, clever bullies simply become more secretive or turn to anonymity online or on mobiles. It could be argued that using sanctions does not change the victimising behaviour or the prejudice if this is present, but ends up driving it underground. Bullies may even use another pupil's phone to pretend that the cyberbullying is coming from someone else. In some cases it has even driven face-to-face bullying to become cyberbullying.

Rigby, in an article on different approaches to intervention, points out that 'Generally, it [this approach] requires a high degree of surveillance, which is often impossible or difficult to maintain. In cases of very violent or criminal behaviour, or in cases for which counselling approaches prove unsuccessful, this approach is more readily justified.'[147]

Aggressive retaliation by victims

When pupils retaliate, teachers often respond by punishing or excluding the immediately visible aggressor, but this does not deal with the anger or teach the pupil how to behave in another way. It also fuels the pupil's sense of grievance and her sense that whatever she does is justified because of her position as 'victim'. While no aggression can be condoned, it is important to consider what messages are being sent out when a sanction is being handed down – the action may be correct according to the rules, but is it complete if it does not address the original aggression itself? You should ask of each intervention:

- Are the pupils safer as a result of your actions?

- Have you taught this person another more acceptable 'assertive' way to act?

- Would a restorative approach be more constructive?

- Has the original perpetrator also been dealt with?

- What outcome do you/they ideally want? This may be to get the two of them to improve their behaviour towards one another, or to leave each other alone.

- Many children want things to 'be the way they were before'. How will this be managed?

After all, the children will both inhabit your classroom for months to come. Some schools train victims to react with 'fogging' or agreeing/joking tactics instead. Children who are not verbally dextrous can be helped to practise some good 'witty' replies to have at their disposal, such as 'You're so ugly' – 'Yes, that makes two of us.'

Aggressive parents

If parents were bullied as children themselves, they might react emotionally upon hearing that their child is now experiencing bullying. They can feel overwhelmed by these emotions. It can be important to acknowledge their pain when working with the parents – they feel an added helplessness as they have failed to protect their child. Sometimes this all translates into anger directed at the bullies, the school and quite possibly, you as the teacher, personally.

Stephen's case

(It should be noted that this case has been anonymised and it reflects some details from more than one case.)

Stephen was an only child. He was repeatedly bullied, beaten up and threatened in the first weeks of his first term at secondary school. His parents became so angry they caused scenes at the school, kept him home for weeks and even went to the press. They believed that the headteacher had failed to protect their son, even after the bullying was reported to him.

Hostility developed between the parents and the school, making a solution harder to find. Stephen was at home alone for six weeks, not socialising with children his age and falling behind in his schoolwork. He became depressed and felt that he had brought all this trouble upon his family. He felt increasingly helpless because his parents to whom he had turned had failed to solve the problem; indeed, it was worsening. It seemed to affect his entire family. Pupils carried on bullying him via his mobile phone and on Facebook. His parents were out all day carrying on this battle with the school while he was alone reading the messages from the bullies.

The school considered banning Stephen's father from the premises after he shouted at a member of staff. The parents went on local television to tell their story. The headteacher said Stephen had failed to identify the names of the perpetrators and he could only act if bullying was reported in full to him. But Stephen was new at the school and did not know the names of the older boys. Everyone was retreating to their fixed positions, while Stephen was being overlooked. To make matters worse, a 'no win no fee' law firm contacted Stephen's parents after the media stories, suggesting they could sue the school for a lot of money. As they didn't have much money and were angry, they accepted.

This was time for an outsider to negotiate some solutions. After notifying the school and the local council, I met with the parents and listened to their story. I asked how Stephen was and where he was at that time, then explained how worried I was about him and how there are risks to a lonely child, isolated due to bullying (a number of suicides had been reported in the previous months) – did he need to talk to someone? The parents were given a few helplines and online services. Perhaps he could be helped to be with other children his age such as his cousins, or at a youth club or another group, to be less isolated? How could he be helped to feel liked socially? Could he have schoolwork sent to him to reduce the amount he was falling behind? Would he like to talk to me? All the discussion was repeatedly brought back to Stephen. He was within his rights to allege assault for the original incident – what evidence did they have of his injuries? Had he seen a doctor? Had it been reported? How could he be made safe in his neighbourhood if these school pupils lived nearby? Should we speak to a community safety officer? What steps were they taking to address the cyberbullying? (I suggested a few steps we could take to identify who was sending these messages.)

My hope was that the parents would downgrade their public protests and go home and look after Stephen – perhaps take him to a film and forget the problem for an hour or two while we got the next steps underway. We discussed resilience and how it takes time to rebuild confidence after an incident like this – there is a lot parents can do to help their child feel loved and capable.

Turning to litigation is not a good solution. If parents are involved in a lawsuit with the school over bullying, the child is required to remain for months, even years, as Exhibit A, a victim. There can be no question of the child being happily reintegrated socially with his peers, as that would undermine the case. Most young people simply want the bullying to stop and to be happily reintegrated with their peers. Any prolongation of the case intensifies their isolation and ostracism. It is also humiliating to be labelled a victim.

I asked what the parents' plans were for Stephen's future – did they want to transfer to another school? To my surprise, they wanted Stephen to stay at his current school. 'We chose it,' they said, 'because it is the best around here with the best results.' I pointed out that the school may not want to retain them after all the media activity and picketing they had done, as well as the fact that Stephen's father was now virtually banned from the school. This was a sobering thought. They went home to Stephen and we agreed to speak again in a couple of days.

I then approached the local authority and the school, first, to notify the correct services and to try to trigger some support for Stephen at home via the educational welfare officer and second, to discuss with the behaviour support service how we might help the school deal with the case.

The school was rather unresponsive, but gradually the case was resolved with excellent help from the behaviour support service, and Stephen returned to school with increased support. His parents ceased talking to the press and threatening to sue the school. They agreed to work with the school on a new plan of action. Stephen was provided with a support group of older pupils and work was done with his year group.

What should have been done earlier?

The school should have had plans in place at the start of the new academic year with a new intake of Year 7 pupils. If good peer support is in place, it is common for the trained peer supporters to make themselves known to the new pupils at the start of term and to offer help of all kinds. Older mentors can help younger newcomers. Advice about the school's approach to bullying should be included in welcome packs. Teachers should have been alert. Whole-school work should be ongoing and embedded in the life of the school so that it is totally unacceptable to terrorise new pupils in the youngest class.

A persistent multi-pronged approach

All the stages of a full prevention strategy are required (see Figure 9.1). This involves good policies and strategies, full engagement of pupils, staff and parents, regular sessions to address how we treat one another and pupils' rights to be safe. In Stephen's case, he was cyberbullied even when he was no longer in school, but the school took no steps to stop this.

Support for the victim may take many forms, from peer support to clubs or small groups, or counselling. A support group based on the method outlined by Robinson and Maines[148] would help Stephen get to know supportive pupils who were volunteering ways in which they could support him. A restorative approach might have helped Stephen if the perpetrators had been identified and if both parties agreed. In this approach the perpetrators are asked to reflect on the harm they have caused and act to restore the damage or make amends.

Another approach that requires identification of the perpetrators is the method of shared concern, often named after its creator Pikas, in which individual meetings are held with the perpetrators.[149] The teacher explains that there is a concern about someone (the victim), and asks for ideas on how to help with this problem. They volunteer to do something. Then a meeting is held with the victim to explore whether the victim has provoked the behaviour in some way. Everyone is asked to make progress in the ways agreed, and further meetings are set up to monitor how they are getting on with the goals agreed. If the school has a menu of approaches available and some training in picking the right one for the particular case, there is a greater chance of success.

Transition

It is good practice to prepare pupils for transition from primary to secondary school (or high school), and schools choose different ways to do this, with increasing use of technology alongside personal visits. Myths abound that children will be bullied in high school or secondary school, and children may end up fearing this all summer. These myths and rumours need to be scotched early.

Older pupils could visit feeder primary schools to talk about their school before the summer term ends, and show their faces as supportive older peer befrienders. They could prepare a short 'Welcome' video clip or PowerPoint presentation. They might create a small handbook for new pupils, welcoming them to the new school.

Innovative use of webcams can help prospective pupils view the new school and become accustomed to it. Pictures of sports and drama events can be shown to pupils the term before they are due to join the new school, to foster a sense of excitement and belonging.

Induction should include a mention of bullying and how it is not acceptable at the school, along with an explanation of how to report it, for pupils and parents. Primary schools should alert the receiving school to any particularly vulnerable pupils if they feel this might be necessary.

Where the primary feeder schools are in a cluster with the secondary school, they should all align their anti-bullying practice so that it is seamless and consistent across the cluster, as recommended by the Bullying Intervention Group (BIG).

Bullying prevention management

Whole-school anti-bullying work should take place whether or not the names of the perpetrators are known. Many schools hide behind saying, 'Bullying is not tolerated here, but unless we know about it there is nothing we can do,' in other words, laying the responsibility on the victims to report it, just as Stephen's headteacher did. However, he could have had the senders of the offensive text messages traced when cyberbullying developed at a later stage, but by then, Stephen was no longer coming into school.

Most bullying takes place in front of an audience, and other pupils could have reported it on Stephen's behalf if good systems were in place. Investigations could have taken place to ascertain what had happened. Many schools have CCTV. Above all, preventative work should be ongoing with the whole pupil body in the first term of the academic year.

There are children and young people who are not able to report bullying – they may have language difficulties or other special needs. Like Stephen, they may simply not know the names of their tormentors. They may have been threatened, or simply be too scared. Children believe, and often rightly, that it will make things worse if they tell.

Much can be done to ensure the safety of new pupils in the first year of secondary school:

- Peer support schemes could provide some older pupils to take a special interest in newcomers and to provide support from the first day of term.
- The school's reporting systems must improve.
- Within the class, anti-bullying prevention work should be undertaken with the entire year group, from the start of term.

The city where Stephen went to school uses safer school police officers and one was notified of the case – these officers have a close watch on the neighbourhood and work in some schools. Any threats of violence after someone has already been assaulted could be a police matter. The officer came into school and ran an e-safety session for Stephen's year group. He mentioned cyberbullying and the law, and highlighted making threats. Stephen and his classmates were asked to retain any evidence of bullying in future, and to report it if they saw it happen to someone else.

Many pupils came forward to offer Stephen support after a circle time session. Some new friendship groups were encouraged. Some of the suspects who were never named by Stephen were traced via the cyberbullying messages and made to understand the harm they had caused. Sanctions were applied. They apologised. The class developed its own agreement on 'how we want to be treated'.

Stephen was allowed to come into school a little later than the other pupils to help him feel safe on the way to school. His parents were given the names of other boys who lived near them and Stephen chose to travel home with two of them. He was encouraged to join some supervised clubs at lunchtime. His strengths were emphasised and developed – chess was one example. As his confidence grew, he began to teach others how to play chess within the club. E-safety sessions were held regularly to enable pupils to problem-solve what to do in certain situations.

WHEN THE BULLYING INCIDENT BECOMES A SERIOUS CASE

It is often said that there are too many procedures and protocols for schools, but this is one instance where having a Serious Incident Procedure or Protocol is vital. This document should set out clearly what might be considered a serious incident and what to do if faced with one (for an example, see Chapter 11).

There should be a designated teacher within the school to whom concerns around child protection should be reported. One of the school governors should be responsible for safeguarding matters.

If a multi-agency response is required, the Common Assessment Framework (CAF)[150] may be a useful mechanism. Schools should feel supported by the other agencies and able to trigger the all-round response that the child needs.

However, some cases are too complex for a school to deal with alone, such as these examples:

Ashley's case

(It should be noted that this case has been anonymised and blends characteristics from more than one case.)

In common with many primary schools, School A was inundated with parents complaining about bullying taking place among pupils on Facebook, even though they were under 13. The school had already written to parents reminding them that their children were too young to be on this SNS, and that they had a responsibility to see that their children acted safely. However, one Monday, ten-year-old Lisa's parents came into school with examples of death threats their daughter had received via Facebook from another pupil in her class. Ashley had been bullying Lisa for some time. Lisa's parents were understandably angry and upset and insisted something be done at once.

Ashley, however, had been receiving special support in school for more than two years. Her parents were known to be addicted to illegal drugs and home life was chaotic. Furthermore, the headteacher explained, Ashley had been seen leaving the flat of a person on the sex offenders register. She was 'known to services'. But these death threats were so serious the school was considering excluding Ashley. They felt they had already done everything that was reasonable to help her. Now they were at a cross-roads. But if Ashley was excluded for a week or ten days it would be impossible to assure her well-being. Anything could happen to her and she would not be seen.

The school had a responsibility to make Lisa safe, however, which would be difficult if Ashley and Lisa were still in the same class every day. Lisa might stay away from school in fear. Consequently, a number of supports were put in place around Lisa, including a nurture group.

Legally the school has powers to act on incidents occurring off the premises, involving pupils. The Education and Inspections Act 2006 provides for such a situation.

I suggested that the local authority anti-bullying coordinator and child protection team be informed and a request for support be triggered with the educational welfare service. Could Ashley be offered some intensive support and education in a different setting – a PRU or perhaps intensive short-term fostering to provide her with some stable home life? Various options were canvassed and the case was left with the designated child protection officer who knew the family.

However, the school was in a small town where everyone knew each other and there were other considerations. Was the headteacher safe? Ashley's family had been violent in the past and they knew where she lived. They might take it out on any of the staff. Decisions are required in instances like this – should the police be notified? Should staff take special precautions? Perhaps the teachers' union could provide advice?

The school was also urged to write to all the parents once again, reminding them that they had written before to draw attention to the number of children using Facebook at age ten, and telling them that due to a distressing incident they were writing to them once more about parents' responsibilities around appropriate use of websites for young children.

It is obvious in a case like this that good record keeping is essential and that the school would now find itself under a duty to collaborate with partner agencies in the decisions made about Ashley. In the course of these procedures, they would be called upon to provide evidence.

Upon following up, the local authority gave assurances that this case had been addressed and they were not under any obligation to divulge further details to an outside regional adviser, other than to assure me that both girls were safe and that appropriate steps had been put in place.

Shana's case

(It should be noted that this case has been anonymised and blends characteristics from more than one case.)

A teacher wrote in to ask for help. Her school had a young girl in Year 9 called Shana who had become an internet sensation overnight. Her uploads had gone viral, with negative posts flooding in. She had uploaded many videos over the past year, mainly of herself singing songs. One had suddenly attracted over 200,000 viewers and the tide of unpleasant hate and abuse was like an assault. There had been a few Facebook 'burn' pages set up in the previous months in England but this occurred on YouTube. (This case might be considered a serious incident and require the formal steps of the protocol in Chapter 11.)

Shana loved uploading her songs, but her 'audience' did not know that she had special needs, was on the autism spectrum and was having to see a psychologist. The hate posts had seriously upset and destabilised her. Matters were serious.

Shana needed a lot of support and some recent videos had begun to appear saying they thought the hate messages were bad and they thought Shana had courage. Shana probably couldn't keep from looking on YouTube even though it would be good if she left it for a while. A few friends could post some supportive messages there as she would probably keep looking.

It was possible to block people who harassed her – the school was sent a short YouTube video of how to do this. Offensive messages that could be violating the terms of service of the YouTube community can be flagged and then the system looks at them and decides whether to take them down or block the sender. They would have to be hate messages that violated the express terms of service – a copy of the terms of service were sent to the school.

Shana would have to be asked if any of the hate messages originated from people she knew. If they were from within the school this must be dealt with as very serious behaviour. Her friends may know.

If not, it should be pointed out to Shana that the comments were made by people who did not even know her and were trying to be funny online; they were not personal to her. Some people think they are clever if they criticise others. If we put ourselves 'out there', in the public gaze, we risk getting abusive messages.

The important message is to work on self-esteem and confidence, and to formulate a plan with the Child and Adolescent Mental Health Services (CAMHS) worker that the school and Shana's family could all work towards in a coherent way.

The police might need to become involved; they could help negotiate with YouTube. Sometimes they are able to trace the individuals involved and warn them to remove the material.

Although Shana had been posting songs and videos on YouTube for a long time (she clearly enjoyed this and found it empowering), she needs some intensive support and advice on e-safety – it would be very sad if she lost all the opportunities the internet could offer. We often see people who struggle with friendships in the real world turning to the internet for validation, intimacy and escape. If this is the case, they might take risks and often become almost addicted to online life. That is why it is vital that such people be given intensive e-safety advice and steered towards safer activities.

The universal advice to most pupils is not sufficient in these situations. Shana was a webcam user, and specific advice on what is appropriate to post is urgently required – she was at risk of posting inappropriate images and clearly in need of intensive levels of support and e-safety education. She could be encouraged to post instead on a Facebook page, with privacy settings set to friends only.

Possible solutions

The wider school community: it would be a good time to do some new work on e-safety and what sensible digital citizenship looks like, and to do further work against discrimination with a focus on people with special needs.

Parents: perhaps a letter to all parents about the risks of their children posting on YouTube and other sites would be a timely reminder.

Shana's parents would need intensive support and advice, and the school should work in tandem with the parents to carry out a plan that the psychologist put in place with Shana. Telling Shana to avoid going online may not be the most useful advice as she would, in all likelihood, be drawn to do so. It would be more helpful to help her enjoy the internet safely in future, with appropriate help and support.

KEY MESSAGES ON RESPONDING TO INCIDENTS

- Avoid labelling someone as a victim; everyone has a right to be safe and the term can be negative or humiliating.
- Avoid saying they have been bullied; many young people do not classify themselves as 'bullied' even though they may be reporting something.
- Bully and bullied are often not two distinct categories, the boundaries may be blurred; focus on changing the behaviour rather than working out who started it, if this is not clear.
- Ensure evidence is saved and if necessary, a computer put out of use.
- Take steps to ensure the young person's safety.
- Build resilience, react calmly and do not over-react; ensure the response is proportionate.
- Take prompt steps to report abuse on websites/services if appropriate or get images removed. If required, contact the police or your local child exploitation online service (CEOP in the UK) following a Serious Incident Protocol. Notify the designated person for child protection if necessary and the internet safety lead teacher.
- Ensure there is a record of the incident and actions taken.
- Check back a few times to ensure there are no further incidents, retaliations or new cyberbullying actions by others.

IN CASES THAT ARE BEYOND CYBERBULLYING

When we talk to children and young people about how we all want to be treated and what is inappropriate behaviour, we may find ourselves dealing with a disclosure – abuse or domestic violence may be disclosed. Alternatively, allegations might be made against a member of staff in a position of trust within the school or service. The school should have a designated person for child protection issues and this lead person should deal with any disclosures. The network manager of the school's ICT systems should be involved if the incident took place via the school's system. (See Chapter 11, the Serious Incident Protocol, that describes steps to take.)

RESOURCES

In Chapter 11:

Example of an Acceptable Use Policy.

Cyberbullying Incident Form.

Example of a Serious Incident Protocol.

Lesson plans.

Short activities.

Staff Training Needs Questionnaire, which can also be used to measure confidence levels before and after training.

Communication tools for pupils with special needs.

In Appendix 2:

The law relating to cyberbullying and traditional bullying.

Government guidance England:

Department for Education (2011) 'Dealing With Allegations of Abuse.' London: The Stationery Office. Available at www.education.gov.uk/publications/standard/publicationDetail/Page1/DFE-00061-2011, accessed on 27 April 2012. Department for Education (2011) 'Screening, Searching and Confiscation.' Available at www.education.gov.uk/publications/standard/publicationDetail/Page1/DFE-00024-2012, accessed on 27 April 2012.

Chapter

10

PROTECTING TEACHERS AND STAFF

SYSTEMS ARE VULNERABLE

A teenager recently hacked into his school's website and exposed personal details of as many as 20,000 people. The 15-year-old pupil from Gosport, Hampshire, in the UK, exposed personal details of past and present pupils as well as confidential details of about 13,000 adults to a few of his friends. Was this a copycat mini WikiLeaks in the year in which the leaks were in the news for months? We cannot know, but the message we need to take from this is that the school was found to have breached the Data Protection Act by compromising the privacy of those on the database because it used the same password for the website.

Such attacks do not always come from pupils or parents, however. In Birmingham in the West Midlands, a primary school teacher used his access to the school's system to hack the personal passwords of other teaching staff. He then sent emails purporting to be from other staff members. These emails contained 'offensive, bullying and racist messages,' the hearing of the General Teaching Council (GTC) subsequently heard.[151] He was found guilty of unacceptable professional conduct and a serious breach of trust. He was also cautioned by the police for obtaining unauthorised access to computer material with intent to commit a criminal offence. The case was only uncovered when an email appeared to be sent by a staff member who had not accessed their email account during the holidays.

A further case involved a teacher who had been sacked from a private school in Dubai in the United Arab Emirates. He aired his grievances on Facebook where he had befriended pupils, and in no time his angry complaints were circulating among pupils and parents.[152]

These situations reveal internal system weaknesses, and individuals who see cracking the system as a challenge. Although it is impossible to know from which direction an attack may come, these cases show how vital it is to have good security systems in place and not to be naïve about data protection.

CYBERBULLYING BY PUPILS AND PARENTS

Teachers are at risk in other ways. Just a decade ago it would have been unthinkable that teachers would have to protect themselves against mass attacks by the parents of the children they teach – only the odd angry parent being difficult in a face-to-face meeting had to be appeased and calmed. Parents of a child who had committed a serious offence might have been difficult to deal with if they denied what their child was alleged to have done, and at worst parents might have started a whispering campaign. But today, in this digital age, parents who dislike a teacher are able to take this a step further than a furtive chat with other parents at the school gate.

A school in the West Midlands described how some parents had created a page on Facebook on which they invited other parents to post ugly and defamatory messages about a teacher they disliked. In the time it took to find out about it and have the page removed, many people had already seen it. The impact on the teacher was enormous, and may have constrained other teachers in their approach for fear it could happen to them.

This behaviour is increasing fast in the UK. In 2010 the ATL reported that more than one in seven teachers had been a victim of cyberbullying by pupils or parents. They reported that students had set up 'hate' groups on SNS calling for specific teachers to be sacked, and they had even created fake profiles in their names containing defamatory information. One head of department at an independent (private) school told the ATL study that his experience of cyberbullying had been the worst week of his career. A secondary school teacher said he had been upset and worried about being a source of ridicule among students after a video of him in the classroom was posted on YouTube.

The ATL survey of 630 teachers and support staff found that 15 per cent had been bullied online, with tactics ranging from abusive messages to hate sites and photographs or videos being posted.[153] By 2011, Andy Phippen, Professor of Social Responsibility in IT at Plymouth University, found that as many as a third of teachers said they had been subjected to online bullying, on Facebook and on Twitter.[154]

In his study for the UK Safer Internet Centre, Phippen found that more than a quarter of those targeted said the abuse had come from parents, with one headteacher driven to the brink of suicide by a year-long online hate campaign. One parent had even set up a Google group and asked others to join in the abuse. It seems that parents might take this action even for imagined slights, if they considered that their child deserved a higher grade, or simply if they disliked the teacher.

On top of the abuse from pupils and parents, one in ten teachers said they had been a victim of another teacher's cyberbullying. Commenting on Phippen's results, the National Association of Head Teachers' General Secretary Russell Hobby suggested that Facebook, Twitter and other social media sites pose 'a devastating threat to schools and are a bigger fear than Ofsted' (Ofsted is the education inspectorate in England). Hobby continued: 'Increasingly, social media are being used to fuel campaigns against schools and teachers. Twenty per cent of our members have received threats or abuse online – parents or ex-pupils being the most common source. The results can be devastating.'[155]

RATE MY TEACHER SITE

Other threats come from sites such as Rate My Teacher, a US-run site that invites pupils to comment on their teachers, allowing them to 'grade' teachers as well as to criticise them. Teachers may not know for a while that they are the target of this behaviour, and by the time they react and get the offensive material removed, many people will have already seen it. Their professional reputation is damaged. Furthermore, they may not know which pupil has instigated it. Faced with their class, they may then feel uneasy and nervous.

Even when access to this site is banned in school, it can be accessed from home. Kathy Wallis, a senior teacher from Cornwall in the UK, told the BBC[156] that she had to talk a young colleague out of resigning over comments posted by her pupils on Rate My Teacher. 'The teacher in question burst into tears and said "Well if that's what they think of me I might as well give up teaching now", she recalled. '[Her students] had said that her preparation was dreadful, she had no classroom control and they made other unfounded malicious comments. Basically they just pulled her apart. It took two days for me to talk her out of resigning.' Wallis said that it took nearly three weeks to remove the malicious allegation against another colleague, even after he was cleared by an investigation by the school's governing body.

In a brief visit to the site in August 2011, I found the following posts within seconds:

'Everyone hates her.'

'A tube [slang for vagina] of the highest order.'

'Aye, she'd get it…can't teach though.'

'She's the worst teacher I ever had. She has no patience and she is not good at helping us.'

'Worst teacher ever! Why is this woman teaching Higher let alone Mathematics at all?'

'She obviously is the man in her relationship she has with Mr M. A true beast!'

'He's a bit weird, hard to get on with.'

'He's a complete waste of space and money, just too [sic] think our tax's [sic] pay his wages!'

'Don't let yourself be alone with him!'

There was far worse.

Of course, some left positive posts or rated their teacher highly, but there are many teachers who have a negative emoticon next to their name as a result of only one person posting a rating as long as two or three years ago. At a cursory glance, it appears that they are rated as bad teachers and this could be online for lengthy periods.

The whole concept of rating teachers might seem harmless until something professionally damaging or indeed defamatory is posted. And the use of slang, especially sexual terms, is widespread, with a misogynistic flavour. A pupil in Scotland took a more direct approach. He filmed himself shouting abuse at a teacher and uploaded the film clip on YouTube. He was charged with breach of the peace and suspended for ten days. The teacher was off work after the incident.[157]

Teachers are warned via their unions not to befriend pupils on Facebook, but pupils are increasingly gaining access to potentially embarrassing images of teachers. This can be very simple to do – if you live in a small town or village, a party or wedding might result in a flood of photos online and a pupil's older sibling or their parent might be included in the list of those who can share the photos. In a matter of minutes an image is downloaded and shared – possibly altered or given new captions.

Headteachers and governors are also increasingly using the internet to search for information on potential employees and staff. In April 2010, at the annual conference of the National Union of Teachers, members were warned that the line between private and professional life had become blurred because of social media. It had recently issued guidance warning teachers not to befriend pupils on SNS and to let school management know if they had befriended parents or ex-pupils.

Karl Hopwood, an internet safety consultant and himself a former headteacher, warned teachers to watch out for unguarded comments.[158] He gave the example of a teacher who posted the status update: 'OMG got to stop pissing about and get my maths boosters planned as I got to teach kids it in about one and a half hours!!!' While posted jokingly (how many of us pretend we have not worked all that hard and have to rush to meet a deadline?) this post could be viewed negatively by a headteacher or parents. Hopwood also gave the example of a deputy head who found that an image of him in a Superman outfit had appeared on the school's bulletin board. Taken by a friend at a birthday party, this picture had spread through his friendships with pupils.

Teachers also need to be aware and wary of sites such as Formspring on which users can post comments and questions anonymously, and Tumblr where users post text, images, videos, links, quotes and audio to their tumblelog, a short-form blog.

What worries teachers is that much of the cyberabuse falls somewhere between what is illegal and what is socially acceptable or professionally comfortable. This makes it even more challenging to resolve, as police will not act unless an actual law is broken. If a complaint is received by an SNS, they tend to remove certain types of material deemed offensive, but not every personally hurtful post, unless it is breach of the terms of service the site has set out for users (See Chapter 11). In addition, once material is 'out there' it can be circulating on the web even if the offending item is removed from the original site.

So teachers may feel that they have nowhere to turn and senior management teams may feel helpless unless this behaviour is explicitly outlawed within the school's Behaviour Policy and both parents and pupils are warned that it will result in punishment or expulsion.

BEFRIENDING PUPILS

More than one in ten school teachers accused of misconduct in 2011 had used SNS and email to forge inappropriate relationships with their pupils. Facebook, Twitter, online chatrooms and emails were used to befriend children in 43 of the cases brought to the regulator, the GTC, in 2011. Eighteen teachers were given prohibition orders and struck off, while 14 were suspended. In all, the GTC heard 336 cases of 'unacceptable professional conduct'.[159]

These cases underline the risks in befriending pupils online in this way. There are enormous difficulties because many teachers explain that it is also possible to keep in touch with a vulnerable young person through social networks, IM or email. They can provide advice and comfort, or review a CV or even signpost someone to a helpline. But if any teacher is providing support to a particular pupil, this should be agreed by the school, carried out on the school's system, where it can be checked and the discussions reported to the internet safety officer in regular debriefing sessions. Teachers should avoid using personal SNS pages or emails.

WHAT IS NEEDED?
A robust approach

A robust approach and strong links with the parent body from the start of every child's school life are needed. Internally, AUPs should be 'live' and active rather than a few sheets of paper gathering dust on a shelf. Staff should be regularly consulted to keep the AUP up to date and it should be adapted to new technology development.

Good practice bullying interventions involve both prevention and response. The school should already be working proactively to counter all forms of bullying and aiming to make the ethos supportive and respectful. Within the prevention of bullying work, there should be an emphasis on equality and diversity that applies to every member of the school community. E-safety education should be continuously delivered within the school and it should also apply to teachers, with some clear guidelines reminding teachers not to befriend pupils on SNS or to give out personal contact details.

Governing bodies should appoint a lead governor to oversee this work. Parent/ school partnerships or agreements should be entered into when a child first starts at a school, and in this agreement parents could be asked to comply with the school's efforts to keep every member of the school community safe and free from victimisation. There are very few parents who would object to a request couched in these terms.

Policy

It is true that there are some policies that are not worth the paper on which they are written, and this is because they are seldom if ever reviewed and lie dormant, not contributing to the life of the school. However, a policy used well can be a useful tool, guiding staff, shaping the ethos of the whole community and giving parents, teachers and pupils reassurance and a framework within which to operate if they need to report incidents.

But a policy without accompanying training is an empty gesture, as Phippen's findings show. He found that among 355 education professionals, the vast majority of respondents (81%) worked in an institution where AUPs were in place for both staff and students. Sixty-eight per cent of respondents had guidance available on the use of social networking by staff for personal and professional use. Fifty-eight per cent had received some level of training on such issues in the last year. This means that over 40 per cent of respondents had not received any training. Almost one in five did not have or know of an AUP, and as many as 25 per cent did not know who they should approach if they were subject to online abuse in their professional role.[160]

It seems that if a policy mentions all the different forms of bullying it is more likely that these forms will be reduced,[161] which is why it should take care to mention bullying in the real world or online, or via mobile phones. It should also clearly mention prejudice-driven bullying linked to homophobia, racism or sexism, and bullying targeting those with a disability or special educational needs. And it should be clearly stated that this policy applies to every member of the school community.

Apart from a school policy that covers students and their relationships with staff, a policy and advice are also needed for staff, which everyone should receive on induction. Staff should also be trained in how to act if a case of such bullying is reported or discovered.

Policies should be developed in consultation with the entire school population including support staff, pupils and parents, with reviews undertaken, at a minimum, every two years.

An exciting aspect of developing such a policy is the discussion to be held around a vision statement, which is when the concept is 'sold' to everyone as they debate what the statement should say. If people have a stake in it they are more likely to 'own' it. The vision statement encapsulates the very essence of the policy. Pupils could design logos or posters to illustrate this vision of a school, where pupils feel safe from bullying.

Anti-Bullying Policies are often stand-alone documents with a child-friendly version, as well as versions for parents and staff. The teachers' version includes procedures and protocols to follow in serious cases or when child protection is required, and recording of incidents can be explained within it. The parents' version, on the other hand, tells them how they can report any concerns and what might happen if there are allegations against their child. Without a stand-alone Anti-Bullying Policy this material could be incorporated into a Behaviour Policy, which is legally acceptable in England, but it is my view that it is in danger of being reduced to a couple of paragraphs and lost to view. The Anti-Bullying Policy should cover cyberbullying, while aspects of e-safety and behaviour relating to the use of the school's systems should be included in the AUP.

An AUP can only cover behaviour using the school's computer system, while behaviour outside school that affects someone in the school community can be covered by a Behaviour and an Anti-Bullying Policy. Procedures should be in place should this type of action happen. Who will tackle it? How will they get the offensive material removed? What is the reporting procedure within the school? If procedures are in place, action can be much quicker. In 2011 the government issued advice on how schools should handle malicious allegations in England,[162] and teachers' unions are also entering this debate with advice for their members (for an example, visit www.atl.org.uk).

One lesson that has been learned since the arrival of the internet is that attempts at suppression or censorship are often fruitless. However, membership of a community or school can be made contingent on compliance with the standards and agreed behaviour set out in the policies of the school. This is easily effected, and provided an agreement by pupils, parents and staff has been entered into, it is easier to enforce.

But looked at another way, it is democratic to allow learners to comment on those who teach them. If this could be managed in a moderated way, the school could learn a great deal about staff without having every comment openly available to the world audience of Rate My Teacher. Perhaps the presence of this site will challenge schools to come up with better 'listening schemes' to allow their pupils to air concerns or grievances in a reasonably polite way within school.

OTHER WAYS TO KEEP DEMOCRACY ALIVE!

Consider a forum discussion on 'How we treat one another' that ends with 'Three ways my classroom experience could be improved' (no names are allowed to be mentioned or personal attacks made). Or 'What is the best aspect of my class or school?' and 'What I like least about my class or school.'

Another problem with the Rate My Teacher site is that many of the comments had been there for a long time. Furthermore, many were marked 'pending review', which suggests there had been complaints about them and the text was subsequently removed. However, if a teacher has a number of these 'pending review' signs, it could be inferred that the messages were nasty and this could colour the visitor's view of the person.

Some pupils are clever enough to write their comment in local slang or patois that eludes adults, although a quick referral to an online slang dictionary can help to clarify if the term is insulting or not. (When I did this, the terms were invariably insulting.)

Advice for teachers

The steps below are reproduced here with the kind permission of the ATL.

Step 1: If you discover that arising from your employment as an education professional a website contains incorrect, inappropriate or inflammatory written material relating to you, or images of you which have been taken and/or which are being used without your permission, then this should be immediately reported to a senior manager at your school.

Step 2: The senior manager (who may be your headteacher or principal) should conduct a prompt investigation.

Step 3: If, in the course of the investigation, it is found that a pupil or student submitted the material to the website, then that pupil should be disciplined in line with the school's disciplinary procedures.

Step 4: Where appropriate, the senior manager should approach the website hosts to ensure the material is either amended or removed as a matter of urgency, that is, within 24 hours. If the website requires the individual who is complaining to do so personally, the school or college should give their full support and assistance. Checks should be carried out to ensure that the requested amendments or removals are made.

   If the website(s) will not cooperate, the senior manager should contact the internet service provider (ISP). An ISP has the ability to block access to certain pages and, in exceptional cases, can close down a website. Even though pages may be removed from a particular website, they are stored (that is, 'cached') by search engines and can be retrieved, for example, by carrying out a Google search. Consequently the senior manager should ensure the website takes steps to 'uncache' the offending page(s). Google provides instructions on how to uncache material through the 'webmaster' help service on their home page.

Step 5: If the material is threatening and/or intimidating, then senior management should, with the member's consent, report the matter to the police. Mindful of their health and safety duty of care, management should offer the member of staff support and appropriate stress counselling.

WHAT SHOULD A HARASSMENT AND BULLYING AT WORK POLICY CONTAIN?

- A statement of intent.
- Equal opportunities statement of commitment.
- Who the policy applies to.
- Definition and effects of bullying.
- The school's approach to bullying and harassment.
- How to complain about harassment or bullying.
- Responsibilities of governors and staff (including complainants).

Bullying is characterised as aggressive, intimidating, malicious or insulting behaviour or abuse or misuse of power through means intended to undermine, humiliate, denigrate or injure the recipient. What may emerge as a concern initially categorised as 'harassment', 'intimidation' or 'aggressive management' may, upon investigation, be considered to be a case of bullying. A person who is subject to bullying may suffer from physical and/or emotional symptoms, for example, disturbed sleep, feeling sick, sweating, shaking, depression or loss of confidence and motivation. Additionally, they may suffer in other ways, for example, loss of training and development opportunities, and missed promotion opportunities.

RESOURCES

Example of an Acceptable Use Policy (Chapter 11).

Cases to use in staff training sessions (Chapter 11).

The law relating to cyberbullying and traditional bullying (Appendix 2).

Department for Children, Schools and Families (2009) *Cyberbullying: Supporting School Staff.* London: The Stationery Office. Available at www.digizen.org/downloads/cyberbullying_teachers.pdf and www.atl.org.uk/Images/DCSF%20Cyberbullying%20guidance.pdf, accessed on 21 March 2012.

Chapter
11

USEFUL TOOLS

EXAMPLE OF AN ACCEPTABLE USE POLICY (AUP)

Date .... Last reviewed .... When next to be reviewed.....................

School or college name..

Who does this policy apply to?

Our policy applies to all students, staff, governors and volunteers associated with the school.

What does it relate to?

The use of information and communications technology (ICT) in all forms, current and emerging.

This policy is part of the School Development Plan and relates to other polices including those for: ICT, Behaviour, Anti-Bullying and Child Protection. It has been written by the school and approved by staff and governors with pupils' participation.

Our vision

We want every member of the school community to be safely using the opportunities offered by digital technology.

Everyone has a right to be free of bullying and discrimination, exploitation or harassment.

Our objectives

- To inform every member of our school community on how they can be safe on the internet and using mobile phones and handheld devices.

- To set up clear boundaries and agreements on the acceptable use of ICT, the school's systems and those used by every individual. Our Acceptable Use Policy sets out clear rules for the use of ICT for both staff and pupils.

- To make staff, pupils, parents and governors our partners in the delivery of an e-safe school.

There are five main areas of this policy:

1. Current digital technologies

2. Teaching and learning

3. E-safety risks

4. Strategies to minimise risks

5. How complaints regarding e-safety will be dealt with.

There are two agreements:

- Staff school computer and internet use policy

- Pupil school computer and internet use policy.

1. Current digital technologies

ICT in the 21st century has an enabling, creative and essential role in the lives of children and adults. New technologies are rapidly enhancing communication and the sharing of information, images, music and film. We want our students and staff to benefit from the opportunities this represents but we acknowledge there are risks. Current and emerging technologies used in school and outside of school include:

- the internet, accessed by a wide range of devices

- intranets, virtual learning environments (Moodle)

- telephone text messaging, email, BlackBerry Messenger

- IM

- SNS (Facebook)

- video broadcasting sites (YouTube)

- chatrooms

- webcams

- blogs

- Twitter

- podcasting

- gaming sites

- music download sites

- image sharing sites

- virtual worlds (Second Life)

- mobile phones with camera and videos

- games consoles with internet communication

- smartphones with email and web functionality.

2. Teaching and learning

- The internet is an essential element in 21st-century life for education, business and social interaction. The school has a duty to provide pupils with quality internet access as part of their learning experience.

- The internet use is a part of the statutory curriculum and a necessary tool for staff and pupils.

- Internet use will enhance learning.

- School internet access will be designed expressly for pupil use and will include filtering appropriate to the age of pupils.

- Pupils will be taught what internet use is acceptable and what is not and given clear objectives for internet use.

- Pupils will be educated in the effective use of the internet in research, including the skills of knowledge location, retrieval and evaluation.

- Pupils will be shown how to publish and present information to a wider audience.

- Pupils will be taught how to evaluate internet content.

- The school will ensure that the use of internet-derived materials by staff and pupils complies with copyright law.

- Pupils will be taught the importance of cross-checking information before accepting its accuracy.

- Pupils will be taught how to report unpleasant internet content.

- Pupils will be partners in carrying out this policy. They will be consulted and their views and experiences will be taken into account.

3. E-safety risks

E-content:

- Exposure to age-inappropriate material – such as violence or pornography.

- Exposure to inaccurate or misleading information.

- Exposure to socially unacceptable material, such as that inciting violence, hate or intolerance.

- Exposure to coercive websites, that is, that promote suicide or anorexia.

E-contact:

- Grooming, using the internet and phones, leading to sexual assault.

- Harassment and stalking.

- Unwelcome contact of any kind.

E-commerce:

- Exposure of minors to inappropriate commercial advertising.

- Exposure to online gambling.
- Commercial and financial scams.
- Pressurised selling to children.

E-culture:

- Bullying via mobile phones/social networking/websites or other forms of digital communication, including untruthful, hurtful and abusive comments, rumour spreading, humiliating or inappropriate imagery intended to denigrate or humiliate another person or group.
- Illegal downloading of copyrighted materials, that is, music and films.
- Plagiarism.

4. Strategies to minimise risks

General:

- Our Acceptable Use Policy Agreement signed by all parents and students.
- All staff will be trained in e-safety and responding to incidents.
- Parents and pupils to provide consent before publication of photographic images.
- All parents will be regularly sent briefings on e-safety.
- E-safety advice will be displayed throughout the school/college.
- E-safety will be taught to all pupils and continually updated as age-appropriate.
- Guidance on cyberbullying will be given in assemblies and classroom activities.
- Sanctions for inappropriate use of the internet will be communicated widely.
- Log-on screen for all students and staff has a tick box indicating acceptance of the school Internet Policy.
- Filtering systems to prevent access to inappropriate material.
- Use of RMTutor, in class monitoring of computer use by teachers.
- Surveillance software monitoring all computer use within the school.
- Mobile phone use within school will be limited.
- Staff will use safe search engines when accessing the internet with pupils.
- All staff sign a Computer and Internet Acceptable Use Policy.
- The school will ask all parents to sign the parent/pupil agreement at the start of each school year or when children are admitted in the case of in-year admissions.
- Child protection concerns will be reported to the designated staff member.
- E-safety concerns are reported direct to the deputy headteacher responsible for ICT systems.

- Regular anonymous surveys of our pupils will help evaluate the effectiveness of our strategies and identify any new concerns.
- We will reflect and review our approach regularly.

Published content and the school website:

- Staff or pupil personal contact information will not generally be published. The contact details given online should be the school office.
- The headteacher will take overall editorial responsibility and ensure that content is accurate and appropriate.
- Photographs that include pupils will be selected carefully so that individual pupils cannot be identified or their image misused.
- Where possible group photographs will be used rather than full-face photos of individual children.
- Pupils' names will not be used in association with photographs anywhere on the school website or other online space.
- Pictures and work will only be shown on the website if parents/carers have signed the consent form issued at the start of each school year.
- Parents will be clearly informed of the school policy on image taking and publishing, both on school and independent electronic repositories.

Social networking and personal publishing:

- If they are to be used, the school will control access to SNS, and consider how to educate pupils in their safe use.
- Newsgroups will be blocked unless a specific use is approved.
- Pupils will be advised never to give out personal details of any kind that may identify them, their friends or their location.
- Ideally pupils would use only moderated SNS.
- Pupils and parents will be advised that the use of SNS outside school brings a range of dangers for primary aged pupils.
- Pupils will be advised to use nicknames and avatars when using SNS.
- Under normal circumstances, no member of staff should engage in direct communication (in or out of school) of a personal nature with a pupil who is not a member of their direct family, by any means, for example (but not limited to) SNS, SMS text message, email, instant messaging or telephone. Should special circumstances arise where such communication is felt to be necessary, the agreement of a line manager should be sought first and appropriate professional language should always be used.

Managing videoconferencing and webcam use:

- When available, videoconferencing and webcam use will be appropriately supervised for the pupils' age.

Managing emerging technologies:

- Emerging technologies will be examined for educational benefit and a risk assessment will be carried out before use in school is allowed.

- Staff note that technologies such as mobile phones with wireless internet access can bypass school filtering systems and present a new route to undesirable material and communications.

- Mobile phones will not be used during lessons or formal school time. The sending of abusive or inappropriate text messages or files by Bluetooth or any other means is forbidden.

- The use by pupils of cameras in mobile phones will be kept under review.

- Games devices including the Sony PlayStation, Microsoft Xbox and others have internet access that may not include filtering. These may not be used in school.

5. How complaints regarding e-safety will be dealt with

- Complaints will be taken very seriously by senior staff and responses will be swift.

- Where possible we will assist pupils and staff to have defamatory, humiliating or abusive material taken down.

- Sanctions will be given in accordance with our Behaviour and Anti-Bullying Policies.

- Incidents will be logged and our practice monitored.

- Our Serious Incident Protocol will apply in any case where there is cause for concern about the safety of an individual or group. This can trigger child protection procedures.

- If there is concern that a serious incident has taken place, the evidence must be kept and any computer within school sealed and retained for further investigation.

Liability: Due to the global scale and linked nature of internet content, the wide availability of mobile and digital technologies and speed of change, it is not possible to guarantee that no unsuitable material will ever appear on a school computer or mobile device. Neither the school nor the local authority can accept liability for material accessed, or any consequences of internet access. Schools cannot control whether or not children access websites below the recommended age, when they are off site therefore they cannot be held liable if children do so and come to harm. However they do have powers to discipline pupils for behaviour beyond school premises especially if it impacts pupils or the school generally.

All school network, internet and managed learning environment systems are monitored and we reserve the right to examine any area of these systems.

STAFF SCHOOL COMPUTER AND INTERNET ACCEPTABLE USE POLICY

All staff having access to the networks must sign a copy of this Computer and Internet Acceptable Use Policy and return it to the senior administrator.

The computer network is owned by the school and is made available to staff to assist their professional development. This Computer and Internet Acceptable Use Policy covers use of digital technologies in school, that is, email, internet, intranet and network resources, learning platform, software, equipment and systems and has been drawn up to protect everyone. Staff are asked to agree to the following:

Usage

- I will only use the school's digital technology resources and systems for professional purposes or for uses deemed 'reasonable' by the headteacher and governing body.

- I will only use the school's approved, secure email system(s) for any school business.

- I will not allow unauthorised individuals to access email/internet/intranet/network, or other school/local authority systems.

- I will not connect a computer, laptop or other device (including USB flash drive) to the network/internet without up-to-date anti-virus software, and I will keep any 'loaned' equipment up to date using the school's recommended system.

- I will use the school's Learning Platform in accordance with school and Local Grid for Learning advice.

- I will ensure that any private SNS/blogs, etc. that I create or to which I actively contribute, are not confused with my professional role and are secure against access by uninvited users, that is, students both current and former.

- I will not engage in any online activity that may compromise my professional responsibilities.

- I agree and accept that any computer or laptop loaned to me by the school is provided solely for professional use.

- I will only use local authority systems in accordance with any corporate policies.

Inappropriate material

- I will not browse, download or send material that could be considered offensive to colleagues.

- I will report any accidental access to, or receipt of, inappropriate materials, or filtering breach, to the appropriate line manager/deputy headteacher responsible for ICT systems.

- I will not download any software or resources from the internet that can compromise the network, or are not adequately licensed.

Data and image protection

- I will ensure all documents are saved, accessed and deleted in accordance with the school's data protection procedures.

- I will not use personal digital cameras or camera phones for transferring images of pupils or staff without permission.

- I will not remove any data from the school's system to a memory stick or laptop without the appropriate level of data protection and encryption.

- I will ensure any confidential data that I wish to transport from one location to another is password protected, even within the school premises.

- I understand that the Data Protection Policy requires that any information seen by me with regard to staff or pupil information, held within the school's information management system, will be kept private and confidential, EXCEPT when it is deemed necessary that I am required by law to disclose such information to an appropriate authority.

E-safety education and students

- I will ensure I am aware of digital safeguarding procedures so they are appropriately embedded in my classroom practice.

- I will promote e-safety with students in my care and will help them to develop a responsible attitude to system use, communications and publishing.

- I will report any incidents of concern regarding children's safety to the e-safety coordinator, the designated child protection coordinator or headteacher.

Management and disciplinary procedures

- I understand that all internet usage and network usage can be logged and this information could be made available to my manager on request.

- I understand that failure to comply with the Acceptable Use Policy could lead to disciplinary action.

The use of computer systems without permission or for inappropriate purposes could be a criminal offence under the Computer Misuse Act 1990. (The Computer Misuse Act 1990 makes it a criminal offence to 'cause a computer to perform any function with intent to secure unauthorised access to any program or data held in any computer.' Sending malicious or threatening emails and other messages is a criminal offence under the Protection from Harassment Act 1997, the Malicious Communications Act 1988 and Section 43 of the Telecommunications Act 1984.)

- I understand that it is my responsibility to ensure that I remain up to date and read and understand the school's most recent Acceptable Use Policy (at least annually).
- I agree to abide by the school's most recent Acceptable Use Policy.
- I wish to have an email account; be connected to the intranet and internet; be able to use the school's ICT resources and systems.

Signed...

Name .... Date ....

PUPIL SCHOOL COMPUTER AND INTERNET ACCEPTABLE USE POLICY

The school's computers and internet access are to help us learn. These rules will keep everyone safe and help us be fair to others. I agree that:

- I will only access the system with my own login and password, which I will keep secret.
- I will not access other people's files or try to find out their passwords.
- I will only use the computers for schoolwork and homework.

I will not download and use material or copy and paste content which is copyright. (Most sites will allow the use of published materials for educational use. Teachers will give guidelines on how and when pupils should use information from the internet.)

- I will not bring in memory sticks or disks from outside school unless I have been given permission.
- I will ask permission from a member of staff before using the internet.
- I will only email people I know, or my teacher has approved.
- The messages I send will be polite and responsible.
- I will not give my home address or telephone number, or arrange to meet someone, unless my parent, carer or teacher has given permission.
- I will report any unpleasant material or messages sent to me. I understand my report would be confidential and would help protect other pupils and myself.
- I will not send any harmful, unpleasant or bullying messages to other people.
- I understand that the school may check my computer files and may monitor the internet sites I visit.

Signed...

Name .... Date ....

RECORDING A CYBERBULLYING INCIDENT
Cyberbullying Incident Form

Name of person reporting the incident	
Name of staff recording incident	
Anonymous	
Date of report	

Type of cyberbullying incident (please tick all that apply)			
Via mobile or handheld device		Involves internet	
Involves chatroom/s		Involves IM	
BlackBerry Messenger		Involves SNS	
Involves photographs		Friendship feud?	
Persistent teasing/sarcastic remarks		Demanding money/valuables	
Name-calling		Ridicule/humiliation	
Threats		Coercion	
Spreading rumours		Encouraging others to join in	
Unpleasant/hurtful email/texts/web posts combined		Provocative/sexist taunts	
Plans to isolate someone		Linked to bullying in school?	
Other			

Racist*		Cyberbullying	
Homophobic		Due to disability	
Sexual		LAC	

* If racist report it to your local authority.[163]

Name of victim/target	

Class/form/age		Year group/house	

Name of perpetrator(s)		1)
2)		3)
Class/form/age		Year group/house

Date(s) of incidents	Day		Month		Year	
Approximate time(s)	Before school	Morning	Afternoon	After school	Weekend	

How long has this being going on?	
Has any intervention been tried?	
If abusive, has this been reported to the service provider or website?	
Does this case require the Serious Incident Protocol to be activated? Has the CEOP report abuse button been used?	
Do the police need to be informed?	
Does a device need to be confiscated or a computer isolated as evidence?	
Does material need to be taken down?	
Have parents been alerted?	
Who has taken responsibility for the above steps?	

If you are not sure what steps to take talk to your e-safety lead in school (see Appendix 1) or within the local authority. The school has the powers to search and confiscate a phone (EIA 2006).

Follow-up	
Has the cyberbullying stopped? Does the student (target) feel safe?	
Is further action required?	
Have those involved changed their behaviour/acknowledged the harm caused?	
Has the case contributed to the learning of the class/year group in some way?	
Have passwords been changed, privacy settings checked and friends list cleaned?	

Any further notes, such as the impact of this incident or recommendations

If you have triggered the Serious Incident Protocol (see the following page), that will take precedence over anything in this document.

Signed.. Date................................

Illustration of a Serious Incident Protocol

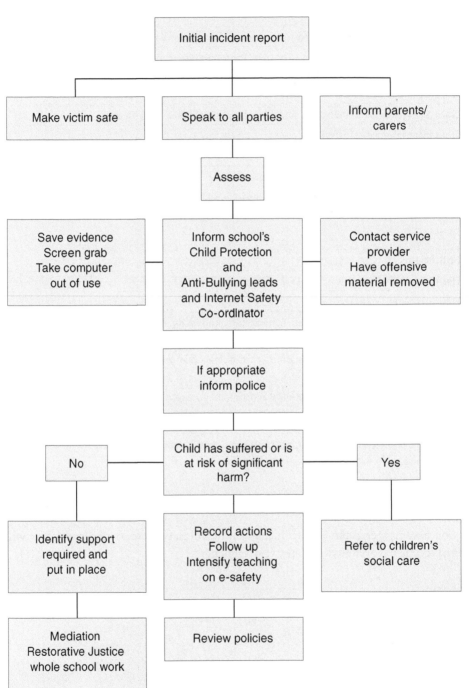

When the incident violates the terms of service of a website

Websites and service providers have terms of service that usually include a prohibition on abusive messages or activities. You would need to show how and when these terms of service were violated. Read the terms of service carefully and note any that are relevant to the case.

If the actions of the perpetrator violate these terms of service with that site or provider, the user may lose their account or be banned from a chatroom. Temporary bans are also used.

This is usually the best way to have material removed from a website if you cannot have the originator take it down. Check whether or not it contravenes the terms of use or terms of service.

Use the report abuse button or the instructions on how to report a contravention of the terms of service.

Your evidence needs to be clear and collated. Some sites consider the first approach with caution. Few sites act as fast as you would like. This is because they may have to investigate. They need to be certain that the evidence is genuine. They have to check that the cyberbully is not posing as a victim to harass someone else. They will be dealing with huge numbers of reports and yours may not be at the top of the pile. Make your report clear and concise but ensure it carries all the information needed. Explain any steps you have already taken to try to address the situation.

Useful tips

- Copy yourself in to any emails you send, so that you have a record of what you sent and the date. Save this on your computer.

- Follow the rules the provider sets out for a report of a terms of service violation.

- Include screen grabs of the offending material with date and time.

- Include the full URL of newsgroups or bulletin boards where offensive postings have appeared.

- If appropriate, add a time line.

- If it is via a mobile phone do not delete the evidence. Note the date and time. You can photograph it with another phone and email it to yourself.

Recently on Tumblr a student found that a girl she knew had posted humiliating photos of her accompanied by nasty remarks. The two were students on the same course. This meant that classmates all saw it. In this case the perpetrator had clearly violated the terms of service and was inviting other people to comment and post hate-filled messages. The victim wanted it removed as soon as possible. However, it is realistic to explain that this may take a little time. It is obviously quicker if the perpetrator can be called in and asked to remove it. Meanwhile the report to the website should be prepared and sent.

CYBERQUIZZES FOR KEY STAGES 2 AND 3
Could I be a cyberbully?
Have you ever...

1. Used/stolen someone else's password?

2. Sent a nasty message using someone else's phone?

3. Pretended to be someone else using text, IM or BBM?

4. Teased and scared someone using IM?

5. Forwarded a message not meant for others to see?

6. Posted photos of someone without asking them?

7. Altered someone's online photos in order to upset them?

8. Created an online ratings poll about someone else without their consent?

9. Spread rumours about someone in cyberspace?

10. Made threats to someone in cyberspace?

11. Sent rude and abusive material to someone?

12. Used information about someone to harass, scare or embarrass them?

13. Created or forwarded a chain letter with threats if people don't pass it on?

14. Signed someone up for something online without asking them?

15. Altered someone's profile without his or her consent?

16. Created a cruel web page about someone and invited others to comment?

17. Hacked into someone's computer?

18. Sent a virus to someone else deliberately?

19. Insulted players in online games?

20. Joined in with insulting chatroom talk that is racist or abusive about religion or culture?

21. Signed on to a website and lied about your age?

Rough guide

1. If you score above 15, what you are doing could be a matter for the police.

2. If you score 12–15, you could be a cyberbully.

3. If you score 10 you are on your way to being a full-blown cyberbully.

4. If you score 5, take a deep breath and think about where this is heading before it is too late.

5. Did you know that it is against the law to send malicious communications or to incite hatred?

How do I know the website is secure?

Aim

Five questions to find out how much pupils know about secure websites before they use that credit card or enter personal details:

1. What do I look for? Name at least two things to look for when deciding if a website is secure.
2. What is SSL?
3. What is https?
4. What is the lock icon?
5. How do I know whether the lock icon is genuine?

1	
2	
3	
4	
5	

Answers

1. (a) Check the URL is secure (look for 'https' in the URL of the pages where you give information or payment); (b) look for the site seal (a lock sign) and check it is genuine; and (c) make sure that when you pay with a card you have some other security check like a password set up with the bank, or you are using a payment system like PayPal or PaymentSense or WorldPay.

2. SSL stands for secure sockets layer and it encrypts your information as it moves between your computer and the website you are viewing and many sites it passes through. Try it! Visit www.ssl.com. Click the link to 'Log in' to start a secure session. Find the lock icon display in your browser. Click the icon, or double-click and see the security information displayed about the website. If there is no display at the bottom of your browser try clicking 'View' in the main menu and make sure 'Status Bar' is checked.

3. Check the web page URL – if you move to a member's area or a pay area, it should show 'https' in the URL of the page. The 's' stands for secure.

4. Companies that sell security systems to websites (Verisign, GeoTrust, SSL.com, etc.) also provide a 'site seal' to the owners of these websites to show that they are secure. These seals are usually:

   • easy to see – on the webpage, usually at the bottom or corner

   • difficult to copy – difficult for thieves and scammers to copy

   • you should be able to check it – click on the seal or hover your mouse over it to see detailed information about the website you are visiting.

5. Double click on the lock sign and you should be able to see the details of the security on that site. Don't trust the seal alone, but also check for that 'https' in the prefix of the web page address. If everything looks good, the company or individual(s) running that website have provided you with a safe means of communicating your sensitive information. The web page is 'secure'. Browse safely!

For more information visit http://faq.ssl.com/article.aspx?id=10068

True or false?

1. Everything I read on the internet is true.

2. Someone somewhere checks what is put onto websites.

3. Messages or photos posted online can be around online forever.

4. There is a system for rating games.

5. Anyone can legally use material or pictures they find online.

6. Wikipedia is always reliable.

7. My page on Facebook is automatically private.

8. You can use a credit card safely online everywhere.

9. It is safe to click on a link sent to you in an email.

10. There is nothing you can do if you're bullied and you don't know who sent it.

Answers

1. False. 2. False. 3. True. 4. True. 5. False (they could use it but not legally). 6. False. 7. False. 8. False (only on secure websites). 9. False (it could be a fake games site for example). 10. False (the sender leaves a technical trail which a service provider could identify).

Electronic footprint activity

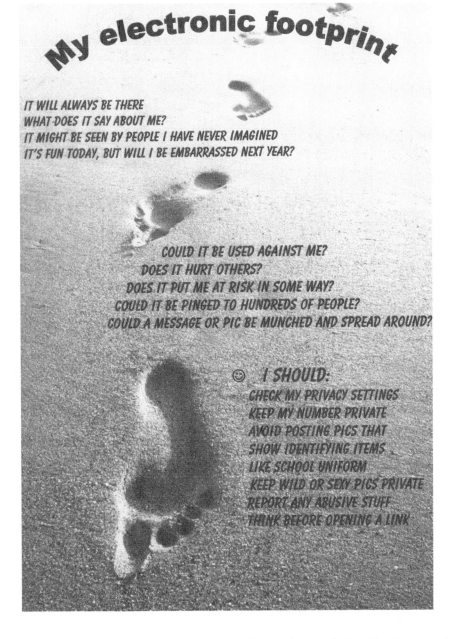

Invite pupils to develop their own posters to be used around the school. Agree the messages to convey and use comuter graphics, art or photography.

LESSON PLAN: STEREOTYPES

Key Stages	2–3
Aim	To challenge stereotypes.
Time taken	40 minutes

Curriculum links

Key Stage	3
PSHE	3a: About the effects of all types of stereotyping, prejudice, bullying, racism and discrimination and how to challenge them assertively. 1b: To respect the differences between people as they develop their own sense of identity. 3b: How to empathise with people different from themselves.

Approach

A definition of a stereotype is needed. Begin with a discussion: What is a Stereotype? Some suggested definitions are shown below:

For Key stage 2 (a child-friendly definition is required)
What is a stereotype?
It is when we decide we don't like people or make fun of them simply because of one thing about them without event trying to get to know them. We put them into a set in our minds. (Games shown below can be played to illustrate this).

For Key Stage 3
What is a stereotype?
It is an oversimplified or exaggerated idea about a group of people pre-judged because of just one aspect of who they are. It suggests that all the people who are similar, are the same. It is a lazy and often cruel way of criticising or judging people.

1. Why do you think this could be a dangerous thing to do?

2. How could people who think like this, lose out?

3. Have you ever felt judged by one aspect alone?

4. Why is it lazy to judge people as a whole group?

Write a short story starting 'It was because of his hair', which shows how mistaken a person can be when judging someone only by a superficial aspect like their hair.

Games

Call out common characteristics such as 'blue eyes' or 'brown shoes'. If any pupil has any of these characteristics they jump into the middle of the circle. They may have nothing in common but brown shoes, but how different they are. We are all unique and special. If we judged people just by one characteristic or saw them as a group, we would be missing out on so much they have to offer. Repeat three or four times with very simple characteristics.[164]

LESSON PLAN: CYBERBULLYING AND GENDER

This activity on how girls and boys experience different kinds of bullying uses material from Chapter 5.

Key Stage	3
Aims	To reduce cyberbullying behaviour that peaks in mid to late teen years. To improve understanding of why these gender patterns are appearing. To improve the quality of support provided if someone does report it.
Time taken	1 hour
Links to curriculum	Behaviour, Citizenship, PSHE, ICT

Approach and rationale

This lesson is based on a youth participation approach to explore the different ways in which young men and women are cyberbullied and how they respond if it happens.

The aim of this approach is to encourage them to take ownership of plans to address this behaviour.

When students learn of the behaviours reported by large numbers of students their age, victims realise that they are not alone. Bystanders tend to be shocked and are empowered to come forward with ideas to address it.

By exposing the patterns of abusive and aggressive behaviour reported by other young people, students become aware of the wider picture and it brings home to them how hurtful and damaging this can be for everyone. They are slightly distanced from these messages from other young people and can objectively examine the situation without involving personal stories.

This exercise engages students to take responsibility and plan strategies for the school. They take charge of the plans and can help deliver them to younger students.

These discussions help the school by revealing valuable information about your own local school population and their experiences of cyberbullying.

Resources

- Cards. Each card should be one line, either describing a type of cyberbullying listed below or using items from your own school survey results:

1. People talking about you nastily online.

2. Messages that try to make you do something you do not want to do.

3. A message from a stranger asking you to meet up.

4. A message with racist names or comments.

5. A message with insults calling you gay whether true or not.

6. Rumours behind your back.

7. Name-calling.

8. A message with unwanted sexual threats, jokes or suggestions.

9. A humiliating photo of you sent around to upset you.

10. Bullying carried on from your life in school.

11. Bullying message linked to my disability.

Method

1. Ask students to get into groups of no more than five.

2. Set ground rules: no names are to be used, that is, nobody will be labelled a bully or a victim. This is not about personal vendettas or telling tales about anyone – we are talking about the bigger picture that we have learned about from other young people.

If anyone is upset by what is discussed here today they can come and talk to teachers or peer mentors at any time. Helplines will be given out on a sheet.

Task 1

Hand out a set of cards to each group.

10 minutes: Young people tell us that these are common types of behaviour that happen online and on mobiles. They each happen more to one group – either to girls or to boys. Discuss these in your groups and decide whether you think the behaviour described on the card is more common among girls or boys and why.

5 minutes: Share the decisions and reasons with the wider group. Project the actual results in slides.[165]

5 minutes: Explore why students think this is happening across three years of surveys in the UK or their own school survey results.

Task 2: Exploring reporting

Show a PowerPoint slide illustrating how few report that they have been cyberbullied, and how few of those that do so actually get help (see Figure 11.1).

10 minutes: Ask the groups to discuss why many cyberbullied people do not report that they have been cyberbullied, and if they do not choose to do so, what other alternatives are open to them.

Prompts:

• Is it not worth it for them?

• Are there risks of retaliation?

• Are they dealing with cyberbullying that is not related to school life?

- Could people be better supported if they do come forward and what would they consider helpful support?

- Would better support encourage people to come forward?

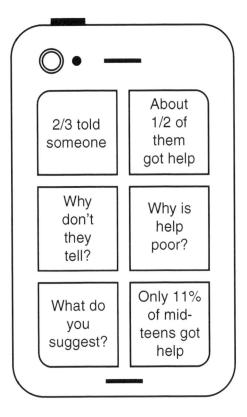

Figure 11.1 Reporting cyberbullying and getting effective help

Task 3

15 minutes: Working in groups, the class plans ways to tackle the most common forms of hurtful behaviour in their school community. They also plan to deliver this to younger pupils.

10 minutes: Each group presents their ideas to the class. Plan on implementing the best ideas and form a group to do it.

LESSON PLAN:
CYBERSAFE DIGITAL PHOTOGRAPHY AND BULLYING

Key Stages	2–3 – adapt as required.
Aims	To prompt pupils to consider the opportunities and risks of using digital photography. To reduce bullying using humiliating or hurtful images. To promote ownership of an agreement on acceptable use of digital images among pupils in line with the AUP of the school.
Time taken	40 minutes plus 15 minutes extra time to develop the agreement.

Curriculum links

Key Stage	3
ICT	1.4b: Recognising issues of risk, safety and responsibility surrounding the use of ICT.
Citizenship	1.2a: Exploring rights and obligations and how these affect the individual and communities.
PSHE	1.4a: Understanding that relationships affect everything we do and that relationship skills can be practised.

Background

Pupils could be asked to research old cameras for homework and then present to the class.

Resources

- Flipchart paper, markers, worksheet and images from www.licm.org.uk (Living Image Camera Museum). There is a very useful timeline on this site showing the history of photography by Philip Greenspun

- A copy of the school's Acceptable Use Policy (AUP) for pupils

- Blank worksheets, with a four-column grid

After this lesson

Pupils will have an understanding of how to keep their own photos private, they will understand the risks of putting images into cyberspace and they will understand that photo misuse can be hurtful to others. They will also know that some behaviour is against website terms of service, and possibly against the law. They will be aware that the school has an Anti-Bullying Policy that we all agree to abide by and an AUP that governs how we use ICT within school.

Pupils will have drawn up a clear agreement in their own words.

Key points

- Digital photography has changed our relationship with photos.

- Some people use photos to bully or humiliate/embarrass others.

- Some people generate photos of themselves which could cause them distress in the future.

- Copyright law protects people's work. Law also prevents malicious communications.

Method

Introduction: How new/old is digital photography? Who knows what the first use of it was? (In the 1960s NASA converted from analogue to digital signals in space probes.) The ease with which we can take, alter and send or upload large numbers of images means we have to develop new rules about our privacy, our use of images and our respect for other people.

1. Ask the learners to list all the ways of capturing an electronic image on today's devices (digital cameras; mobile phones; webcams; pictures taken from websites; pictures taken from friends' Facebook pages; screen grabs).

2. Ask them to put the name of each one into the worksheets (grid with four columns).

3. Show photographs or slides of some early cameras (available on www.licm. org.uk) and explain how limited and slow the process of developing and making prints once was, from the first glass plates to 127mm and then 35mm film. Once there were only eight images on a roll of film and later 12, 24 and 36. We had to wait several days and return to the chemist to collect our prints. When was digital photography first used? Use timeline and images.

4. In pairs, the group discusses the main ways in which handling photos was different in 1950 and now.

   Background information: News photos can be sent immediately where once they appeared in the newspaper days later, especially if from a faraway country. Fewer shots were taken and images were carefully selected because there was a cost to printing each one. The Kodak Brownie, thought of as the first camera for the masses, took only eight shots per film. You would carefully remove the film and put it into a black case avoiding the light, then take it to the chemist for developing and fetch it days later. The photos were your personal images, unless they fell into the hands of someone else or the negatives were lost or stolen. You then controlled which ones to give or show friends, or tear up.

   People carefully made albums of their own personal photos. Now we can take unlimited numbers of shots, video clips and screen grabs. We can transmit these instantly across the world making news or sharing a personal event. We can edit our images easily whereas only experts could edit before. Feed back to the group.

5. Digital photography frees us up in so many ways but it can also carry risks. What might these be? (List these on the worksheets alongside each type.)

    Prompts: Photos uploaded to the internet can be around forever. They are impossible to get back. Share with someone and they can ping your images around to their friends and the world. Misuse of your photo is more likely once uploaded. Someone can pass your photography off as their own work. Risks include: identity theft and bullying using photos.

    Images uploaded could affect your job prospects one day (recruiters increasingly search the net for information on candidates). If you pose for a webcam, you do not know how that might be used and by whom.

6. In this new world of digital photography we need to develop new agreements about how we handle images of ourselves and of other people. In small groups draw up the key points for an agreement. Rank these points in order of priority. Vote and agree. Draw up an agreement beginning: We agree that it is not acceptable to use or share photos in the following ways:

    Suggestions:

    • To deliberately hurt or humiliate another person or group.

    • To alter images in a cruel or unpleasant way.

    • To pass on an image received from others wishing to hurt another person or group.

    • To misuse a personal photo shared by two people who were once in a relationship.

We will:

• check our privacy settings when we upload photos

• clean our friend lists on SNS to keep only real friends

• think twice before uploading images of ourselves or friends online.

• We will treat images with care, this includes pictures made by us, made by other people or found accidentally.

Useful background information

• 1878 Dry plates being made commercially (Gelatin and silver bromide on glass)

• 1880 First half-tone photo in a newspaper

• 1888 First Kodak camera 20mm roll of paper

• 1889 Kodak camera with film instead of paper

• 1900 Kodak Brownie box roll film camera

• 1924 First quality 35mm camera, Leica

• 1932 Technicolor for movies introduced

- 1939–45 World War 2: Multi-layer colour negative film

- 1948 First polaroid instant film

- 1951 First video tape recorder

- 1975 Eastman Kodak builds first digital camera

- 1985 First autofocus single lens reflex

- 1991 Kodak first digital SLR for professionals

- 1992 First photo CD

- 1994 First digital camera by Apple for consumers, worked with a computer via serial cable

- 1996 Sony Cybershot

- 1999 Nikon 2.74 megapixel DSLR $6000

- 2004 Kodak ceases production of film cameras

- 2005 First consumer priced digital SLR Canon price US$3000

- Today we have digital cameras, cameras in phones, webcams and Skype

In the 1960s NASA converted from using analogue to digital signals in space probes to map the surface of the moon by sending digital images to earth. Computers were developing and they used computer technology to enhance the images sent by space probes. Digital imaging was also used for spy satellites. Did you know that the first filmless electronic camera was patented in 1972, so it is relatively recent that digital cameras were available for all?

Source: Thanks to 'History of Photography Timeline' by Philip Greenspun.[166]

LESSON PLAN: WHAT DO I DO ONLINE?

Key Stage	4
Aim	To enable students to take ownership of keeping themselves safe online.
Time taken	40 minutes

Facts

By the age of 14–15 29 per cent of pupils say they always follow the e-safety guidelines they have been taught. We want to explore how to make the e-safety advice more relevant to the activities they do online and to improve their ability to find out for themselves.

Background

In order to be prepared, teachers can search on the following sites for advice on privacy settings or ask pupils to do a preparatory search for homework: the Cybersurvey research, Symantic, Google Safety Centre: Good to know, Facebook privacy settings, UKCCIS.

Method

10 minutes: Have an informal discussion about the *skills* people have. How many know how to:

- block senders

- report abusive messages to the website

- report abusive material to CEOP

- react if they have received a nasty or bullying message; name three actions you could take: for example, save evidence, report it to someone you trust, seek help from cybermentors or other services, talk in confidence to a helpline, clean friends list

- change password, block the sender.

List on a sheet (or whiteboard) the activities students do online. Then explore whether there are any risks attached to these activities. The aim is to find out what simple steps could be taken to avoid harm. Some examples are below. The idea is to make the session relevant to the group of pupils and therefore finding out what they do first is helpful. The solutions are then tailored to their activities and they recognise this as relevant. Together you may have to search for some answers; this enables them to learn how to help themselves in future.

It is not intended that this session scares people, but rather it should empower them to be resilient and protect themselves while using the technology.

	What might the risks be?	What steps can I take?
Search for information	If I accept the first choice listed by my search engine I may be getting incorrect information.	Look to verify information in more than one location. Do not believe everything you read. Retain a healthy scepticism. Learn to cross-check information and select with discernment.
	Google will give me more of what I already like, reinforcing one view.	What seems to be a free service may be possible because information on users is sold to advertisers. Be aware of this when using free sites. Details about your browsing, shopping or personal details may be shared.
Contact people/ friends via SNS (Facebook)	Someone wants to befriend you but they are not who they say they are.	Contact with friends is enjoyed by everyone. But take simple precautions – admit as friends only people you know. If you are not sure about a new request, check someone is genuine by doing a search.
	Your profile is public and information about you falls into the wrong hands.	Keep your profile and your address and phone number private. Having huge friends lists to look popular is a sure way to get into difficulties. Remove from the list people you are no longer friends with.
	Someone you met online wants to meet up.	Avoid meeting up with people you only know online but if you insist on meeting – take a friend with you or meet in a public space and tell someone where you are going and when.
	You are bullied by a former friend on Facebook.	Keep the evidence. Do not reply. Remove the sender from your friends list. If the behaviour breaches the terms of service of the website, report it to the SNS site. Talk to a person you trust.
	Someone gets your password and changes your profile or sends messages as if from you.	Keep your password safe, always opt for two-stage verification when offered and change your passwords from time to time. Always log out and shut down your browser if you walk away from the screen.
Arrange social plans	It is possible to find out where you are going to be and when. This could get into the wrong hands.	When you reply to a group message check who is in that group.

	What might the risks be?	What steps can I take?
Visit chatrooms	Sometimes people who are not feeling good about their social life or their relationships at home may seek that friendship and intimacy in chatrooms. It can lead them into dangerous situations or into being bullied.	Students who use chatrooms heavily have told us that they are cyberbullied more than other people. This suggests you should take great care about the groups you join and the chats you have. You may also get drawn into a group looking to involve young people and you should be very alert to deliberate grooming. Operate with all your antennae on full alert! Get out of an unpleasant situation by logging out. Use a nickname or change names. Stay in charge – your personal profile should not have your address or phone number, or even your real photo. Tell a parent or carer if something makes you worried. Learn how to keep a conversation in chat in case you need this evidence to report something. Check out how to report on the site or through the CEOP button.
Gaming	When gaming, why is it dangerous to play on a third party site rather than the originator site? A friend might send you an email with a link saying you must try this game. Would you click on that link?	Many amateur sites also host a game. These can be risky or malicious. Play only at the game site. Some games require Active X or JavaScript controls to let your computer interact to a greater extent. These can be useful to hackers, so turn these controls off in the configuration menu when you are finished. Symantic recommends you have a separate user account for online gaming with only a web browser installed on it. When finished gaming, you switch back to the full user account.
Shopping	How would you protect your personal and credit card details when shopping online? What could you do to guard against phishing?	Consider opening an email address only for shopping. Use Hotmail or Gmail for a spare address. Use your bank's verifying service or PayPal to verify the card – this is an extra layer of security. Check the site is genuine. Never follow a link a friend has sent you but search for the store's internet address yourself to check it is authentic. Check what they will do with your data and do not agree to it being used for promotions or sold to other parties. Watch out for phishing – online fraud – where someone tries to trick you into giving them personal details. Never enter your password after following a link in an email from someone – go onto the website via your own search first.
Sharing music and files	You could be illegally downloading music or other material.	Join a legal music downloading site and make sure your music is downloaded from this site.
Share jokes	By passing on a 'joke' am I joining in the bullying of someone?	Think twice before pinging on a joke if it is about someone or some people.
Share photos	Would I be embarrassed if one day this photo came up when I was in a job interview or my nan saw it?	If you upload photos to Facebook you can now choose a privacy setting for each one. Keep some personal. Be careful what you share with friends or make public.

LESSON PLAN: PROACTIVE LESSONS TO PREVENT CYBERBULLYING

This example has been used with Years 9 and 10 but could be adapted for younger pupils.

Key Stages	3-4
Aims	To reduce cyberbullying. To reinforce e-safety messages and encourage their use. To explore the impact of prejudice-driven bullying.
Time taken	90 minutes broken into three sessions or three separate short sessions.

Curriculum links

Key Stage 3	
PSHE – from Personal Well-Being Key Stage 3 programme of study	'…the impact of prejudice, bullying, discrimination and racism on individuals and communities.'
ICT programme of study	'Exchanging and sharing of information.' Pupils can be alerted to the safety issues of using email, chatrooms, IM and any other 'direct contact' communications device, along with the importance of keeping personal information private.
Citizenship – knowledge and understanding about becoming informed citizens	Pupils should be taught about their right to privacy and the responsibility to protect the privacy of others by not disclosing information when using the internet.
Developing skills of participation and responsible action	This teaching point provides a good opportunity to discuss the issues relating to communication using ICT. The safety issues of using email, chatrooms, IM and text messaging can be discussed, alongside the problems of cyberbullying, which are often associated with these forms of technology.
Key Stage 4	
PSHE – from Personal Well-Being Key Stage 4 programme of study	'…the diversity of ethnic and cultural groups, the power of prejudice, bullying, discrimination and racism, and the need to take the initiative in challenging this and other offensive behaviours and in giving support to victims of abuse.'
ICT programme of study – reviewing, modifying and evaluating work as it progresses	Pupils should be encouraged to adopt safe and responsible behaviours regardless of the technology they are using.
Citizenship – knowledge and understanding about becoming informed citizens	Pupils should be taught about their right to privacy and the responsibility to protect the privacy of others by not disclosing information when using the internet.

Curriculum links developed from Becta, 'Signposts to Safety: Teaching E-safety at Key Stages 3 and 4'. Available at http://webarchive.nationalarchives.gov.uk/20101102103654/publications.becta.org. uk//display.cfm?resID=32422, accessed on 30 April 2012.

Approach

- To explore important messages gathered from Cybersurvey responses from young people (or your school's own survey), in order to respond more effectively to their e-safety needs. This knowledge will inform a resource for schools.

Resources

- Some statistics from your own school survey, or those from the Cybersurvey in this book.

- A feedback leaflet or sheet telling students relevant results from your school survey and where they can get help.

- You will need worksheets (pp.185–187), spare pens and introductory slides explaining the session.

- Possible film clips: Roger Crouch's interview at www.youtube.com/user/lgfonline. Roger was a father who was devastated by the loss of his son, Dominic (note: this film is distressing).[167] *Or* Irish advertisement against homophobic bullying at www.youtube.com/watch?v=lrJxqvalFxM.

Method

1. Introduction: 5 minutes.

2. First group session seated in groups with 'scribes': 20 minutes.

3. Show film clip: 5 minutes.

4. Second group session: 20 minutes.

5. Dragons' Den activity to design a new approach to delivering e-safety to pupils: 40 minutes.

6. Everyone hands in their message to the teacher leading the session on cyberbullying and e-safety in the form of a tweet.

Suggested structure for the activities

1. Introduce the project and explain that students are going to look at what other young people have said about cyberbullying and e-safety. After some discussion, develop new ways of addressing this issue. Form pupils into groups of five. Provide either the worksheet from p.187 for information, or a sheet of your own school data. Emphasise the fact that not enough people follow the e-safety advice they have been given and that many victims of cyberbullying do not report it.

2. Each group nominates a 'researcher' for their group.

3. Each group discusses these messages on cyberbullying and e-safety from young people and examines them from different angles. The researchers write

down what is said in the boxes on the 'E-safety education' worksheet given below. Their job is to capture as much of the debate as they can.

4. Show the film clip.

5. Group session 2. Discussions about homophobic bullying using the 'Homophobic bullying online and on mobiles' worksheet from p.186 and the questions on 'Reporting cyberbullying' on p.187. Again, the 'researcher' writes down the discussion.

6. A group of 'dragons' is chosen to form a panel. It is useful to have senior management team staff on this panel, including people such as the anti-bullying and e-safety leads, as well as pupils. They get together to discuss the criteria they will apply to pitches for e-safety ideas. The remainder of the pupils work in three groups to develop their pitches on 'Cyberbullying and e-safety: What should be taught and how should it be delivered?' (Note: if one table finishes early there are some extra questions provided on p.188.)

7. The dragons convene and listen to each pitch. They score them and announce the winners.

8. Pupils can create a tweet to send to the headteacher with a key message on the issue of cyberbullying and e-safety.

E-SAFETY EDUCATION

Student researchers: Please collate answers in these boxes. Use the exact words of group members where possible.	
Why do people stop following the advice as they get older? (Is it still relevant and if not, why?)	
What would make e-safety education more useful to your age group?	
What age should it start?	
What should it include that is now left out?	

HOMOPHOBIC BULLYING ONLINE AND ON MOBILES

This form of bullying is high, starting at age 10. Why do you think the UK has such a high level of homophobic bullying?	
Do you think people use cyberbullying to say things they would not say face to face? Why is this?	
What do you think would reduce it? Is it something that can change? What should schools do about homophobia?	
Why do you think so many people at your school said they took it as a joke? (Prejudice survey)	
58% knew people it had happened to. How might this affect the atmosphere of a school? Does it have an effect on students in any way?	
People are often homophobically bullied in chatrooms and on SNS sites. Yet they go back. Why, and what advice would you give them?	

REPORTING CYBERBULLYING

What percentage do you think reported it?	
What percentage of those people do you think got help?	
What do you think could make reporting more worthwhile and responses more successful?	

WORKSHEET FOR EACH TABLE: FIVE QUICK QUESTIONS

1. What do we mean by cyberbullying?

2. What types of *online experiences* did we ask about?

A message:

- where the sender was not who they said they were
- that tried to make you do something you did not want to do
- from a stranger suggesting you meet up
- that showed people were talking about you nastily online
- that contained threats
- with unwanted sexual suggestions, jokes or threats
- with insults calling you gay (whether true or not)
- calling you racist names or comments.

Guess what percentage of all students had experienced one or more of these?

3. What types of *mobile experiences* did we ask about?

- A humiliating photo of you deliberately sent round to upset/embarrass you... not shared joke.

- Insults because of disability/insults calling you gay whether true or not.
- Unwanted sexual words, threats or suggestions.
- Racist words or comments.
- Unpleasant name-calling.
- People text you about where to meet, then deliberately change the place without telling you.
- Bullying carried on from your life in school.

Guess what percentage of all the students had experienced one or more of these?

4. Cyberbullying

We asked if they thought it was cyberbullying. Guess what percentage said that what had happened to them was cyberbullying?

What percentage of those who were cyberbullied said it was carried on from their life in school?

5. Homophobic bullying online and on mobiles

What percentage do you think suffered this type of bullying?

Are you surprised by the answers or was it what you thought?

Answers: 1. Cyberbullying is an aggressive, intentional act using electronic forms of contact, repeatedly over time, to hurt or humiliate someone or some people. 2. 48%. 3. 32%. 4. 18%. 5. One-quarter received messages with insults calling them gay, but only 8 per cent actually said they were homophobically bullied, often many times a day several times a week. Why do you think so few wanted to describe their experience as homophobic cyberbullying? Should people be helped without having to report it?

Extra questions if people finish early

Thirty-seven per cent of 10- to 11-year-olds and 80 per cent of 12- to 13-year-olds say they have a Facebook or other SNS page. The age at which you are now allowed to join is 13.

- At what age do you think it is safe for children to use Facebook and why?
- What conditions if any would you put in place if you were a parent of a ten-year-old wanting to join?
- If you were facing a class of ten-year-olds, what would your message be to them about using SNS?
- Please give any suggestions on using SNS safely that you would tell a ten-year-old.

CASES TO USE IN STAFF TRAINING SESSIONS

'...they text you...make you think they're gonna do something bad to you.'

Shola

Shola is 15 and attends a unit attached to a mainstream school. She has cerebral palsy and limited use of her arms and legs. She uses assisted technology in class and to communicate. Shola really enjoys using IT equipment and is a keen member of a number of SNS. The school set up its own intranet for learners to use and Shola was on the school planning group who designed and built the site. To launch the site the school used an assembly. When Shola approached the stage to do her bit of the presentation another student shouted out a derogatory remark. The remark was not challenged by staff. Soon after the intranet went live, pictures of Shola began to appear with comments about her physical appearance and her personal life.

Response

The school had a software program enabling the IT department to identify the person who posted these pictures. They traced the student and promptly removed the pictures. The student's parents were immediately called in and the law of harassment was explained to them. The school also reminded them of the school's code of conduct for anyone using the intranet signed by all pupils and parents. This had clearly been breached in this case so the school acted upon its written policy and excluded the boy for one day.

It was agreed via discussion with Shola, her parents, the student and his parents, that he would prepare an assembly in which he would demonstrate the achievements of learners with disabilities and their use of technology to the whole school. Shola was consulted on this and was able to give her own views. The police community liaison officer was invited to the school to talk to learners about the seriousness of harassment.

The headteacher also began a review of staff training to make sure all staff felt confident in challenging discriminatory language and bullying in the school. Proactive sessions were planned to promote an inclusive attitude towards disability.

Are you clear on what the law is on harassment?

How does this case illustrate observance of the duties under the Equality Act 2010?

Jason

Jason had taunts and death threats from four other pupils posted on his home page on the popular teenage chat site Bebo. It was clear that people who knew him well were doing this. Jason had split up with his first girlfriend weeks before. She had started a whispering campaign about him online. Now four other students had picked this up and began threatening him and saying he should die. Jason, being 13, had little experience of relationships and was devastated and scared. Then he became angry. He thought he would teach them a lesson and escape it all through one violent action in an attempt to take his life. Impulsively Jason posted a message saying he was going to die. He was determined. It was only the quick action of a friend who saw the message online that saved Jason from damaging himself severely.

Notes

Fortunately Jason was rescued but this is a case for the Serious Incident Protocol to be used. The police need to be advised and intensive counselling and support provided for Jason. If exclusion is chosen for the perpetrators it is not clear how they will helped to change their behaviour nor what will restrain them from harassing Jason again online or in the neighbourhood. Steps must be taken to ensure they are legally restrained from doing so. If they are sent to a Pupil Referral Unit (PRU), liaison is recommended between the school and the PRU to ensure that the programme devised for these young people is rigorous and addresses all the components involved.

They might face criminal proceedings for trying to incite someone to take their life. Jason's parents might sue the school if they feel that not enough had been done to safeguard pupils. They can also trigger an inspection of the school. In such a case the school would need to provide evidence of the procedures in place and what actions they had taken to safeguard pupils and teach them about cyberbullying and digital citizenship. In particular, if Jason had complained to the school that he was being bullied, they would need to show evidence of their response. The school's behaviour management would come under detailed scrutiny.

It is likely that Jason's parents would consider moving him to another school, but this is only successful in some cases. Being a traumatised newcomer is not going to make it easy for Jason to integrate socially and he might have some good friends at the first school. He might require a period of home schooling. The education welfare and education psychology services should help provide support if this is a local authority school. When he is ready to reintegrate, a support group of young people should be put around him and trained peer supporters used to help him settle.

The school would need to review all its anti-bullying practice and plan an intensive programme to communicate it to all pupils. This might include a pledge. Inviting a community safety officer to visit and make clear that behaviour of this kind can be illegal does have a strong impact. The school should notify all parents, alert the governors and retrain staff. This should include how to recognise signs of distress or depression in young people. Pupil surveys should be undertaken at regular intervals to explore the extent of cyberbullying within the school.

The school or police should contact Bebo and have the offensive material removed.

Patrick

'I am 15, a bit quiet in class and you see, the thing is, I am not all that interested in sport. I had a girlfriend for a few weeks but she told some people that she dumped me because I am "frigid" and "weird". She cuts me dead now.

I got anonymous messages on MSN calling me "gay boy" and stuff – making threats. Then my Facebook page was hacked into with sexually explicit pictures and tags. Some of this stuff is so awful and it keeps getting worse.

On my way home from school, someone threw a condom filled with horrible dirty liquid at me.

I'm scared of what will happen if I tell someone and the bullies find out, it will get worse 'cos they'll kill me if they find out. I don't know what to do about the rumours that I am gay and some of the pictures and messages are all about sex, so I can't show anyone. It is all getting worse.'

Comments

The risks to Patrick if he does report this campaign of victimisation are high. He faces difficulties telling his parents as he has not discussed sexual orientation with them at any time and he feels that if he tells a teacher, the issues will all escalate even further. In addition he attends a faith school where homophobia is never referred to and there have never been any sessions on homophobic bullying or anyone saying this behaviour is wrong. Patrick has not fully recognised his own sexual orientation and feels 'bounced' into doing so now.

He thinks that because the messages are anonymous nothing can be done. The nature of some of the messages is such that he would not want any adult seeing them either. He has developed a feeling of total helplessness as the weeks have gone by. Gradually he has become more depressed and begun to think about taking his own life. Increasingly he is convinced there is nothing anyone can do.

As a last resort he rang a helpline. It offered privacy and even anonymity and avoided any face-to-face awkwardness.

What could be done to help Patrick?

- Provide a support group of trained peers around Patrick, possibly older pupils – do not tell them too much about his case.

- Thank him for coming to report this problem.

- Support him by creating a safe space for him to talk and be heard.

- Use effective listening techniques.

- Ensure he is not at risk requiring child protection measures, or at risk of assault.

- Do not humiliate him by announcing that he has become a victim.

- Invite him to help decide what should be done from a menu of choices.

- Arrange 'secret' ways of checking with Patrick on how things are via non-visible signals or emails.

Meanwhile ask him to:

- block senders

- keep evidence

- help him get offensive material taken down by contacting service providers/ trace senders or internet provider address where possible

- report to the CEOP if content suggests it is necessary.

Within the school:

- Do whole school prevention of bullying work on diversity.

- Do small group and class work on 'How I want to be treated'

- Re-negotiate the Anti-Bullying Policy with staff and young people so that it is a live strategy – find out why pupils think it has been ineffective.

- Work with the whole school, including staff, on the Equality Act 2010.

- Do the exercise on electronic footprints (p.171) to show that the messages left by these senders could be traced in years to come by colleagues, workplaces and friends, reflecting badly on them.

When the ground is prepared, consider showing some of the powerful films made by groups such as Stonewall, but also show a film on bullying of another type such as *Make Them Go Away* (special educational needs) or *Let's Fight it Together* (cyberbullying) so that homophobic bullying is one strand of several.[168]

Patrick's sexual orientation is not something that needs to be discussed at all. It should be made clear that any form of bullying is unacceptable, including homophobic messages, whether the target is gay or not. Because of the growing use of homophobic insults generally in schools, this language should be challenged.

If the senders of the offensive messages can be traced they could be made to understand the harm caused and work to make amends. Alternatively they may not be responsive to restorative approaches and sanctions will need to be applied. Draw to their attention that under the Malicious Communications Act their behaviour might be unlawful.

Natalie

(Story reported on BBC Newsbeat, last updated on 05:13 GMT, Friday, 19 August 2011, and adapted for staff training.)

Natalie is 15 and is one of those young people who have had problems with Formspring. At first, she thought it was a great idea. She said:

'I thought, "It would be cool, a new thing, why not go on it?" It looked really cool. It was like join today, then people ask you questions. I was like, "Oh my god yes, people are going to ask me questions, get to know me. How exciting."'

'It turned bad,' she admitted. 'I started getting hate, people were telling me to go kill myself, that I was ugly, fat, everybody hated me and was better off without me.'

Natalie has now left the site because she didn't like the kind of messages she was getting.

'I get more abuse in person, so I was kind of used to it,' she said. 'I was just like, "Oh my gosh. It's happening at home, I can't escape. I go to school I get abuse, I come home, I get abuse. What do I do? Where do I go? I don't feel safe anywhere."'

This case involves being bullied both in school and online. Natalie needs an urgent and total intervention coordinated by her school.

Formspring.me is an SNS on which users ask and answer questions. It is growing popular with teenagers. Users subscribe or 'follow' the answers to questions published by other users, rather as people follow Twitter posts. But the default settings for accounts on Formspring allow questions to be asked anonymously on a user's profile by fellow users who conceal their identity as well as by those without an account. The site is popular, but the ability to pose anonymous questions to users has inevitably led to incidents of cyberbullying and harassment.

Some measures can be taken to help users protect themselves when using Formspring:

- changing privacy settings preventing anonymous questions from being asked
- choosing 'Protect My Account' so that only approved users can follow your answers and ask questions
- blocking rude or abusive users, preventing them from asking you any further questions
- reporting incidents of cyberbullying to Formspring.

CEOP has provided some simple step-by-step instructions on how to stay safe when using Formspring:

1. Customise your settings using the tab at the top of the page.

2. When you are in the 'Settings' area select your privacy settings by choosing 'Privacy'.

3. Select 'Protect My Account' box to ensure that you have full control over which users follow you. If this option is selected only pre-approved users will be able to ask questions and view answers.

4. Choose not to receive anonymous questions by selecting 'Don't receive anonymous questions.'

5. Block users if you do not like what they are asking you when viewing questions waiting to be answered. Users are asked why they are blocking that user and will need to select a reason.

6. Reporting users. The sending of bullying questions and messages violate Formspring's Community Rules. These incidents can be reported to Formspring for investigation and they will take the appropriate action, that is, disabling the user's account and removing the offending content (abuse/harassment on Formspring can be reported here: http://formspringme.zendesk.com/anonymous_requests/new).

Within school a whole programme of intervention should be in place addressing bystanders and providing support to Natalie from peer supporters, teachers and outside counsellors. Natalie should be able to give a slight signal to a teacher indicating that she is alright during the day. If she does not do this the teacher can interpret this as 'Natalie is having problems.' This would avert the issue of Natalie constantly having to seek out a teacher to report cyberbullying and being seen by others.

When it isn't a legal issue, could it be contractual?

Ben's parents came into school to report that the parents of a classmate had posted comments on an SNS about their child after the children had fallen out.

Most of the parents in that class of eight-year-olds would see these comments and they were hurtful. Ben's parents were very upset. It was true that the boys had a history of fighting/arguing and bullying. Sometimes each boy alleged that the other had done something to him. This could not always be substantiated.

Accusations flew about who was to blame over an incident in school the week before. But nothing was proven.

What can or should the school do?

They should remind parents that...

- The school has a duty of care to keep pupils safe.

- The school should have an Anti-Bullying Policy.

- In order to do the work of keeping all children safe, the school has asked parents to support the work of the school when they first enrol their children.

- It is inappropriate to name other people's children online; these are young children who need to learn to behave well.

- The school can call upon all parents to support them in the work that they do to improve social relationships and create a respectful caring environment.

- If parents model bullying behaviour it makes the work of the school doubly difficult.

Aims

- To improve the relationship between these two pupils as they are going to have to live together in this school.

- To teach all the children what is acceptable or unacceptable behaviour.

Actions

The school writes to every parent of a pupil at the school to notify them that any online naming and shaming of other people's children will not be supportive to the work of the school and they ask them as part of their home/school agreement to take every care with their online communications.

The headteacher invites the parents who have posted the message to a meeting and makes it clear that this is inappropriate – there is a duty of care to every pupil and the school would like this taken down. If all parents were to behave in this way chaos would follow. Explain that to be a parent at this school is to agree to support the school's behaviour strategy and that this involves not attacking any child verbally or otherwise.

The headteacher then sees Ben's parents and explains the actions taken to date and the plan to improve the behaviour and relationship skills of both boys as the feuding has been going on too long.

The school sees both boys separately and works to agree a behaviour agreement with each one. Together a teacher and each pupil agree that they will focus on achieving five goals and create a week-by-week plan. The school agrees to help each of the boys to achieve their goals. The extent to which they have achieved their goals is measured over the week and involves positive reinforcement. If their behaviour improves they get a reward. Over the weeks if they improve their behaviour it will add up to being able to go on the school trip at the end of the term. If they do not manage to improve their behaviour, the trip will be denied them. The boys will be helped to deal with anger, impulsive behaviour and physical aggression. They will be encouraged to deal with social situations, be less sensitive to every imagined slight or incident and stay away from one another if necessary. They will also be helped to make other friends and get on with their lives. It is hoped that they will learn to recognise when they feel anger build up and learn ways to calm themselves down.

Throughout the remaining weeks of term both sets of parents are given regular reports on the behaviour of their children and are asked to carry on the agreement at home. They are encouraged to build their child's confidence and seek ways of dealing with rages.

STAFF TRAINING NEEDS QUESTIONNAIRE (ADAPT TO SUIT)

Dear colleague,

Thank you for your help with these questions. This is to help us understand your training needs and to aid us in reviewing policy and strategy relating to e-safety and the use of our ICT systems.

Please circle the number of the statement that most closely reflects your view of the school's Acceptable Use Policy (AUP).

1	I have seen it but not used it
2	I have seen it and used it
3	I have seen it but not fully understood it
4	I saw it a long time ago
5	I don't think it applies to me
6	I have not seen it
7	I refer to it frequently in my role
8	I teach it to pupils
9	I teach it to staff
Other:	

If you have seen it or used it, please answer the following (1 = least, 5 = most).

How well does it suit our purpose?	1	2	3	4	5
Is it still up to date?	1	2	3	4	5
Is it comprehensive and thorough?	1	2	3	4	5
Is it easy to understand and act upon?	1	2	3	4	5
Please tell us of aspects of the AUP that require reviewing or updating:					

	Yes	Maybe	No
Would you be willing to be involved with a policy review?			
Would you be willing to lead pupils in a policy review?			
Would you be able to lead staff in a learning session?			

	Not at all				Very
How confident are you in the following actions?	1	2	3	4	5
Reporting abuse					
Putting Serious Incident Protocols into action					
Teaching e-safety					
Demonstrating privacy settings to pupils					
Tracking incidents/monitoring					
Responding when pupils report cyberbullying					

	Not at all				Very
How aware are you of the following?	1	2	3	4	5
Advice to staff on contacts with pupils via SNS or email					
Advice to staff on contacts with pupils via SNS or email					
Protecting your own privacy from students					
Handling school-related calls to a mobile					
Protecting data/encryption/removing data from school premises					
Taking photographs of school events within the guidelines					
Keeping evidence if a pupil reports incidents of bullying or harassment					
Keeping evidence if a pupil reports incidents of bullying or harassment					
The risks of location software					
The issues surrounding plagiarism and copyright					
The Equality Act 2010					

MY TRAINING NEEDS (STAFF)

Please identify your priorities for training on a scale of 1–5 (1 = of interest, 5 = priority need).

	1	2	3	4	5
Updates in e-safety advice (such as handheld devices and games consoles with internet access)					
Trends we have noticed within the school and how we might respond					
How to respond to cyberbullying incidents, with case examples					
E-safety for staff					
Embedding our AUP					
Training in our Anti-Bullying Policy and strategies					
How to help students with special needs or disabilities to use the internet safely					
Appropriate responses to cyberhomophobia and other prejudice-related bullying					
Appropriate responses when pupils access sites encouraging anorexia or suicidal activities					
Discussions following pupil surveys or incident monitoring results, for example, 'How effective is our strategy and how do we know?'					
How to work with parents – our proactive approach and how to respond when incidents occur – real-life cases					
My own digital skills need a brush up					
Training in the Serious Incident Protocol					
Please add any other topis you think should be covered:					

Thank you for your response. We will respond within X weeks.

SHORT ACTIVITY 1: WOULD YOU DO THIS?

This is one of several short activities to explore decision making in cyberspace. These activities can be used regularly with different questions as 15-minute recap sessions or longer exploratory sessions.

Aims

- To increase pupils' awareness of risk and to improve how they assess risk.

- To identify any gaps in understanding and reiterate learning.

Key Stage

- Key Stages 3–4

This activity can be used to measure before and after session changes in people's positions. Count and record how many stood at 'Yes' or 'No' before the lesson and again afterwards, to see how much they have understood.

Time

- 15 minutes

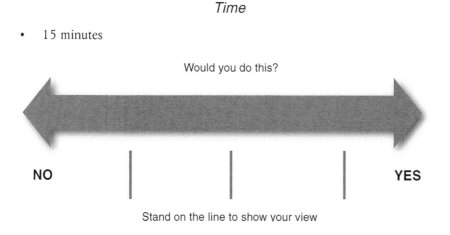

Figure 11.4 Would you do this?

SHORT ACTIVITY 2: IS IT OKAY TO…?

Aim

- To measure pupils' understanding of e-safety and create a baseline measure.

Key Stage

- This can be adapted for any stage between 2–4.

Time

- 15 minutes

Below is a worksheet to explore the actions pupils report. Ask them to consider each action and judge it according to the tabs across the row. Add up everyone's responses. Discuss what can be done about behaviours considered 'not OK', 'cruel' or 'illegal'. Agree some plan of action. The actions could be changed according to age and to reflect what is shown in your school survey. Re-run this activity after a few weeks of e-safety education to monitor any changes in attitude. Change the questions to suit.

In this exercise you can explore relationship behaviour such as dumping a friend via text or by changing your status on a Facebook profile. Alternatively explore what is cruel and what is actually illegal. Choose your actions for the left hand side of this grid and vary them from week to week. Invite pupils to decide the answer for each action.

Is it OK to...	It's brilliant	It's OK	It's not OK	It's cruel	It's illegal
dump someone by text?					
post untrue rumours about someone?					
share someone's private pictures with others?					
use someone else's work as your own?					
keep pestering someone maliciously?					

SHORT ACTIVITY 3: ONLINE ACTIVITIES – WHAT IS SAFE?

Aim

- To explore common actions to decide if they are safe or risky.

Key Stage

- Key Stage 4 and upper ages of Key Stage 3.

Time

- 15 minutes

Materials you will need

- Blank cards and the diagram below drawn larger.

Ask students to name activities they do online and write each one on a card – one action per card, such as shopping with a credit card online or accepting someone you don't know as a friend. Shuffle all the cards in a box. Invite students to pick one and allocate the cards to a position on this Venn diagram drawn on a large sheet or board. Discuss their decisions and why some might be safe in certain circumstances, such as if the website is secure. If an action is safe sometimes, place in the centre. Discuss.

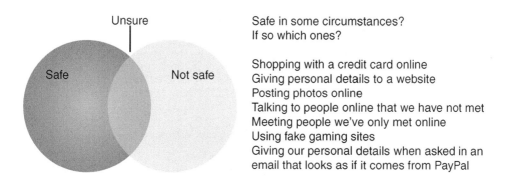

Unsure

Safe   Not safe

Safe in some circumstances?
If so which ones?

Shopping with a credit card online
Giving personal details to a website
Posting photos online
Talking to people online that we have not met
Meeting people we've only met online
Using fake gaming sites
Giving our personal details when asked in an
email that looks as if it comes from PayPal

Figure 11.5 Online Activities: what is safe? Venn Diagrams

SHORT ACTIVITY 4: SAFETY MATRIX

Aim

• To explore the situations that might be safe in certain circumstances.

Key Stages

• Key Stages 3–4

Time

• 20 minutes

This is a slightly more nuanced, sophisticated exercise to learn to assess risk and manage it. Working in groups, pupils are asked to think of three actions for each square. They then explore the actions that are safe only if the website is safe and those that are safe in some circumstances. The teacher should have a list of possible actions ready to prompt if necessary, that is, it is only safe to pay by credit card and give personal details on a safe website. Why is this and how does anyone know it is a safe website?

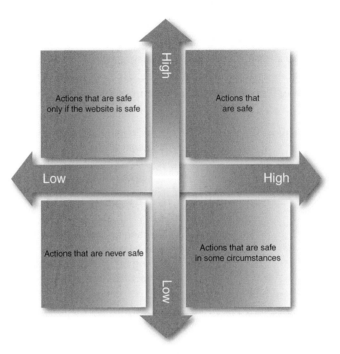

Figure 11.6 The Safety Matrix

SHORT ACTIVITY 5: SOLUTIONS TO COMMON PROBLEMS ONLINE

Invite pupils to put 'problems' onto post-it notes and put them up on flipchart sheets on the walls. Look at the problems they have posted and try grouping them into types. Perhaps put pop-ups and unwanted selling emails together. Group notes that link with personal details together. Once you are all agreed on the categories – the sorts of problems people encounter often – the next step is to problem-solve what to do.

COMMUNICATION TOOLS FOR PUPILS WITH SPECIAL NEEDS

	Resources
Mencap www.mencap.org.uk	'Am I making myself clear?' – advice on using text and images when communicating with people with learning difficulties
NSPCC www.nspcc.org.uk	'How it is' – an image vocabulary for children about feelings, rights and safety, personal care and sexuality; CD provided
Persona Dolls www.persona-doll-training.org	'Understanding bullying' is a sensitive resource on how to use these remarkable dolls to support children who are bullied and challenge those who bully
Autism and Aspergers Publishing Co. www.aapcpublishing.net	A wealth of publications that are useful including 'Strategies at hand'
www.includemetoo.org.uk	A communications passport has been developed for use by young people with disabilities

	Creative ideas
Story boarding	Draw 4–6 frames. Create a cyberbullying or e-safety scenario and ask the children what they think should happen next or what the characters should do now. What would they like to see happen? What do they worry might happen? Explore choices and agree together
Cartooning	Body language: everyone draws a simple cartoon character. Ask: So how would he look if he were scared? How would he look if he felt brave? (They draw him.) How can we look brave even when we are nervous? It does not tell bullies we are scared which can make them bully us more
One time use cameras	Ask the children to take pictures of where they feel safe and happy or where they do not feel safe in school. Investigate why they do not feel safe in some locations. Discuss with group what to do
Using sticker dots	Coloured sticker dots are useful for agreeing/disagreeing (red or green) with statements on a flipchart sheet and especially useful for mapping hotspots on a large drawing of the school

	Creative ideas
'What is a friend?' on YouTube_www.youtube.com watch?v=wZHmsVRshwU	Use a video clip first. 'What is a friend?' is from notebookbabies, a series of clips by a teacher, Tony Dusko. Then discuss friendship. Create a human figure and children use post-it notes to attach the qualities they look for in a friend. A friend is someone who…
'True friends' www.youtube.com/watch?v =PJDOcr0P8cY&feature= related	Created by teacher Tony Dusko these endearing clips are short. They set the tone for classroom discussions. Discuss how people can support one another and set up a 'Good to be kind' star chart. Older pupils might create clips for you
Art, drama and computer graphics plus signing, Makaton, Braille www.Makaton.org	Employ every method at your disposal. Drama – acting out scenarios and how to get help – is vital. Posters, screen savers and graphics raise awareness. Promote positive images of disability. Paralympics pictures etc.

Chapter

12

ABOUT THE CYBERSURVEY

This book draws extensively on the findings from the Cybersurvey, and for those interested in how this survey was carried out, I provide some more detail below.

The Cybersurvey is an online survey tool used to gather information from young people on cyberbullying and e-safety education. The aim was to use a standard questionnaire and develop baseline data, after which the survey could be repeated. This would help frontline practitioners in local authorities and schools to evaluate their interventions and e-safety education and to compare responses between areas.

The Cybersurvey was designed and managed by Adrienne Katz, with thanks to Graham Tilby, Shirley Hackett, Rebecca Calnan, Toni Brettell, Katriona Lafferty of Dudley Metropolitan Borough Council and Diane LeCount of Essex County Council. Thanks to Rennie Thompson and Jo Brown of Oxfordshire County Council for early advice and suggestions. Our sincere thanks go to the young people of Dudley Decision Making Kids (DDMK), the Dudley youth shadow safeguarding board and the 158 young people in Essex who piloted the questionnaire. The Reach Project has made it possible to expand the survey and to explore cyberhomophobia.

To date, 9290 young people have completed it in various locations.

Participating local authorities

- Birmingham City Council

- Dudley Metropolitan Borough Council

- Essex County Council

- Herefordshire

- Oxfordshire County Council

- Solihull Metropolitan Borough Council

- Suffolk County Council (eSafer Suffolk)

- West of England group

Statistical analysis was carried out by Emma McManus, Mark Lovelace, Cath Dillon and Jack Morris. Survey design, project management and reports were by Adrienne Katz. Youthworks Consulting Ltd hold copyright for the questionnaire. Including the questions from the charity EACH (Educational Action Challenging Homophobia).

Development: principles of youth involvement

As with any exploration of young people's behaviour it was vital to develop the questions with young people. This was for a number of reasons. First, to find out the issues they thought should be covered and second, to check that the questions worked for them. A question can be understood differently by young people or on occasions the wording is challenged by their age group. Furthermore, given enough time and 'safe' space they often suggest a question that turns out to be a revealing or pivotal one.

For the young people to have a stake in the survey and to feel that it is worth undertaking, they need to be involved from the start in a development process that is both respectful and inclusive. This means consulting people of different abilities and those often called 'hard to reach'. In this endeavour I received dedicated help from the Dudley Metropolitan Borough Council youth participation team who worked tirelessly in a very inclusive way to give young people of all abilities the opportunity to give their views. Each subsequent wave of the survey has included a number of people with special needs or disabilities; Suffolk also did pioneering work with vulnerable adults.

This survey is not something adults simply administer to young people – it is made clear to all that it was developed with young people for other young people. Post-survey workshops have been held to discuss the findings and to hear what young people think about the statistics. This consultative process is in accordance with Article 12 of the UN Convention on the Rights of the Child:

> States Parties shall assure to the child who is capable of forming his or her own views the right to express those views freely in all matters affecting the child, the views of the child being given due weight in accordance with the age and maturity of the child.[169]

Respondents are told the purpose of the survey, that young people were involved in developing it and that the results are intended to help other young people. Although we want their answers, they have the right to withdraw from any question if they wish to do so.

Once the Cybersurvey questions were devised they were approved by adult professionals, a safeguarding e-champion and colleagues from a community safety team and several professionals in youth participation and anti-bullying across four local authorities. The proposed questions were also submitted to the young people's group, Dudley Decision Making Kids (DDMK) and the young shadow safeguarding board. The survey was then piloted in Essex with 158 young people through the anti-bullying lead and further amended.

Administering the survey

The survey is online. Codes are provided to each local authority for their schools. Young people answer anonymously. For the 2011 survey for the Reach Project in the west of England, some new questions were added to explore the extent of homophobic bullying in cyberspace, as earlier surveys indicated that this was a growing concern.

Young people answer anonymously, but the internet provider (IP) address, date and time of each entry are logged. On rare occasions we have had to contact a school or local authority due to concern about a young person. In such cases we use these identifying details, and child protection procedures would be invoked if necessary. Some useful helplines are given at the end of the survey in case a respondent needs subsequent support.

Feedback to young people has been provided to schools with ideas for discussion in classrooms along with some staff training and conference presentations. A series of information gathering events organised by Reach provided opportunities to explore the results with young people and to ask for their ideas and explanations for the key messages emerging from this data.

Table 12.1 Sample breakdown

Survey	Year	Boys	Girls	Age group					Total sample
				10–11	12–13	14–15	16+	17–18+	
West Midlands original	2009	1544	1775	912	1318	840	202	131	3348
Oxfordshire original+	2009a	1415	1007	428	836	969	189[a]	–	2521
Essex	2010	726	726	447	672	284	42	7	1452
Reach+ Suffolk	2011a,b,c	916	901	681	611	259	266	–	1969
Total		**4601**	**4409**	**2468**	**3437**	**2352**	**699**	**138**	**9290**

a. Age = 16+ years, includes age 17.

In each wave a few respondents skipped the age or gender question.

Oxfordshire administered additional questionnaires on paper and changed one or two questions. These responses are not referred to in the figures in this book.

Appendix 1

USEFUL TERMS

What is...?

An avatar: a digital figure or icon that you choose to represent you in a virtual world such as Second Life.

Acceptable Use Policy (AUP): covers all aspects of an agreement by users, staff and pupils, about responsible use of computer networks.

BBM (BlackBerry Messenger): a secure and private way to chat to people admitted to your BBM group. The system indicates if your message has been received and read.

Blog: an informal online journal or diary.

Bluetooth: a shortwave transmission used for sending files between digital devices.

Child Exploitation and Online Protection Centre (CEOP): apart from their work in addressing crimes against children, CEOP produce and deliver a range of training and e-safety education materials and film clips. Thinkuknow offers an array of resources (www.ceop.police.uk; www.thinkuknow.co.uk).

Defamatory Blogs: blogs in which the writer posts defamatory statements about someone, either through malice or negligence. If directed at a teacher this can damage their professional reputation.

Digital footprint: this is the digital trail of your activities in cyberspace. It can include photos or emails, texts, webpage content, chats and social networking site pages.

E-safety lead or champion: this person usually works within the safeguarding board and is a specialist in electronic abuse and e-safety matters.

'Fogging': a technique taught to some victims of bullying to defuse the situation. If the statement is true the recipient says, 'It's true' or 'That's right' or 'So you noticed?' If the statement is not true the recipient says, 'You could be right' or 'It could be true' or 'It's possible' or That's what you think.' It can serve to calm the situation and the bully does not get the reaction they seek.

Flame: it is flaming when someone sends nasty messages or posts to another, usually escalating into an angry row.

Forum: an online space where people can share common interests.

Frape or fraping: this word, made from a blend of Facebook and rape, describes the act of 'raping' someone's Facebook profile when they leave it logged in. The fraper often changes profile pictures, status, sexuality and interests. Fraping can include the poking or messaging of strangers from someone else's Facebook account.

Gamer: a player of electronic games, who will have a gamertag, the username they are known by.

Global Positioning System (GPS): allows the position of the phone to be locaed and the user pinpointed. (A GPS receiver calculates its position using asatellite signals.) Many games include a GPS locator that can show where a player is, something players often do not realise.

Griefer: in an online multiplayer game, a griefer is a player who deliberately irritates, disrupts and harasses other players.

IM (Instant Messaging): messaging in real time, using text or multimedia short messages.

Internet safety coordinator (ISC): the person within the school with responsibility for internet safety.

Local authority designated officer (LADO): deals with child protection cases.

Munch: a screen grab. This might be of a photo or a BlackBerry screen or Facebook page. Conversations or images can be captured and then posted direct on Twitter. Popular BlackBerry Messenger munch apps are used by young people.

Network manager: the person who manages the school's ICT system.

Pan-European Game Information (Pegi): Pan European Game Information rating scales indicate the ages for which a game is suitable (www.pegi.info/en/index). There are five age categories:

- 3 rating is suitable for all ages (green).
- 7 rating is suitable only for age 7 and older (green).
- 12 rating is suitable for ages 12 and older – mild action violence and suggestive themes (yellow).
- 16 rating is suitable for ages 16 and older – moderate to strong action violence, references to drugs or gambling and rude humour (yellow).
- 18 rating suitable for ages 18 and older is equivalent to adult only – graphic violence and strong sexual content (red).

Ping: to send off a message or photo, or re-send it to others.

Poke: a feature of Facebook used to get the attention of someone. The recipient receives a 'poke alert' which shows who has sent the poke.

Senior designated person (SDP): refers to the senior designated person in your organisation who deals with child protection.

Skin: a skin is a design wrapped around a website that can be used to change the way it looks, fooling the user into thinking it is genuine for example (that is, fake game sites).

SMS (Short Message Service): a short message service, such as texts. Increasingly phones can add multimedia attachments to text messages, such as phones or video clips.

Troll: a troll is someone who posts inflammatory, irritating, or off-topic messages in an online community, a forum, chatroom or other group. Their pleasure derives from upsetting people.

UK Council for Child Internet Safety (UKCCIS): the body promoting the safety of children on the internet.

Appendix 2

THE LAW RELATING TO CYBERBULLYING AND TRADITIONAL BULLYING

This is not an exhaustive or definitive description of the legal position, and it covers only England, Wales and Scotland – schools should take advice on their legal obligations. For readers outside of the UK, I recommend checking the law of your own country – there are some useful organisations and websites listed in Appendix 7 that may provide a useful starting point.

The intention here is to alert schools to the relevant legal instruments and what they should bear in mind.

For England and Wales

There are a number of Acts that have a bearing on schools in relation to cyberbullying and e-safety. This responsibility was formerly shared between state schools and the local authority, but schools in England are currently undergoing a major change in the way they are owned and run, so the legal position of many is changing as they become academies or free schools, moving out of the local authority system. Unlike a local authority-controlled school, academies have further functions as employers and as landowners. An Academy Trust has become the legal entity responsible for the running of the school. New responsibilities arise from this change in addition to those obligations to safeguard children already in place. It has also been pointed out that headteachers could find themselves taking several different roles within the organisation, each of which may carry specific legal responsibilities. Legal advice may therefore be necessary to clarify the position and questions relating to the insurance required.

The following relate to all schools, however:

- Education Act 2002
- Education and Inspections Act 2006
- Children Act 2004

- Human Rights Act 1998
  - Equality Act 2010
  - Education Act 2011
  - United Nations Convention on the Rights of the Child 1989.

Safeguarding children and young people

Section 175 of the Education Act 2002 places a duty on local authorities, the governing bodies of maintained schools and of further education institutions, to ensure that they safeguard and promote the welfare of children. 'Safeguarding' covers more than the contribution made to child protection in relation to individual children. It encompasses issues such as pupil health and safety and bullying, about which there are specific statutory requirements.

Under the Children Act 1989 a bullying incident should be addressed as a child protection concern when there is 'reasonable cause to suspect that a child is suffering, or is likely to suffer, significant harm.'

Governing bodies have a duty to promote 'well-being', defined in the Children Act 2004 in terms of:

- physical and mental health and emotional well-being
- protection from harm and neglect
- education, training and recreation
- the contribution children make to society
- social and economic well-being.

These have been expressed as the five *Every Child Matters* outcomes:

- being healthy
- staying safe
- enjoying and achieving
- making a positive contribution
- achieving economic well-being.

It has long been argued by those working to reduce discrimination and victimisation that children cannot achieve the five outcomes if they are bullied. Increasingly research on the impacts of bullying shows this to be so. Pupils must be protected from harm and neglect and schools are required to put in place appropriate measures to keep them safe in school, including when using the school's ICT system. The governing bodies of academies are also expected to keep under review how their academy contributes to these outcomes.

Participation

The Children Act 2004 and the United Nations Convention on the Rights of the Child provide for the views of children to be taken into account in matters affecting them. From this has developed a culture of youth participation that forms the bedrock of anti-bullying work.

Behaviour

Section 88 of the Education and Inspections Act 2006 requires every governing body to ensure that its school pursues policies designed to promote good behaviour and discipline among pupils. In particular it requires governing bodies to:

- make and review a written statement of principles to guide the headteacher in determining the measures that make up the school's Behaviour Policy; this must be communicated to all pupils, staff and parents

- consult the headteacher, members of staff, parents and all pupils on this statement of principles.

Under the Education and Inspections Act 2006, headteachers, with governors and staff, must identify and implement measures to promote good behaviour, respect for others, and self-discipline among learners, and to prevent all forms of bullying. This includes the prevention of cyberbullying.

The Act outlines some legal powers that relate quite directly to cyberbullying. Headteachers have the power 'to such extent as is reasonable' to regulate the conduct of learners when they are off-site or not under the control or charge of a member of staff. This is of particular significance to cyberbullying, which is often likely to take place out of school but which can impact very strongly on the school life of those learners involved.

The Education and Inspections Act 2006 allows for situations where a staff member needs to confiscate items from learners. This can include mobile phones when they are being used to cause a disturbance in class or otherwise contravene the school Behaviour/Anti-Bullying Policy. (The Department for Education has issued guidance to teachers on confiscating items such as phones.)

The Education Act 2011 includes legal powers to:

Help teachers root out poor behaviour, tackle underperformance, and improve the way in which schools are held to account.

Provisions in the Act include:

- power for schools to search pupils without consent for any dangerous or banned items

- new pre-charge reporting restrictions on allegations of criminal offences made by pupils against teachers at their school

- re-focusing routine school inspections on four key areas that matter most to parents (behaviour, including bullying, is one of the four).

Under the Equality Act 2010, new duties on schools and other public bodies came into force in April 2011. The Act strengthens and simplifies existing equality legislation and brings together existing duties not to discriminate on grounds of 'race', disability and gender. It extends these to include duties not to discriminate on the grounds of age, sexual orientation, religion or belief, and gender re-assignment. It places a requirement on governing bodies and proprietors of schools to eliminate discrimination and promote equal opportunities. It applies to school policies for tackling prejudice based bullying and has a stronger emphasis on the need to take proactive steps than previous legislation.

Civil and criminal law

Although bullying is not a specific criminal offence in UK law, there are criminal laws that can apply in terms of harassment or threatening behaviour, including threatening and menacing communications. Some cyberbullying activities could be criminal offences under a range of different laws. This information is given here not to encourage criminalisation of children, but to assist in developing a concept of responsible citizens who understand what is not acceptable or legal.

Academies should obtain advice on the Law of Negligence as it relates to their new entity. They should be aware that even where tasks are delegated they have the ultimate legal responsibility.

The Protection from Harassment Act 1997 is relevant for incidents that have happened repeatedly. Section 1 prohibits behaviour amounting to harassment of another. Section 4 provides a more serious offence of someone causing another person to fear, on at least two occasions, that violence will be used against them. A civil court may grant an injunction to restrain a person from conduct which amounts to harassment and, following conviction of an offence under Sections 2 or 4, restraining orders are available to protect the victim of the offence.

Section 127 of the Communications Act 2003 covers all forms of public communications, and subsection (1) defines an offence of sending a 'grossly offensive... obscene, indecent or menacing' communication. Subsection (2) defines a separate offence where for the purposes of causing annoyance, inconvenience or needless anxiety, a person sends a message that that person knows to be false (or causes it to be sent) or persistently makes use of a public communications system.

Section 1 of the Malicious Communications Act 1988 makes it an offence to send an indecent, grossly offensive or threatening letter, electronic communication or other article to another person with the intention that it should cause them distress or anxiety.

Section 5 of the Public Order Act 1986 makes it an offence to, with the intent to cause harassment, alarm and distress, use threatening, abusive or insulting words, behaviour, writing, signs or other visual representation within the sight or hearing of a person likely to be caused harassment, alarm or distress. This offence may apply where a mobile phone is used as a camera or video rather than where speech writing or images are transmitted.

It is an offence under the Obscene Publications Act 1959 to publish an obscene article. Publishing includes circulating, showing, playing or projecting the article or transmitting that data, for example, over a school intranet. An obscene article is one whose effect is such as to tend to deprave and corrupt persons who are likely to read, see or hear the matter contained or embodied in it.

When cyberbullying takes the form of hacking into someone else's account, then other criminal laws might come into play, such as the Computer Misuse Act 1990, in addition to civil laws on confidentiality and privacy.

Defamation is a civil 'common law' tort. It applies to any published material that damages the reputation of an individual or an organisation, and it includes material published on the internet. A civil action for defamation can be brought by an individual or a company, but not by a public authority. It is up to the claimant to prove that the material is defamatory. However, the claimant does not have to prove that the material is false – the burden of proof on that point lies with the author/publisher, who has to prove that what they have written is true. If teachers are defamed online by parents or pupils in campaign this may be considered.

Statutory guidance for schools, issued by the Department for Education

- Guidance for Governing Bodies on Behaviour and Discipline (www.education. gov.uk/aboutdfe/statutory/g0076647/behaviour-and-discipline-in-schools-guidance-for-governing-bodies)

- Dealing with Allegations of Abuse Against Teachers and Other Staff: Guidance for Local Authorities, Headteachers, School Staff, Governing Bodies and Proprietors of Independent Schools (www.education.gov.uk/aboutdfe/ advice/g0076914/dealing-with-allegations-of-abuse-against-teachers-and-other-staff)

Advice

- Preventing and Tackling Bullying: Advice for School Leaders, Staff and Governing Bodies (www.education.gov.uk/publications/standard/ publicationDetail/Page1/DFE-00062-2011)

- Screening, Searching and Confiscation: Advice for Headteachers, Staff and Governing Bodies (www.education.gov.uk/aboutdfe/advice/f0076897/ screening-searching-and-confiscation)

- Guide for Heads and School Staff on Behaviour and Discipline (www. education.gov.uk/aboutdfe/advice/f0076803/behaviour-and-discipline-in-schools-a-guide-for-headteachers-and-school-staff)

- Use of Reasonable Force: Advice for Headteachers, Staff and Governing Bodies (www.education.gov.uk/aboutdfe/advice/f0077153/use-of-reasonable-force-advice-for-school-leaders-staff-and-governing-bodies)

For Scotland

What does the law say?

In Scotland pupils have the right to be educated in an atmosphere that is free from fear. The United Nations Convention on the Rights of the Child, the Children (Scotland) Act 1995 and the European Convention on Human Rights apply. Assault, harassment and intimidation are offences, regardless of the age of the perpetrator or victim.

Although there is no law which states that Scottish schools must have a specific Anti-Bullying Policy, this is strongly recommended in the document *Action Against Bullying* (1992) and further endorsed by local authorities, the Scottish Office and its successor, the Scottish Executive.[170]

The development of the *Cyberbullying Guidance* (2009) relates directly to the commitment in *Strengthening the Highlands*: 'People are, and feel safe from crime, disorder and danger.' The Guidance accompanies the revised Education, Culture and Sport Service Anti-Bullying and Anti-Racism Guidelines and Procedures.[171]

Cyberbullying and the law

Incidents of cyberbullying are not specific criminal offences in Scottish Law. However, there are laws that may be relevant in terms of harassing or threatening behaviour, or menacing and threatening communications. Some cyberbullying activities may constitute offences under a range of different laws, for example:

- Protection from Harassment Act 1997

- Communications Act 2003, Section 127

- Malicious Communications Act 1998

- Criminal Law (Consolidation) (Scotland) Act 1995, Section 50A.

Some aspects of cyberbullying may also constitute a common law breach of the peace. At present, behaviour in Scotland that might be described as harassment or stalking is usually prosecuted as a breach of the peace.

The respect*me* website can provide further information on how these Acts relate to bullying, and specifically to cyberbullying (see www.respectme.org.uk). If the bullying behaviour is based on sexual, racial or religious grounds, prosecution could be sought through anti-discriminatory laws.

When bullying occurs

In Scotland there is a culture of collaborative working together to address school bullying that attempts to respond quickly to diminish the serious impacts to the young people involved. Parents, pupils, teachers and the whole school community are encouraged to develop effective reactive strategies that can provide this quick response and only rarely is the legal system involved.

Nevertheless there may be cases in which it is appropriate to call in the police. It may be because other efforts have failed or because the case itself is so serious.

Any person can make a complaint about bullying to the police. The website www.antibullying.net states that:

> Teachers, parents or other members of a school community may decide to do so if:
> - a bullying incident could have serious consequences for the victim
> - other strategies have failed or are considered to be inappropriate because of the seriousness of what has happened and
> - there is a reasonable possibility that making such a report could make the bullying less likely to recur and produce an outcome that helps the victim.

If bullying takes place both in and out of schools it is considered vital for teachers and parents to work with the police and other appropriate agencies. If a cyberbullying incident occurs establishments should contact the Highland Council via a dedicated email address (below) when the incident is first reported, and a team of professionals will be able to provide advice and support where necessary and appropriate.

Any case where a child may be at risk, must be reported to the designated child protection officer, who will follow Highland child protection guidelines.

Teachers should be aware of GTC Scotland's *Code of Professionalism and Conduct* that sets out the key principles and values for registered teachers in Scotland.

Important numbers

- The Scottish Child Law Centre 0131 667 6333, www.sclc.org.uk
- The Law Society of Scotland 0131 226 7411, www.lawscot.org.uk
- The Children's Legal Centre 01206 873820, www.childrenslegalcentre.com
- Anti-Bullying Network 0131 651 6100, www.antibullying.net
- Highland Cyberbullying Support: cyberbullying@highland.gov.uk
- Scotland's anti-bullying service www.respectme.org.uk

Appendix 3

BACKGROUND CONTEXT IN THE UK

UK background context

At times it is easy to forget what life was like before we had fast WiFi everywhere, and smartphones, apps and tablets that are capable of so many functions. But when we look back it is a shock to realise that the headlong pace of the past digital decade has delivered a total change in how life is lived in a remarkably short time. It is not surprising that those researching risks to children and strategies to keep them safe are playing catch up.

UK practice is described by the Family Online Safety Institute (FOSI) in its country reports as 'a good mix of industry self-regulation and collaborative government oversight; pioneering and successful initiatives lead by the Internet Watch Foundation (IWF) and Child Exploitation & Online Child Protection Centre (CEOP) in areas such as illegal online child abuse content and the creation of the UK Council of Child Internet Safety (UKCCIS)'.[172] An example of this is a call by a cross-party parliamentary inquiry for the government to initiate a formal review of an Opt-In filter to access adult material on the internet. The group recommended that:

- The government should press for accelerated implementation plans for 'Active Choice' – the content filtering system proposed for new internet customers by the largest ISPs.

- Within 12 months, ISPs should roll out 'single account' network filters that provide one-click filtering for all devices connected to the same internet account.

- A single regulator should take lead responsibility on internet safety.

- Public WiFi networks should have a default adult-content bar.

- Government and industry should draw up new guidelines to publicise existing safety settings on computers and internet-enabled devices.

- ISPs should provide more support and signposting for internet safety education.[173]

The cross-party group noted that 'Many parents report feeling left behind by the evolution of technology, and that they lack the knowledge and skills to educate their children about internet safety. Parents are also concerned about many other forms of disturbing internet content, including cyberbullying, extreme violence, self-harm, suicide and pro-anorexia websites.' Government reviews have also examined the commercialisation and sexualisation of children via all media and internet industry leaders have met with the Prime Minister to discuss these issues.

Despite the government's efforts over the past decade, governments change and the long delays and upheaval that inevitably result before new measures and personnel are in place can mean that, for a period, things stand still while the digital world moves on at a faster pace than ever. The challenge is not to get stuck delivering old messages or talking only to the industry, parents and educators. To date the voices of young people have often been drowned out.

It can take a lengthy period to develop and embed new advice into all schools. Early adopters take it on at once and then the majority follow. But a few schools had not even fully adopted the 2007 guidance by the time it was withdrawn three years later despite a very efficient delivery programme. Currently there is a policy of giving schools as little advice as possible, in order not to 'burden' them, despite schools wanting guidance on this topic.

On the ground, meanwhile, successfully delivering messages to young people about digital citizenship in a fast-changing scenario requires acting faster than bureaucracy can manage. It needs adaptation, adjustment and attention to various influences and changes. Some of these changes will be due to exciting new developments in technology, while others will be because young people have flocked to some new social network or fashionable site. These are 'foreground' changes. They all take place against the 'backdrop' where the pace of change is slower, but significant none the less. This backdrop includes changes in our local communities, and actions by government and providers.

One of the 'backdrop' factors is population change. If the following population patterns and literacy levels are borne in mind, we can design e-safety delivery to be targeted, appropriate and enjoyable for all. The UK population has been growing increasingly diverse. The fastest change in the population can be seen in the under 16 age group in England. London schools are thought to contain people speaking around 300 languages. For over 33 per cent of London children English is not their first language, resulting in a rich linguistic heritage in which large numbers of children speak several languages. Many are accustomed to translating for their parents on a daily basis. Some of these parents may struggle to understand how to help their children stay safe online unless supported effectively, while others will be extremely adept, but in their own language.

Another backdrop feature is the diminishing but still present digital divide. While a small number of people remain unskilled at using new technology or too impoverished to have access, there are many who are unskilled at the basics too.

The Literacy Trust has pointed out that:

- One in six people in the UK struggle with literacy. This means their literacy is below the level expected of an 11-year-old.

- The number of children achieving the expected levels for reading at age 11 is 84 per cent in 2011.

- The number of children achieving the expected levels for writing at age 11 is 75 per cent in 2011.[174]

Consequently, as with the design of any effective learning, account must be taken of the diversity – including ethnicity, culture and religion – of children and young people in the school population. Children come to school with very different experiences and knowledge – including use of mobile technology, facility in the use of English, parental knowledge and involvement. Parents' reading skills can also vary markedly, which suggests that relying on print materials targeted at parents on e-safety messages for their child may not be successful. Instead, practical demonstrations and other media will be more effective. Diversity is a strength and brings innovation and fresh vibrant thinking, but to do justice to all pupils and their families it is necessary to reconsider materials and sessions on e-safety advice regularly and make the relevant changes or adopt different approaches to relate to local families. Pupils with special needs or disabilities also need a range of dedicated e-safety materials and resources. Digital literacy cannot be disentangled from multilingualism, culture, poverty and opportunity, or reading skills. Safe access to the internet and all that it offers can be viewed as an equality issue as, without this access, people will be left behind and job prospects harmed.

Targeted programmes

This book has attempted to outline some groups of children and young people who appear more vulnerable than others online. This is further explored by a UKCCIS report, 'Identifying Vulnerable Children Online and What Can Be Done To Help', which states that 'vulnerability online needs to be understood in the broader context of children's lives'. This broader context is likely to include their families. The report also reminds us that 'vulnerability is not a static issue but one that needs contextualising within the emotional, psychological and physical developmental stages of childhood'.[175] Without a doubt, this is an area for future research which will contribute to discussions on how to deliver some targeted programmes. Schools can try to ensure that they effectively reach the families of vulnerable pupils and support the latter intensively in school.

What your local community means for e-safety education

Your local neighbourhood population is an important consideration when delivering e-safety education to children and their families. If you are an e-safety educator you will need to be aware of this changing population, just as you would when delivering any bullying prevention strategy. What local feuds are being played out on estates? Who is the dominant local group? Are the delivery methods you propose appropriate and easily understood? Community Safety Officers can provide this knowledge. Sessions for parents should be sensitively planned to suit the local population groups. This calls for creative ideas. Who does not attend? Who is hard to reach? Who needs a session on a different day or time?

Furthermore, all bullying prevention work is concerned with tackling racist bullying, or as we tend to describe it: bullying linked with race, religion or culture. This means protecting the rights of everyone. Newcomers may bring with them bitter prejudice or fear of another group, especially if fleeing war. Ideas about respect and honour are often poorly understood by practitioners if the group are new to the country. Examples of this have been seen among some newer populations for whom violent retaliation was seen as honourable. They might believe retaliatory attacks are a form of respect for their 'insulted' friend or sibling. We need to teach and provide other routes through which they can maintain honour and respect. If we simply discount their beliefs and feelings they could feel a lack of respect and simply take their revenge battles beyond the school gates.

Some community groups bring with them myths about other immigrant groups. When I visited a group of young people who had recently arrived in North London to find out if they experienced bullying at college, they replied 'No, nothing like that' adding, 'we run the place'. This alerted me at once. Upon enquiring further, they reassured me everything was 'going well, no problems'. Only later in the discussion did they reveal strong prejudices about another ethnic group of students whom they described as 'all rapists'. The college now had a group who considered that they 'ran the place', controlling the student union and holding discriminatory views towards another group of students. There was much work to be done!

If gangs increasingly use Facebook to organise fights, work has to be done on the ground with the young people rather than only focusing on headlines and panic around the technology. A 15-year-old boy, Sofyen Belamouadden, was knifed to death in broad daylight in in the ticket hall of Victoria Station in London by a large mob of school boys in front of shocked commuters. Police discovered that one boy had called on mates to bring knives and the attack was orchestrated on Facebook. Twenty boys were arrested. Here the SNS site is purely a tool for the intention to harm. It does leave an evidence trail for the police to use, but it is not in itself the motivator. There is often a panic-driven focus on the technology that blinds us to the behaviour and the fact that there had been simmering tension between the gangs for some time. It seems that blind loyalty demands that even bright students make poor decisions when called on to support their mates. Specialist work is needed to diffuse such hostility as early as possible and multiple partners are needed from local agencies including youth services, police and conflict resolution specialists. Preventing young people from using Facebook, while not actually possible, would not reduce the tension between the groups.

Poverty and the digital divide

For 3.5 million children growing up in poverty in our country it is harder to deliver effective digital literacy. Recent research by the OECD revealed that these UK children are least likely to be able to escape deprivation when compared with their counterparts in other rich countries. Britain's social mobility was the lowest when compared to 12 other advanced western countries.[176] The internet could help them bridge the knowledge gap, which is all the more reason why children and young people should be safe online so that they can take advantage of the gateway to their future it represents. While growth has been rapid, a digital divide remains.

Rural areas

In rural areas there are different challenges. There is a drive to get the country digitally connected, but it takes more than simply providing broadband or WiFi to far flung spots – people need to be educated in safe use. Work is being carried out in the county of Suffolk (UK) to explore the cyberbullying experiences of its young, often rural, population. They are also designing support for rural vulnerable adults. It is hoped that information gathered using the Cybersurvey in this county will shape e-safety messages and strategy in the future.

Reaching parents

Some parents stay away from a school session on e-safety, for fear of revealing that they do not understand English or perhaps do not use the internet. Other parents feel uneasy in schools due to their own unhappy past experiences. Some simply do not turn up, presenting challenges to the effective spread of e-safety advice. But does it always have to take place in a school?

Muslim women may prefer sessions on their own and it can be helpful to provide a crèche if sessions for mothers are held during the day. A large turnout was achieved for a meeting on educational issues, by holding the event in a local community centre in Bradford with a play area for toddlers and Halal food provided. Mothers very often do not have babysitters and cannot leave their toddlers with anyone in order to attend. This centre was regularly used by locals and they felt comfortable there, which made it a good choice. Translators were on hand to help, but after a while we found they were barely needed as everyone relaxed and began to use the English they had, without being nervous and with a lot of enjoyment and laughter.[177]

Some way should be found to reach all communities in a sensitive manner with *practical* demonstrations. One of the recommendations of the EU Kidsonline study is that there should be greater availability of age appropriate positive content for children, especially in small language communities.[178] Early years settings are ideal for the first steps towards learning for both parents and children. They offer a way in for parents who are not digitally expert without feeling embarrassed because the level is geared to young children. Starting early can engage parents to continue to learn alongside their children.

Holding a session with local partner agencies in their premises, rather than at the school, can open doors to parents who attend that service but seldom come into school. It pays to remember that some parents are not comfortable in the school setting if they have memories of failure in their own school days. Children's centres may offer possibilities.

National Anti-Bullying Week, an annual focus on bullying, offers an ideal opportunity to invite parents to learn how they can help their child stay safe. But too many schools report that they put on e-safety evenings and few parents attend. It seems those that are very technically savvy stay away because they think they know it, while those who feel ashamed that they don't understand or are not digitally literate may stay away because they fear looking stupid if they come. The secret can lie in the title of the event – for example titles such as 'Keeping our children safe' or 'The right of your child to be safe' usually work better than 'Addressing cyberbullying'. If parents think their child is popular and not cyberbullied then titles such as the latter can mean they stay away as they feel it is irrelevant. If they think their child is a perpetrator they will definitely stay away! Research by the Anti-Bullying Alliance and others tells us that parents tend to underestimate the extent of the cyberbullying their child has experienced.

Sessions in which older teenagers teach parents of primary age pupils have been successful in the South West region of England. They were able to demonstrate what chatrooms, SNS pages, MSN and blogs look like, how children and young people interact and how to help them stay safe. These could be in a community or technology college, or a library where there are many computers.

Change is rapid

Over 80 per cent of the population are internet users and mobile phone ownership overtook landline ownership in 2009. Facebook membership is high and according to the *Sunday Times*, Twitter has moved 'from geek street to high street, with one in six Britons now using the service for an average of 12 minutes a day.'[179]

Responses come from a wide range of organisations

The creation of the UK Council of Child Internet Safety (UKCCIS, established in 2008) was a response to the Byron Review of 2008: 'Safer Children in a Digital World'.[180] UKCCIS brings together organisations from industry, charities and the public sector to work with the UK government to deliver the recommendations from Professor Tanya Byron's Report, including the implementation of a Child Internet Safety Strategy.[181] It provides a much admired helpline for professionals and an audit tool.

The voluntary sector is represented by charities such as Childnet International with its range of projects and websites such as Digizen and Know it all. Childnet contributed to the government guidance on cyberbullying that was issued in 2007.[182] This became the standard advice and was widely used as the key guidance on cyberbullying. Childnet now hosts UKCCIS jointly with the South West Grid for Learning.

The Anti-Bullying Alliance brings together a wide range of organisations addressing bullying, either as part or all of their work. Founder members such as the National Society for the Prevention of Cruelty to Children (NSPCC) work on children's safety from cruelty to abuse and host Childline, a national children's phone helpline service which also offers online advice.

The charity Beat Bullying grew rapidly in a few short years and began to offer an online cybermentors service for those young people who were victims of cyberbullying. It trained young people to be cybermentors and provided oversight and support to the programme.

The Bullying Intervention Group (BIG) provides a national award scheme for schools and services that can provide evidence of excellence in anti-bullying practice including cyberbullying.

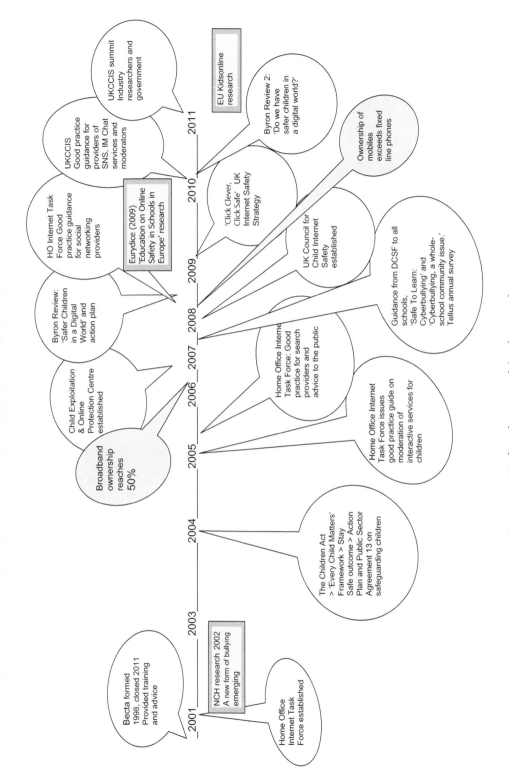

Figure A3.1 Timeline: the connected decade – some key moments

Appendix 4

OFSTED FRAMEWORK FOR SCHOOL INSPECTION ENGLAND

Please be aware that these notes focus only on the way the new framework has an impact on behaviour and bullying.

The framework sets out the statutory basis for inspection and summarises the main features of school inspections from January 2012. Inspections will be slimmed down and focus on four key areas:

- achievement of pupils at the school

- quality of teaching at the school

- behaviour and safety of the pupils at the school

- quality of leadership and management of the school.

Schools that are 'satisfactory' or 'inadequate' are to be inspected more frequently than schools that are 'good' or 'outstanding'. Schools that are rated 'outstanding' will be exempt from Section 5 inspection but will undergo a risk assessment, and schools that are 'good' move to a five-yearly inspection. Changes in pupils' attainment and attendance over time, the views of parents and carers and qualifying complaints or any other significant concerns (including those raised by the local authority) can trigger an inspection.

Section 42 of the document refers to 'The behaviour and safety of pupils at the school' and specifically references bullying. The framework reads as follows:

When evaluating the behaviour and safety of pupils at the school, inspectors will consider:

- pupils' attitudes to learning and conduct in lessons and around the school

- pupils' behaviour towards, and respect for, other young people and adults, including freedom from bullying and harassment that may include cyberbullying and prejudice-based bullying related to special educational need, sexual orientation, sex, race, religion and belief, gender reassignment or disability

- how well teachers manage the behaviour and expectations of pupils to ensure that all pupils have an equal and fair chance to thrive and learn in an atmosphere of respect and dignity
  - pupils' ability to assess and manage risk appropriately and to keep themselves safe
  - pupils' attendance and punctuality at school and in lessons
  - how well the school ensures the systematic and consistent management of behaviour.

In considering the overall effectiveness of the school, inspectors will look at:

…how well the school provides positive experiences for all pupils by promoting the pupils' spiritual, moral, social and cultural development through planned and coherent opportunities in the curriculum and through interactions with teachers and other adults.

Ofsted considers that equality is intrinsic throughout.

The former self-evaluation document has been scrapped but schools are expected to have their own evidence of self-evaluation and should be able to demonstrate that they have dealt with behaviour effectively over time. (They will also be expected to show how they are monitoring and evidencing their progress across all of the other key areas.)

Inspections will include parent, pupil and staff surveys. Parents will also be able to report their comments via Parent View online (http://parentview.ofsted.gov.uk).

Monitoring will change so that an equivalent measure is used for all children regardless of deprivation or context.

The main focus will be on narrowing the gap between the most disadvantaged and those doing well. (Bullying has been shown to reduce attainment.)

There is still an emphasis on school leadership working with the community and adjusting the curriculum to meet needs.

The risk assessment process will take into account current attainment, progress and attendance as well as any parents' complaints and concerns.

Source: www.ofsted.gov.uk/resources/draft-framework-for-school-inspection-january-2012

Appendix 5

BACKGROUND CONTEXT IN THE USA

There have been some seminal turning points in thinking about bullying in the USA. These events and the reactions to them have contributed to the debate about how children's use of new media is viewed and managed.

In the midst of sensational or tragic news stories, moral panics about crime against children, state legislation and policies, schools are trying to find practical ways to address cyberbullying and e-safety. How do they integrate what they do with all of these influences and requirements, alongside a child's life at home and away from school? Some argue that schools' efforts to restrict, ban or control the use of digital media by children and young people have gone so far as to make education fall behind other industries in its use of technology.[183] Young people are seen on the one hand as skilled digital players, yet on the other hand as in need of extensive protection. It may help to consider these seminal turning points in order to understand what drives the fears about risk and responses to it.

Bullying comes under a spotlight after Columbine

The shooting at Columbine High School in the late 1990s and a spate of similar incidents launched a national soul searching into bullying and its relation to violence. Extensive research on bullying behaviour and links with violence or crime followed.[184]

In 2002, the US government released a report on school violence, detailing its findings that almost 71 per cent of attackers involved in the 37 incidents reviewed felt 'persecuted, bullied, threatened, attacked or injured by others prior to the incident.' As the report explains:

> In several cases, individual attackers had experienced bullying and harassment that was long-standing and severe. In some of these cases the experience of being bullied... appeared to have been a factor in [the attacker's] decision to mount an attack at the school. In one case, most of the attacker's schoolmates described the attacker as 'the kid everyone teased.'

In a number of the incidents it emerged that the attackers described being bullied in terms that suggested that these experiences 'approached torment'. They told of behaviours that, if they occurred in the workplace, would likely meet legal definitions of harassment and/or assault.

Much of what followed in the wake of this cataclysmic event can be traced back to this pivotal moment in which bullying changed from being seen as simply a part of growing up, to being thought of as a serious precursor to violence. In the work that followed, the links with depression and mental health were also outlined, and bullying maintained a high profile over the next decade. Bullying prevention came to be viewed as crime prevention, and efforts were made to understand and avert its impacts on emotional health. But the decade that followed also saw the phenomenal growth of mobile phone technology and with it the development of cyberbullying.

Internet and mobile users

Change has been rapid. In June 2010 there were 239,893,600 internet users in the USA, or 77.3 per cent of the population.[185] This rose to 78.2 per cent of the population by 2011.[186]

Facebook

Young people are using Facebook below the watershed age of 13, just as in the UK: 7.5 million under-13s used Facebook in 2010,[187] a violation of the site's policies, according to a survey by Consumer Reports' 'State of the Net' survey. More than five million of the users were under the age of 11, and about one million children experienced bullying on the site.

In March 2011, Facebook expanded an existing reporting system that lets users flag content they consider bullying to a parent or teacher. The site also lists tips on preventing cyberbullying, including using a 'block' feature to stop abusive behaviour.[188]

Smartphones

The number of people in the USA who own smartphones jumped 10 per cent to 82.2 million in the three months July 2011, according to a report by metrics company comScore Inc. released on 30 August 2011 – that represents 35.1 per cent of the 234 million people aged 13 and up who use mobile devices in the US.[189]

Cyberbullying has been identified as a mid and late teen problem. As they grow older, young people are more digitally skilled. Their social and sexual lives are also developing an intensity at this age that is lacking among younger children. Their social lives are entirely lived through new technology.

From the Berkman for Internet and Society Harvard Report:[190]

Online harassment appears less frequently among early adolescents (Lenhart 2007; Ybarra and Mitchell 2004a) and children (McQuade and Sampat 2008). It is seemingly highest in mid-adolescence, around 13–14 years of age, (Kowalski and

Limber 2007; Lenhart 2007; McQuade and Sampat 2008; Slonje and Smith 2008; Williams and Guerra 2007).

Tragic cyberhomophobia takes centre stage

A spate of suicides due to homophobic bullying in 2010 promoted another tsunami of anguish and self-examination, prompting calls for more state legislation. A 'summit' was held at the White House in Washington. By mid-2004 16 states had passed anti-bullying legislation aimed at creating safe learning environments. By 2011, partly in response to the outcry these tragic deaths evoked, this had risen to 48 states. But legislation often fell foul of the first amendment when tested in court.

Other intense debates have centred round issues of faith schools being exempted in some states from having to address homophobic bullying. In these tragic suicides two streams of debate coincide. One is how to address online harassment and cyberbullying or abuse, the other is how to promote equality and make homophobia unacceptable. There is currently little agreement on either.

Unintended consequences arise from efforts to control

Educators and legislators with the good intention of preventing incidents of bullying may unintentionally clash with the constitutionally protected rights of students. In fact, in *Saxe vs State College District Area School District*, the Third Circuit struck down a school district's comprehensive Anti-Harassment Policy as unconstitutionally overbroad under the Free Speech Clause of the First Amendment.

Although this consequence of anti-bullying policies and legislation may be unintended, it emphasises the underlying tension between school safety and student rights that are further explored in a book by Shaheen Shariff.[191] In an analysis of the law, Shariff explores the way cyberbullying raises new contentious areas where rights might conflict, such as between the rights of teachers not to be defamed and pupils' rights of free speech or rights to an education. If a pupil posts something defamatory or professionally damaging about a teacher online, should the pupil be excluded from school and denied the chance to sit a forthcoming exam? How does the teacher achieve redress?

This clash of rights shows how much there is to learn about the law and how it adapts to the online word. Furthermore, professional advice to teachers on interacting with their students online is a sensitive and difficult territory. Some teachers argue that they should never communicate with students by email, Facebook or SMS (Short Message Service) while others argue that some students are acutely in need of support via these very media and the restrictions are preventing them from doing their jobs. Policies can overstate the problem or blame the technology, thus making the school anti-technology rather than anti-the behaviour. The state of Missouri's 2011 Amy Hestir Student Protection Act came to be known as the 'Facebook law', illustrating how technology is seen as the foremost cause of the problem (it contained a social networking clause regulating teacher and pupil contact). Vickery discusses how after this bill was passed, confusion, backlash and anger followed.[192]

Where next?

Initially there were fears that online exploitation and victimisation of children and young people would grow exponentially. The Crimes against Children Research Center (CCRC) at the University of New Hampshire conducted two comprehensive national assessments of youth internet safety, five years apart – the first and second Youth Internet Safety Surveys (YISS-1, 2000 and YISS-2, 2005)[193]. They demonstrated dramatic changes showing marked increases in the amount of internet harassment and unwanted exposure to pornography, as well as decreases in unwanted sexual solicitations. They point out that this is a highly volatile environment with dramatic change in a short time frame, and we can expect further changes in their third survey (2010).[194] There have, of course, also been considerable technological and educational developments to address these risks over the past decade.

David Finkelhor of the CCRC attempted to put some perspective on the choppy waters of panic and alarm. He argued that the view that the internet itself is a 'risk-promoting environment or a specially risky environment' is not substantiated if US figures on crimes against children are examined. Warnings from child exploitation prevention agencies and media reports highlight the extreme cases. But Finkelhor proposes that there is no actual evidence that the internet is an amplifier in this way, and in fact the data shows that while this 'anxious narrative has come to dominate,' there have been remarkable improvements in social problem and risk indicators in the USA. He goes on to explore the notion that perhaps this panic by adults is a kind of paranoia about youth, which he terms 'Juvenoia'.[195]

Gradually, greater understanding and stronger data is bringing a more practical approach. The work of Sameer Hinduja and Justin W. Patchin at the Cyberbullying Research Center combined understanding and measuring cyberbullying and its impacts, with useful messages for schools. These led to short briefing papers, such as *Cyberbullying: Identification, Prevention and Response*, in which they advocate creating a peaceful school climate, or guides for educators and parents on electronic dating violence.[196]

In 2010, to answer the challenge they saw as 'the gulf between research and practice,' a working group of 12 'practitioners', including educators, lawyers, public health and mental health experts, a paediatrician, a social worker, a juvenile judge and a youth minister met at Harvard's Berkman Center for Internet & Society exploring possible strategies in the context of current research. Among the issues explored were: sexual solicitation and sex crimes against minors; harassment and bullying; youth-generated problematic content; and access to problematic content. Berkman fellow danah boyd stressed the need to move beyond the hysteria generated by news stories and 'press the re-set button.' The group argues that there are cybermyths and cyberfacts. Michelle Ybarra,[197] who carried out the YISSs, explained that: 'The mistaken perception that things are getting worse stems both from high-profile media reports and from the fact that some research studies skew towards older kids.'[198]

There were also concerns that the behaviour known as 'sexting' would lead to children being arrested for sending self-generated photos to friends. Two new studies from the CCRC suggest that concerns about teen sexting may be overblown. One study found the percentage of youth who send nude pictures of themselves that would qualify as child pornography is very low. The other found that when teen sexting images do come to police attention, few youth are being arrested or treated like sex offenders.

In her work which looked at 1600 young people between the ages of 10 and 15, Ybarra found that 62 per cent hadn't been involved in internet harassment – either as victim or perpetrator – over the course of the previous year. Of the remaining group, 17 per cent had been both perpetrator and victim. Only 3 per cent of harassers had not themselves been victimised, while 18 per cent had been victimised but hadn't harassed anyone themselves.

In the course of any given year, between 33 and 39 per cent of children surveyed reported having been harassed over the three-year period from 2006 to 2008, with the most common incidents including rude or mean comments, online rumours, and threatening or aggressive comments. The slight increase in percentages coincided with the children growing older – not surprising, as bullying, both online and off, tends to peak in middle school (11–14 in the US). On a monthly basis, only about 8 to 9 per cent of those surveyed reported being harassed.

Those who had been harrassed are twice as likely to be white as non-white, more likely to come from affluent homes, and nine times as likely as non-victims to perpetrate harassment themselves, according to Ybarra.

Not surprisingly, children who are bullied online are also more likely to be bullied offline. Ybarra's research shows that victims of internet harassment are more likely than peers to have brought weapons to school in the past 30 days, more likely to abuse alcohol and more likely to suffer from a lack of closeness with primary caregivers. 'Kids don't operate in a vacuum,' Ybarra concluded.

Appendix 6

COMPARING USA SCHOOL GRADES WITH UK SCHOOL YEARS

US grade system	Level	Age	British school year system	Welsh and English National Curriculum Key Stages
Nursery/pre-Kindergarten 3–4	Pre-school	0–4	Nursery/pre-school	Foundation stage (non-compulsory)
Pre-Kindergarten 4–5		4–5	Reception	(compulsory from age 5)
Kindergarten	Elementary	5–6	Year 1	Key Stage 1
Grade 1	"	6–7	Year 2	(Key Stage 1 SATS exams this year)
Grade 2	"	7–8	Year 3	Key Stage 2
Grade 3	"	8–9	Year 4	"
Grade 4	"	9–10	Year 5	
Grade 5	"	10–11	Year 6	(Key Stage 2 SATS exams this year)
Grade 6	Junior high	11–12	Year 7	Key Stage 3
Grade 7	"	12–13	Year 8	"
Grade 8	"	13–14	Year 9	(Key Stage 3 SATS exams this year)
Grade 9	High school: freshman	14–15	Year 10	Key Stage 4 GCSE study
Grade 10	High school: sophomore	14–16	Year 11	(GCSE exams)

US grade system	Level	Age	British school year system	Welsh and English National Curriculum Key Stages
Grade 11	High school: junior	16–17	Year 12	Key Stage 5 GCE A-level (at sixth form or college) (non-compulsory)
Grade 12	High school: senior	17–18	Year 13	(GCE A-level exams)
Junior college	University, technical college or community college,	18–	–	Key Stage 6 higher education at university, technical college, etc.
	"	21+	–	"

In England, 'education' must legally be started no later than *the term of the child's fifth birthday*, whereas in the USA, school begins at age six and may end 'no sooner than the child's 16th birthday,' although the child may continue to receive state education at school or college until the completion of the school year in which the child turns 18.

Australia

The New South Wales school system is very similar to the British one.

- Ages 0–4 – pre-school
- Ages 4–5 – kindergarten
- Ags 5–6 – Year 1, etc.
- Ages 16–17 – Year 12
- Kindergarten – Year 2 – Stage 1
- Years 3–4 – Stage 2
- Years 5–6 – Stage 3
- Years 7–8 – Stage 4
- Years 9–10 – Stage 5
- Years 11–12 – Stage 6

Appendix 7

SOURCES OF HELP

UK RESOURCES
For young people

Chatdanger: (www.chatdanger.com) informs young people about staying safe in interactive areas online.

Child Exploitation and Online Protection Centre (CEOP): (www.ceop.police.uk), or use the CEOP button on many websites to report unsuitable or threatening behaviour online.

ChildLine: Tel 0800 1111 (www.childline.org.uk). For those who are hearing impaired, textphone 0800 400222 in daytime hours.

Childnet International, Know It All: comprehensive advice site (www.childnet.com/KIA).

The Counselling Directory: (www.counselling-directory.org.uk) provides information about counselling and psychotherapy and details of registered practitioners by region.

Crimestoppers: Tel 0800 555111 if you think a crime has been committed.

CyberMentors: a service run by Beatbullying (www.cybermentors.org.uk). Young people can talk to a mentor about a problem with cyberbullying, or talk to them in the chatroom. Counsellors are available for serious concerns.

EACH (Educational Action Challenging Homophobia): provides a national helpline for young people experiencing homophobic bullying. Tel 0808 1000 143.

If U Care, Share: (www.ifucareshare.co.uk) founded in memory of Daniel O'Hare who took his own life at the age of 19 without warning. For care and advice for young people and their families contact Share@ifucareshare.co.uk, Tel 0191 3887186.

The Samaritans: Tel 0845 7909090 (confidential, non-judgemental support 24 hours a day), if you are feeling desperate or depressed or your friend feels this way.

Thinkuknow: CEOP's advice for different age groups: 5–7, 8–10 and 11–16 (www. thinkuknow.co.uk).

Talk CBT: a counselling service for all, based in the north east, but has a specialist suicide prevention programme for young people (http://talkcbt.co.uk).

For parents

Bullying Intervention Group (BIG): help for young people and pages for parents: www.bullyinginterventiongroup.co.uk/bighelp.php and www.bullyingintervention group.co.uk/parents.php

Kidscape: a helpline for parents: Tel 08451 205 204.

Mumsnet: discussion threads on bullying: www.mumsnet.com

National Youth Agency: www.nya.org.uk

The **NSPCC** offers a wide range of advice and support in this area, including what to do when a child may disclose a further problem such as domestic violence or neglect: www.nspcc.org.uk

The **Red Balloon Learner Centre Group:** offers support and education for the recovery of bullied children who are severely affected: Tel 01223 366052; www. redballoonlearner.co.uk

Stonewall: provides information on tackling homophobic bullying: www.stonewall. org.uk

Transforming Conflict: provides information on restorative practices and training: www.transformingconflict.org

For professionals and practitioners

Anti-Bullying Alliance: for a description of ways to enable participation for children and young people with special needs: www.antibullyingalliance.org.uk

BBC Schools: Cyberbullying: UK website links to resources and information on cyberbullying and how to combat it: www.bbc.co.uk/schools

The **Child Exploitation Online Protection Centre (CEOP):** hosts the Young People's online charter and is responsible for safety on the internet. There is advice for parents and carers and for young people: www.ceop.gov.uk

Childnet: for information and materials on a range of online safety aspects such as social networking, being a good digital citizen and cyberbullying, Childnet also offers activities, posters and materials on www.kidsmart.org.uk; see also www. digizen.org/cyberbullying

Department for Education Behaviour: pages carry information and advice on bullying: www.education.gov.uk/schools/pupilsupport/behaviour

EACH (Educational Action Challenging Homophobia): provides training for local authorities to challenge homophobic bullying and an action line: www. eachaction.org.uk

Equality and Human Rights Commission: www.equalityhumanrights.com

Holocaust Memorial Day: for resources to tackle stereotypes and prejudice. Includes educational materials and annual events: www.hmd.org.uk

Instead Consultancy: for professional advice and training on equality and diversity in education: www.insted.co.uk.

Leap: offers training and workshops in confronting conflict and hosts the Academy for Youth and Conflict for formal training leading to qualifications for staff: www. leaplinx.com

Mencap: the Don't Stick it, Stop It! campaign provides stickers and useful materials, such as line animations and video clips, which can be used for training/awareness purposes: www.mencap.org.uk/dontstickit

National Youth Agency: www.nya.org.uk

The **NSPCC:** offers a wide range of advice and support in this area, including what to do when a child may disclose a further problem such as domestic violence or neglect: www.nspcc.org.uk

Professionals Online Safety Helpline: helpline@safeinternet.org; Tel 08443814772

Respectme Scotland: for useful advice on managing bullying and cyberbullying: www.respectme.org.uk/Encouraging-Responsible-Use-of-Mobile-Technologies. html

Show Racism the Red Card: the anti-racism campaign in football, with resources and events: www.srtrc.org/

The **Southwest Grid for Learning Trust:** offers an excellent e-safety evaluation tool called 360 degrees: www.swgfl.org.uk

Stonewall: provides information on tackling homophobic bullying: www.stonewall. org.uk

Transforming Conflict: for information on restorative practices and training: www. transformingconflict.org

Wales 2011: 'Respecting Others: Anti-bullying Guidance': http://wales.gov.uk/ topics/educationandskills/publications/circulars/antibullying/?lang=en

International resources

USA

Kidpower: a non-profit organisation based in the USA offering workshops, training and resources to help people learn personal safety skills and build self-confidence: www.kidpower.org

Mental Health America: bullying pages including information, statistics and guidelines for victims of bullying and their carers: www.mentalhealthamerica.org

Stopbullying.gov: a US Department of Health and Human Services offering games, films and information about bullying and how to prevent it: www.stopbullyingnow. hrsa.gov

Canada

Bullying Canada: an interactive community site for young people with victim stories and a chat forum: www.bullyingcanada.ca

Bullying.org: a website with educational programmes and resources for individuals, families, educational institutions and organisations; it includes online learning resources: www.bullying.org

Cyberbullying.org: a Canadian-based site set up to advice and support young people around preventing and taking action against cyberbullying: www.Cyberbullying.org

Australia

Bullying. No Way! Is a website created by Australia's educational communities to create learning environments where every student and school community member is safe from bullying: www.bullyingnoway.gov.au

Child Safety Australia provides information including helpful advice for children, parents and carers: www.childsafetyaustralia.com.au

The **Kids Helpline** provides information and resources for children, teenagers and young people, as well as for schools, parents and carers: Tel 1800 55 1800; www. kidshelp.com.au

ENDNOTES

1. Ofcom Communications Market report, August 2011. Available at http://stakeholders.ofcom.org.uk/market-data-research/market-data/communications-market-reports/cmr11, accessed on 25 April 2012; Halliday, J. (2011) 'Smartphone sales up as 60% of teenage users confess to being highly addicted.' *The Guardian* 4 August, p.11.
2. Paton, G. (2010) 'Children "more likely to own a mobile phone than a book".' *The Daily Telegraph* 26 May: the National Literacy Trust 'found that 85.5 per cent of pupils had their own mobile phone, compared with 72.6 per cent who had their own books. Among children in Key Stage 2 – aged seven to 11 – 79.1 per cent had a mobile compared with 72.7 per cent who had access to books.'
3. Taken from a YouGov poll for the UK Post Office in 2008.
4. Katz. A. and McManus, E. (2008) *Teasing, Taunting, Touching: What is OK?* For Flame TV for BBC Panorama.
5. Cass, C. and Agiesta, J. (2011) 'Are online slurs OK?' Associated Press, 20 September. Available at http://stlouis.cbslocal.com/2011/09/20/are-online-slurs-ok/, accessed on 16 March 2012. The AP-MTV poll is part of the campaign, The Thin Line, to stop online abuse.
6. 'Deindividuation' refers to the idea in social psychology of one's individual identity being subsumed by a group identity in some circumstances.
7. Laville, S. (2011) 'London teenagers found guilty over Victoria station killing.' *The Guardian* 16 May. Available at www.guardian.co.uk/uk/2011/may/16/london-teenagers-jail-victoria-station-murder, accessed on 16 May 2011.
8. BBC News (2011) 'Boy's Victoria station killing "planned on Facebook".' 25 January. Available at www.bbc.co.uk/news/uk-england-london-12280889, accessed on 15 March 2012.
9. Psyblog (2010) 'Cheating: Does deindividuaiton encourage it?'. Available at www.spring.org.uk/2010/01/cheating-does-deindividuation-encourage-it.php, accessed on 25 April 2012. This is a discussion of Diener, E, Fraser, S.C., Beaman, A.L. and Kelem, R.T. (1976) 'Effects of deindividuation variables on stealing among Halloween trick-or-treaters.' *Journal of Personality and Social Psychology* 33, 2, 178–183. Available at http://psycnet.apa.org/psycinfo/1976-20842-001, accessed on 25 April 2012.
10. Jaron Lanier is a partner architect at Microsoft Research and the innovator in residence at the Annenberg School at the University of Southern California. He is also author of *You Are Not a Gadget: A Manifesto*, Kindle Edition, January 2010 (Allen Lane).
11. Finkelhor, D. (2011) 'Internet Safety: Trends in the US. Some Reflections.' Presentation at EU Kids Online Conference, London, 23 September.
12. Wertham, F. (1954) *Seduction of the Innocent.* Toronto: Clarke, Irwin and Co
13. Bond, E. (2011) 'The mobile phone = bike shed? Children, sex and mobile phones.' *New Media & Society 13,* 4, 587–604.
14. Hammarberg, T. (former Vice Chair of the UN Committee) quoted in Wertheimer, A. (1997) 'Inclusive education, a framework for change, national and international perspectives.' Bristol: Centre for Studies on Inclusive Education (CSIE). Available at www.leeds.ac.uk/disability-studies/archiveuk/CSIE/inclusive%20ed.pdf, accessed on 18 May 2012.

15. Department for Children, Schools and Families (2007) *Safe to Learn: Embedding Anti-bullying Work in Schools.* London: The Stationery Office.
16. This definition is used by the Bullying Intervention Group (www.bullyinginterventiongroup.co.uk).
17. Department for Children, Schools and Families (2008) *Bullying Involving Children and Young People with Special Educational Needs and Disabilities: Safe to Learn: Embedding Anti-bullying Work in Schools.* Nottingham: DCSF Publications, p.22.
18. Consultation By Young Voice and The Council for Disabled Children, with children, young people and parents for the development of government guidance: Department for Children, Schools and Families (2008) *Bullying Involving Children and Young People with Special Educational Needs and Disabilities: Safe to Learn: Embedding Anti-bullying Work in Schools.* Nottingham: DCSF Publications.
19. Craig, W.M. and Pepler, D.J. (1997) 'Observations of bullying and victimization in the school yard.' *Canadian Journal of School Psychology 13,* 41–59.
20. Katz, A. and McManus, E. (2009) *Safe to Play,* Dudley Metropolitan Borough Council.
21. TellUs4 Survey (2009), an England-wide pupil survey www.nfer.ac.uk/nfer/publications/TEL01/TEL01_home.cfm?publicationID=488&title=Tellus4%20national%20report, accessed on 26 April 2012.
22. Equality and Human Rights Commission (2011) *How Fair is Britain? The First Triennial Review.*
23. Carter, H. (2009) 'Teenage girl is first to be jailed for bullying on Facebook.' *Guardian,* 21 August. Available at www.guardian.co.uk/uk/2009/aug/21/facebook-bullying-sentence-teenage-girl, accessed on 16 May 2012.
24. Rivers, I. and Noret, N. (2010) '"I h8 u": findings from a five-year study of text and email bullying.' *British Educational Research Journal 36,* 4, 643–671.
25. Hinduja, S. and Patchin, J.W. (2009) *Bullying Beyond the Schoolyard: Preventing and Responding to Cyberbullying.* Thousand Oaks, CA: Sage Publications, p.49.
26. Wolak, J., Mitchell, K.J. and Finkelhor, D. (2007) 'Does online harassment constitute bullying? An exploration of online harassment by known peers and online-only contacts.' *Journal of Adolescent Health 41,* 6, Supplement, 51–58.
27. boyd, d. and Marwick, A. (2011) 'Bullying as true drama.' *New York Times* 22 September, p.A35.
28. Smith, P.K., Mahdavi, J., Carvalho, M. and Tippett, N. (2006) *An Investigation Into Cyberbullying, Its Forms, Awareness and Impact, and The Relationship Between Age and Gender and Cyberbullying.* DfES Research Report. London: Department for Education and Skills.
29. Ybarra, M.L. and Mitchell, K.J. (2004) 'Online aggressor/targets, aggressors and targets: A comparison of associated youth characteristics.' *Journal of Child Psychology and Psychiatry 45,* 7, 1308–1316.
30. Buchanan, A., Katz, A. and McCoy, A. (1999) *Young Men Speak Out: Factors Associated with Depression and Suicidal Behaviour.* London: Samaritans. In a report for the Samaritans there were strong links between bullying and suicidal thoughts among young men. They often did not want to tell their parents in order to 'protect' them. There were four suicides in three weeks in autumn 2010 in the USA.
31. Katz, A. and McManus, E. (2009) *Safe to Play,* Dudley Metropolitan Borough Council.
32. Raskauskas, J. and Stoltz, A.D. (2007) 'Involvement in traditional and electronic bullying among adolescents.' *Developmental Psychology 43,* 3, 564–575.
33. Hinduja, S. and Patchin, J.W. (2009) *Bullying Beyond the Schoolyard: Preventing and Responding to Cyberbullying.* Thousand Oaks, CA: Sage Publications, p.50.
34. *The Guardian,* Media, 30 July 2007, p.9.
35. Cowie, H. and Colliety, P. (2009) *Cyberbullying – The Situation in the UK. Country Report.* Guildford: University of Surrey.
36. The case studies described in Chapter 3 have been developed from real-life cases in my work for illustrative training purposes and disguised to protect the individuals.
37. Sourced from Cybersurvey 2009, 2010 and 2011.
38. Available at www.careerbuilder.co.uk/UK/share/aboutus/pressreleasesdetail.aspx?id=pr28&sd=1%2f13%2f2010&ed=12%2f31%2f2010, accessed on 15 March 2012.
39. Ofcom (2011) *Communications Market Report.* UK. Available at http://stakeholders.ofcom.org.uk/binaries/research/cmr/cmr11/UK_CMR_2011_FINAL.pdf, accessed on 25 April 2012.

40. Phippen, A. (2009) *Sharing Personal Images and Videos Among Young People.* Exeter: South West Grid for Learning Trust. Available at www.swgfl.org.uk/Staying-Safe/Files/Documents/sexting-detail, accessed on 15 March 2012.

41. Ybarra, M., Diener-West, M. and Leaf, P.J. (2007) 'Examining the overlap of internet harassment and school bullying: Implications for school intervention.' *Journal of Adolescent Health 41,* 842–850 – indicating that over a third of students harassed online also reported being bullied at school.

42. Hayden, C. (2008) *Staying Safe and Out of Trouble.* Portsmouth: University of Portsmouth.

43. Ybarra, M. and Mitchell, K.J. (2004) 'Online aggressor/targets, aggressors and targets: A comparison of associated youth characteristics.' *Journal of Child Psychology and Psychiatry 45,* 7, 1308–1316.

44. Ybarra, M. and Mitchell, K.J. (2004) 'Online aggressor/targets, aggressors and targets: A comparison of associated youth characteristics.' *Journal of Child Psychology and Psychiatry 45,* 7, 1308–1316.

45. Austin, S. and Joseph, S. (1996) 'Assessment of bully/victim problems in 8 to 11 year olds.' *British Journal of Educational Psychology 66,* 447–456.

46. Ybarra, M.L. and Mitchell, K. J. (2004) 'Online aggressor/targets, aggressors and targets: A comparison of associated youth characteristics.' *Journal of Child Psychology and Psychiatry 45,* 1308–1316.

47. Benton, T. (2011) *Sticks and Stones May Break My Bones, But Being Left On My Own is Worse,* NFER – analysis of school bullying within NFER attitude surveys; Williams, K.D. (2001) *Ostracism. The Power of Silence.* New York: Guilford Press.

48. East Sussex County Council Annual Safer Schools Survey 2011.

49. Smith, P.K., Mahdavi, J., Carvalho, M. and Tippett, N. (2006) *An Investigation Into Cyberbullying, Its Forms, Awareness and Impact, and The Relationship Between Age and Gender and Cyberbullying.* DfES Research Report. London: Department for Education and Skills.

50. Noret, N. and Rivers, I. (2006) 'Text Messages as a Form of Bullying: An Analysis of Content. A Qualitative Study.' Presented at the British Psychological Society Annual Conference, University of York, 21 March (20.6 per cent compared to 10.4.)

51. Cross. E.J., Richardson, B., Douglas, T. and Vonkaenel-Flatt, J. (2009) *Virtual Violence: Protecting Children from Cyberbullying.* London: Beatbullying.

52. Institute of Education Sciences (2011) *Student Reports of Bullying and Cyber-Bullying: Results From the 2007 School Crime Supplement to the National Crime Victimization Survey.* Available at http://nces.ed.gov/pubs2011/2011316.pdf, accessed on 1 May 2012.

53. Lenhart, A. (2007) *Mean Teens Online: Forget Sticks and Stones, They've Got Mail.* Pew Research Center Publications. Available at http://pewresearch.org/pubs/527/cyber-bullying, accessed on 14 December 2011.

54. Besag, V. (2006) *Understanding Girls' Friendships, Fights and Feuds: A Practical Approach to Girls' Bullying.* Maidenhead: Open University Press.

55. Andrews, E. (2011) 'Social networking sites "mean young girls are exposed to bullying 24 hours a day."' *Daily Mail* 22 November. Available at www.dailymail.co.uk/news/article-2064566/Social-networking-sites-mean-young-girls-exposed-bullying-24-hours-day.html, accessed on 23 April 2012.

56. MSN Cyberbullying Report (2006) *Blogging, Instant Messaging and Email Bullying Amongst Today's Teens.* MSN UK.

57. Kernaghan, D. (2008) 'An overview of an investigation of Northern Irish 12-15 year old female perceptions, attitudes and experiences of bullying through their online social networks.' Available at www.anti-bullyingalliance.org.uk/.../Donna_Kernaghan_cyberbullying_research.pdf, accessed on 19 March 2012.

58. Katz, A. and McManus. E. (2008) 'Teasing, Taunting, Touching: What is OK?' For Flame TV for BBC Panorama.

59. One-third of boys experienced this in the Cybersurvey 2010 out of recipients of any type of unpleasant message.

60. Cybersurvey 2010 and 2011a.

61. Boys were twice as likely as girls to say they had bullied other people, 15 per cent compared to 7 per cent in Cybersurvey 2011a, and 11 per cent compared to 6 per cent of girls in Cybersurveys 2011a, 2011b and 2011c combined.

62. Experian and the Electoral Commission, 30 December 2011.

63. Byron, T. (2008) *Safer Children in a Digital World: The Report of the Byron Review*. Nottingham: DCSF. Available at http://media.education.gov.uk/assets/files/pdf/s/safer%20children%20in%20a%20digital%20world%20the%202008%20byron%20review.pdf, accessed on 23 April 2012.

64. Katz, A. and McManus, E. (2009) *Safe to Play*, Dudley Metropolitan Borough Council.

65. Atkinson, S. and Staunton, T. (2011) 'The Early Years Online'. Paper presented at the EU Kids Online 2 Final Conference, September 2011, pp.3–10.

66. Sonck, N., Livingstone, S., Kuiper, E. and de Haan, J. (2011) *Digital Literacy and Safety Skills*. London: EU Kids Online, London School of Economics & Political Science. Available at http://eprints.lse.ac.uk/33733, accessed on 25 April 2012.

67. The Schools and Students Health Education Unit (SHEU) (2011) *Young People into 2011*. Exeter: SHEU.

68. Balding, J (2005) Young People in 2004: The Health-related Behaviour Questionnaire Results for 40,430 Young People Between the Ages of 10 and 15. Exeter: Schools Health Education Unit.

69. The charity EACH challenges homophobia. It runs a Lottery-funded programme for young people called Reach. I gratefully acknowledge their kind permission to use items from this project.

70. Davies, T., Bhullar, S. and Dowty, T. (2011) 'Rethinking responses to children and young people's online lives.' EU Kids Online 2 final conference, 22–23 September, London: London School of Economics and Political Science.

71. Vickery, J. (2011) *Why Can't We Be Facebook Friends? Social Networking, Risk and School Policies*. Austin, TX: University of Austin.

72. Hinduja, S. and Patchin, J. (2009) *Bullying Beyond the School Yard: Preventing and Responding to Cyberbullying*. Thousand Oaks, CA: Sage Publications.

73. Juvonen, J. and Gross, E. (2008) 'Extending the school grounds? Bullying experiences in cyberspace.' *Journal of School Health 78*, 496–505.

74. National Pupil Database and Longitudinal Study of Young People in England (LSYPE), wave 3 quoted in Department for Education (2011) *A Profile of Pupil Absence in England*. London: Department for Education.

75. Cross, E.J., Richardson, B., Douglas, T. and Vonkaenel-Flatt, J. (2009) *Virtual Violence: Protecting Children from Cyberbullying*. London: Beatbullying.

76. Katz, A. and McManus, E. (2009) *Safe to Play*, Dudley Metropolitan Borough Council; Department for Children, Schools and Families (2008) *Bullying Involving Children and Young People with Special Educational Needs and Disabilities: Safe to Learn: Embedding Anti-bullying Work in Schools*. Nottingham: DCSF Publications.

77. Katz, A. and McManus, E. (2009) 'Safe to Play.' Dudley Metropolitan Borough Council.

78. Katz, A. and McManus, E. (2009) 'Safe to Play.' Dudley Metropolitan Borough Council.

79. Cullingford, C. (2000) *Prejudice from Individual Identity to Nationalism in Young People*. London: Kogan Page, p.231.

80. Show Racism the Red Card (2011) *The Barriers to Tackling Racism and Promoting Equality in England's Schools*. North Shields: Show Racism the Red Card.

81. Slee, P.T. and Ford, D.C. (1999) 'Bullying is a serious issue.' *Australia & New Zealand Journal of Law & Education 4*, 1, 23–39, p.23.

82. Arseneault, L., Bowes, L. and Shakoor, S. (2009) 'Bullying victimization in youths and mental health problems: "Much ado about nothing?"' *Psychological Medicine. Psychol Med 40*, 5, 717–729.

83. Finkelhor, D., Ormrod, R.K. and Turner, H.A. (2007) 'Re-victimization patterns in a national longitudinal sample of children and youth.' *Child Abuse and Neglect 31*, 479–502.

84. Hayden, C. (2008) *Staying Safe and Out of Trouble*. Portsmouth: University of Portsmouth.

85. Ybarra, M.L., Diener-West, M. and Leaf, P.J. (2007) 'Examining the overlap of internet harassment and school bullying: implications for school intervention.' *Journal of Adolescent Health 41*, 842–850 – indicating that over a third of students harassed online also reported being bullied at school.

86. Kowalski, R.M. and Fedina, C. (2011) 'Cyber bullying in ADHD and Asperger Syndrome populations.' *Research in Autism Spectrum Disorders 5*, 1201–1208.

87. Katz A., Buchanan, A. and Bream, V. (2001) *Bullying in Britain: Testimonies from Teenagers*. Young Voice.

88. Mishna, F. (2003) 'Learning disabilities and bullying: Double jeopardy.' *Journal of Learning Disabilities 36*, 336.

89. Mencap (2007) 'Bullying wrecks lives: the experiences of children and young people with a learning disability.' Available at www.mencap.org.uk/sites/default/files/documents/2008-03/Bullying%20 wrecks%20lives.pdf, accessed on 16 May 2012.

90. Stonewall (2006) *School Report*. London: Stonewall.

91. Equality and Human Rights Commission (2010) *How Fair is Britain? The First Triennial Review.* Available at www.equalityhumanrights.com/key-projects/how-fair-is-britain, accessed on 1 May 2012.

92. Kintree, K. *et al.* (2008) *Young People and Territoriality in British Cities.* York: Joseph Rowntree Foundation.

93. Katz, A., Stockdale, D. and Dabbous, A. (2002) *Islington & You.* Young Voice.

94. These quotations have been taken from my Cybersurveys and group discussions with young people.

95. Katz, A. and McManus, E. (2009) *Safe to Play*, Dudley Metropolitan Borough Council – 38 per cent of badly bullied children in primary schools had experienced homophobic bullying.

96. Stonewall (2007) *School Report*. London: Stonewall.

97. Katz, A. (2001) *The Reach Cybersurvey for Educational Action Challenging Homophobia.* London: Youthworks Consulting.

98. Livingstone, S., Haddon, L., Görzig, A. and Ólafsson, K. (2011) *Risks and Safety on the Internet: The Perspective of European Children.* London: EU Kids Online, London School of Economics and Political Science.

99. Katz, A. and McManus (2008) 'Teasing, Taunting, Touching: What is OK?' For Flame TV for BBC Panorama.

100. Frosh, S. *et al.* (2002) *Young Masculinities.* New York: Palgrave; Mac an Ghaill, M. (1994) *The Making of Men.* Buckingham: Open University Press.

101. Buchanan, A., Katz, A. and McCoy, A. (1999) *Young Men Speak Out: Factors Associated with Depression and Suicidal Behaviour.* London: Samaritans.

102. Warwick, I. *et al.* (2004) *Homophobia, Sexual Orientation and Schools: A Review and Implications for Action.* DfES Research Report RR594, London: Department for Education and Skills; Rivers, I. (2001) 'The bullying of sexual minorities at school: Its nature and long-term correlates.' *Educational and Child Psychology 18*, 1, 32–46.

103. Department for Children, Schools and Families (2007) *Youth Cohort Study and Longitudinal Study of Young People in England: The Activities and Experiences of 16 Year Olds*; Green, R., Collingwood, A. and Ross, A. (2010) *Characteristics of Bullying Victims in Schools.* London: National Centre for Social Research.

104. Katz, A., Stockdale, D. and Dabbous, A. (2002) *Islington & You.* Young Voice.

105. Williams, K. and Nida, S.A. (2001) 'Is Ostracism Worse Than Bullying?' In M. Kern (ed.) *Bullying, Rejection and Peer Victimization: A Social Cognitive Neuroscience Perspective.* New York: Springer; Williams, K.D. and Zadro, L. (2001) 'Ostracism: On Being Ignored, Excluded, and Rejected.' In M.R. Leary (ed.) *Interpersonal Rejection.* New York: Oxford University Press; Williams, K.D. (2001) *Ostracism: The Power of Silence.* New York: Guilford Press.

106. Quoted by kind permission of Kipling Williams from an email on 13 May 2011.

107. Williams, K.D. and Nida, S.A. (2009) 'Is Ostracism Worse than Bullying?' In M. Kern (ed.) *Bullying, Rejection, and Peer Victimization: A Social Cognitive Neuroscience Perspective.* New York: Springer, pp.279–296.

108. Benton, T. (2011) *Sticks and Stones May Break My Bones, But Being On My Own Is A Lot Worse.* London: National Foundation for Educational Research (NFER) – an analysis of reported bullying within NFER attitude surveys.

109. For a list of publications, see www1.psych.purdue.edu/~willia55

110. Association of Teachers and Lecturers (2007) *Doing Gender: ATL Survey Report on Aspects of Sex/Gender Identity and Homophobia.* July.

111. Cullingford, C. (2000) *Prejudice. From Individual Identity to Nationalism in Young People.* London: Kogan Page.

112. Livingstone, S. and Helsper, E. (2010) 'Balancing opportunities and risks in teenagers' use of the internet: the role of online skills and internet self efficacy.' New Media and Society 12, 2, 309–329. Valkenburg, P.M. and Peter, J. (2007) 'Online communication and adolescent well-being: Testing

the stimulation versus the displacement hypothesis.' *Journal of Computer-Mediated Communication 12*, 4, 1169–1182. Ybarra, M.L. and Mitchell, K.J. (2004) 'Online aggressor/targets, aggressors, and targets: A comparison of associated youth characteristics.' Journal of Child Psychology and Psychiatry 45, 7, 1308–1316. described in Livingstone, S. and Brake, D. (2009) 'On the rapid rise of social networking sites, new findings and policy implications.' *Children & Society 24*, 1, 75–83.

113. Buchanan, A., Hunt, J., Bretherton, H. and Bream, V. (2001) *Families in Conflict*. London and Bristol: Nuffield Foundation and The Policy Press.

114. Carrick-Davies, S. (2011) *Munch, Poke, Ping! Vulnerable Young People, Social Media and E-Safety: A Study for the TDA*. Available at www.carrick-davies.com/research/vulnerable-young-people, accessed on 23 April 2012.

115. Carrick-Davies, S. (2011) *Munch, Poke, Ping: Vulnerable Young People, Social Media and E-safety*. London: Training and Development Agency.

116. Kelley, P. G., Brewer, R., Mayer, P., Cranor, L.F. and Sadeh, N. (2011) 'An investigation into facebook friend grouping.' Available at http://patrickgagekelley.com/papers/11interact/Interact11FB.pdf, accessed on 16 May 2012.

117. Ybarra, M.L. and Mitchell, K.J. (2004) 'Online aggressor/targets, aggressors and targets: A comparison of associated youth characteristics.' *Journal of Child Psychology and Psychiatry 45*, 7, 1308–1316.

118. Austin, S. and Joseph, S. (1996) 'Assessment of bully/victim problems in 8-11 year olds.' *British Journal of Educational Psychology 66*, 447–456; Haynie, D.L., Nansel, T.R., Eitel, P., Davis Crump, A., Saylor, K., Yu, K. and Simons-Morton, B. (2001) 'Bullies, targets and bully/victims: Distinct groups of youth-at-risk.' *Journal of Early Adolescence 21*, 29–50.

119. Mishna, F., Khoury-Kassabri, M., Gadalla, T. and Daciuk, J. (2012) 'Risk factors for involvement in cyber bullying: Victims, bullies and bully-victims.' *Children and Youth Services Review 34*, 63–70.

120. Marini, Z., Dane, A. and Volk, T. (2011) 'What's A Bully Victim?' Available at www.education.com/reference/article/what-is-a-bully-victim, accessed on 25 April 2012.

121. Ybarra, M.L. and Mitchell, K.J. (2004) 'Online aggressor/targets, aggressors, and targets: A comparison of associated youth characteristics.' *Journal of Child Psychology and Psychiatry 45*, 7, 1308–1316.

122. Woods, S. and White, E. (2005) 'The association between bullying behaviour, arousal levels and behaviour problems.' *Journal of Adolescence 28*, 3, 381–395. Available at www.psy.herts.ac.uk/res/SW-PUB3.pdf, accessed on 25 April 2012.

123. Stein, J.A., Dukes, R.L. and Warren, J.I. (2007) 'Adolescent male bullies, victims, and bully/victims: A comparison of psychosocial and behavioral characteristics.' *Journal of Pediatric Psychology 32*, 3, 273–382.

124. Glew, G.M., Fan, M.Y., Katon, W. and Rivara, F.P. (2008) 'Bullying and school safety.' *Journal of Pediatrics 152*, 1, 123–128.

125. Unnever, J.D. (2005) 'Bullies, aggressive victims, and victims: Are they distinct groups?' *Aggressive Behavior 31*, 2, 153–171.

126. The Cybersurvey can be commissioned throughout the year at www.youthworksconsulting.co.uk.

127. Smith, P.K., Kupferburg, A., Mora-Merchan, J., Samara, M., Osborn, R. and Bosley, S. (2011) 'A content analysis of school anti-bullying policies: A follow up after six years.' *Educational Psychology in Practice 28*, 1, 61–84.

128. Research conducted by BMRB for the Anti-Bullying Alliance during October 2009 of 1163 parents of children aged 8–14 in England.

129. Ybarra, M.L., Mitchell, K.J., Finkelhor, D. and Wolak, J. (2007) 'Internet prevention messages: Targeting the right online behaviours.' *Archives of Pediatrics & Adolescent Medicine 161*, 138–145. Quotation p.144.

130. Ybarra, M.L., Mitchell, K.J., Finkelhor, D. and Wolak, J. (2007) 'Internet prevention messages: Targeting the right online behaviours.' *Archives of Pediatrics & Adolescent Medicine 161*, 138–145. Quotation p.144.

131. With grateful thanks to the Reach Project run by the charity EACH (Educational Action Challenging Homophobia) for letting me quote from this workshop we delivered together.

132. With grateful thanks to the Reach Project run by the charity EACH (Educational Action Challenging Homophobia) for letting me quote from this workshop we delivered together.

133. i-SAFE National Assessment Center. Statistics retrieved on 24 May 2007 from www.isafe.org/xblock.

134. Livingstone, S., Haddon, L., Görzig, A. and Ólafsson, K. (2011). *Risks and safety on the internet: The perspective of European children. Full Findings*. LSE, London: EU Kids Online. Available at www2.lse. ac.uk/media@lse/research/EUKidsOnline/EUKidsII%20(2009-11)/EUKidsOnlineIIReports/D4FullFindings.pdf, accessed on 25 April 2012.

135. The phenomenon of 'juvenoia' was described by David Finkelhor in a presentation entitled 'The Internet, Youth Deviance and the Problem of Juvenoia' at the EU Kids Online conference at the London School of Economics and Political Science in September 2011.

136. Family Online Safety Institute (2011) *State of Online Safety Report*, p.10.

137. Murray, J. (2012) 'Pupils need to understand computers, not just how to use them.' *Guardian*, 9 January. Available at www.guardian.co.uk/education/2012/jan/09/computer-studies-in-schools, accessed on 17 May 2012.

138. Carrick-Davies, S. (2011) *Munch, Poke, Ping: Vulnerable Young People, Social Media and E-safety*. London: Training and Development Agency – points out that there was an absence of supportive adults in the lives of the pupils in a PRU where he undertook focus groups.

139. Greenwich Board of Education, Connecticut, 'Bullying Prevention and Intervention Procedure'. Draft addition to Policy E-002, Whole Student Development. Reported by Greenwich Patch, available at http://greenwich.patch.com/articles/bullying-5f3cb349, accessed on 24 April 2012.

140. Smith, P.K. and Shu, S. (2000) 'What good schools can do about bullying: Findings from a survey in English schools after a decade of research and action.' *Childhood 7*, 2, 193–212.

141. Katz, A. and McManus, E. (2009) *Safe to Play*, Dudley Metropolitan Borough Council.

142. Beatbullying (2012) *Virtual Violence 11: Progress and Challenges in the Fight Against Cyberbullying*. London: Beatbullying. Based on an average teacher's income per year (£36,200), they calculated teaching hours per week (40 hours).

143. Beatbullying (2012) *Virtual Violence 11: Progress and Challenges in the Fight Against Cyberbullying*. London: Beatbullying.

144. Equality Act 2010.

145. boyd, d. and Marwick, A. (2011) 'Bullying as true drama.' *New York Times*, 22 September. danah boyd is a senior researcher at Microsoft Research and a research assistant professor at New York University. Alice Marwick is a postdoctoral researcher at Microsoft Research and a research affiliate at Harvard University, Cambridge, MA.

146. Cohen, R. (1995) *Students Resolving Conflict: Peer Mediation in Schools*. Tucson, AZ: Good Year Books. Pages 48–49.

147. Rigby, K. (2011) 'What can schools do about cases of bullying?' *Pastoral Care in Education 29*, 4, December, 273–285, p.277.

148. Robinson, G. and Maines, B. (2008) *Bullying: A Complete Guide to the Support Group Method*. London: Sage Publications.

149. Pikas is a counselling-based approach for situations where a group of pupils have been bullying. The bullying children are seen individually and encouraged to recognise the suffering of the victim and suggest a positive way forward. The victim is also seen (and if a provocative victim, encouraged to modify his/her behaviour). The approach works towards a group meeting of the bullies and victim to agree a modus vivendi with some follow-up. It is not suitable for children under 9 years. Class teachers and counsellors require prior training.

150. Used in England to bring together a range of agencies to collaborate on a case in severe cases, or those that reveal other concerns such as domestic violence or other child protection issues, such as drug or alcohol misusing parents.

151. Keogh, K. (2011) *The Birmingham Post* 24 January.

152. EdArabia (n.d.) 'School in Dubai has banned teachers from befriending students on Facebook.' Available at www.edarabia.com/21230/school-in-dubai-has-banned-teachers-from-befriending-students-on-facebook, accessed on 16 March 2012.

153. Williams, R. (2010) 'Teachers suffer cyberbullying by pupils and parents.' *The Guardian* 30 March. Available at www.guardian.co.uk/education/2010/mar/30/teachers-bullied-online, accessed on 17 August 2011; see also www.atl.org.uk

154. Hartley-Parkinson, R. (2011) 'One in three teachers bullied online by pupils AND parents.' *Mail Online* 16 August. Available at www.dailymail.co.uk/sciencetech/article-2026450/One-teachers-bullied-online-parents-pupils.html#ixzz1VIOxxP2I, accessed on 16 March 2012; Phippen, A. (2011) *The Online Abuse of Professionals – Research Report*, UK Safer Internet Centre.

155. Quoted in Warman, M. (2011) 'Teachers fear Facebook more than Ofsted.' *The Telegraph* 17 August. Available at www.telegraph.co.uk/technology/social-media/8704823/Teachers-fear-Facebook-more-than-Ofsted.html, accessed 17 August 2011.

156. James Silver, 'Teachers "bullied by online grading".' Radio 5 Live. Available at http://news.bbc.co.uk/1/hi/uk/6139626.stm, accessed on 15 August 2011.

157. *The Scotsman* 27 January 2007.

158. Hopwood was addressing an NUT conference in April 2011. Reported in *The Guardian* 24 April 2011. Available at www.guardian.co.uk/education/2011/apr/24/pupils-facebook-friends-net-privacy-teachers, accessed on 24 April 2012.

159. Vasegar, J. and Williams, M. (2012) 'Teachers warned over befriending pupils on Facebook.' *The Guardian* 23 January.

160. Phippen, A. (2011) *The Online Abuse of Professionals – Research Report*. UK Safer Internet Centre.

161. Smith, P.K., Kupferberg, A., Mora-Merchan, J.A., Samara, M., Bosley, S. and Osborn, R. (2012) 'A Content analysis of school anti-bullying policies: A follow-up after six years. *Educational Psychology in Practice 28*, 1, 47–70.

162. On the website of the Department for Education (www.education.gov.uk)

163. It is good practice for all types of schools to record racist incidents and in England, since theMcPherson enquiry after the death of Stephen Lawrence, the recommendation to report these to the local authority has been widely followed. There are moves to expand this practice to record incidents affecting all those protected by Equality Act 2010. For Ofsted inspections, schools should show they have a robust system for the recording of prejudice related bullying as evidence of their 'due regard' for fostering good relations and for keeping pupils safe. They will be inspected on the actions they have taken as a result, rather than on the data itself. Richardson, R. (2011) 'Recording and reporting racist incidents in schools – an update on requirements and good practice, summer 2011'. Insted Consultancy. Available at www.insted.co.uk/recording-reporting-2011.pdf, accessed on 25 May 2012; Ofsted (2012). 'Inspecting equalities: Briefing for section 5 inspection'. Manchester: Ofsted. Available at www.ofsted.gov.uk/resources/briefings-and-information-for-use-during-inspections-of-maintained-schools-and-academies-january-201, accessed on 25 May 2012.

164. This lesson has been used by the Adrienne Katz for many years in anti-bullying work and is also used in a booklet written by her to accompany the DVD 'Make Them Go Away' (2009). Available at www.education.gov.uk/publications/standard/publicationDetail/Page1/DCSF-00672-2009, accessed on 29 May 2012.

165. Cybersurvey reports are available at www.youthworksconsulting.co.uk. Schools also frequently do their own surveys of pupils' experiences of bullying and could use these.

166. Greenspun, P. (2007) 'History of Photography Timeline.' Available at http://photo.net/history/timeline, accessed on 17 May 2012.

167. Roger Crouch, the father of Dominic, speaks movingly about the family's loss of a much loved son. Roger campaigned against homophobic bullying after Dominic's death but sadly succumbed to grief and killed himself a year later. This clip is only suitable for older teens with support. Available at www.youtube.com/watch?v=llfW1bhbqWk, accessed on 30 April 2012.

168. Childnet, Lets Fight It Together. Available at www.digizen.org/resources/cyberbullying/films/uk/lfit-film.aspx, accessed on 18 May, 2012; Take One Productions, Make Them Go Away. Available at http://clients.mediaondemand.net/take1flv/dcsf/send/SEND.html, accessed on 18 May 2012. The resource booklet is available at http://clients.mediaondemand.net/take1flv/dcsf/send/send_online/8206-DCSF-DVD%20Booklet.pdf.

169. The UN Convention on the Rights of the Child: www.unicef.org.uk/UNICEFs-Work/Our-mission/UN-Convention.

170. For all the behaviour policies: www.education.gov.uk/schools/pupilsupport/behaviour/behaviourpolicies.

171. Advice for headteachers, staff and governing bodies: www.education.gov.uk/aboutdfe/advice/f0076899/preventing-and-tackling-bullying.

172. www.fosigrid.org/index.php?option=com_content&view=article&Itemid=97&id=30%3Aunited-kingdom, accessed on 26 July 2011 from the Family Online Safety Institute.

173. Independent Parliamentary Inquiry Into Online Child Protection: Findings and Recommendations (2012) Available at www.claireperry.org.uk/downloads/independent-parliamentary-inquiry-into-online-child-protection.pdf, accessed on 22 May 2012.

174. Literacy The State of the Nation, The National Literacy Trust, www.literacytrust.org.uk.

175. Livingston, S. and Palmer, T. (2012) 'Identifying Vulnerable Children Online and What Strategies Can Help Them.' UKCCIS.

176. Save The Children's campaign to end Child Poverty (9th Jan 2008) claims child poverty is the biggest barrier to social mobility and they argued in June 2011 that UK children have the lowest chance of escaping poverty. Save the Children (2011) 'UK children have lowest chance of escaping poverty'. Available at www.savethechildren.org.uk/news/2011/06/uk-children-poverty, accessed on 29 May 2012. Save The Children argued their case by quoting from the 2010 OECD report 'A Family Affair: Intergenerational Social Mobility across OECD countries'. Available at www.oecd.org/dataoecd/2/7/45002641.pdf, accessed on 29 May 2012.

177. Katz, A., Buchanan, A. and McCoy, A. (2002) *Thwarted Dreams: Young Views from Bradford.* Surrey: Young Voice.

178. Livingstone, S., Haddon, L., Görzig, A. and Ólafsson, K. (2011) Risks and safety on the internet: The perspective of European children. Full Findings. LSE, London: EU Kids Online. Available at www2.lse.ac.uk/media@lse/research/EUKidsOnline/EUKidsII%20(2009-11)/EUKidsOnlineIIReports/D4FullFindings.pdf, accessed on 25 April 2012.

179. Harlow, J. (2011) 'What a Lot of Bitter Twitter.' *The Sunday Times,* 31 July 2011.

180. Byron, T. (2008) 'Safer Children in a Digital World' and (2010) 'Do we have safer children in a digital world? A review.' London: DCSF. Available at www.education.gov.uk/ukccis/about/a0076277/the-byron-reviews, accessed on 22 May 2012.

181. www.dcsf.gov.uk/ukccis/content.cfm?id=background_to_the_council, accessed on 26 July 2011.

182. Childnet (2007) 'Cyberbullying: A Whole School Community Issue.' Available at www.childnet-int.org/publications/policy.aspx, accessed on 22 May 2012; DCFS (2007) 'Safe To Learn: embedding anti-bullying work in schools.' Available at http://old.digizen.org/cyberbullying/fullguidance, accessed on 22 May 2012.

183. Vickery, J. (2011) Paper given at EU Kids Online conference, London School of Economics and Political Science, London.

184. United States Secret Service and United States Department of Education (2002) 'The Final Report and Findings of the Safe School Initiative: Implications for the Prevention of School Attacks in the United States.' Washington, DC. Available at www.secretservice.gov/ntac/ssi_final_report.pdf, accessed on 25 April 2012.

185. www.internetworldstats.com (viewed 13 December 2011).

186. www.internetworldstats.com/top20.htm (viewed 13 December 2011).

187. www.consumerreports.org/cro/magazine-archive/2010/june/electronics-computers/social-insecurity/state-of-the-net-2010/index.htm.

188. Family Safety Centre page on Facebook. Available at http://engb.facebook.com/help/safety, accessed on 24 April 2012.

189. www.inman.com/news/2011/08/30/number-smartphone-users-jumps-10, accessed on 13 December 2011.

190. Schrock, A., Boyd, D. and Sacco, D. (2010) Enhancing Child Safety and Online Technologies: Final report of the Internet Safety Technical Task Force to the Multi-State Working Group on Social Networking of States Attorneys General of the United States. Durham: Carolina Academic Press. Available at http://cyber.law.harvard.edu/sites/cyber.law.harvard.edu/files/ISTTF_Final_Report.pdf, accessed 21 May 2012.

191. Shariff, S. (2009) *Confronting Cyber-Bullying: What Schools Need to Know to Control Misconduct and Avoid Legal Consequences.* New York: Cambridge University Press.

192. Vickery, J. (2011) Paper given at EU Kids Online conference, London School of Economics and Political Science, London.
193. Youth Internet Safety Survey (YISS) 1 Publications are available at www.unh.edu/ccrc/youth_internet_safety_survey_publications.html; information and publications relating to the Second Youth Internet Safety Survey (YISS-2) at http://unh.edu/ccrc/projects/second_youth_internet_safety.html, accessed on 24 April 2012.
194. Information about the Third Youth Internet Safety Survey (YISS-3) is available at www.unh.edu/ccrc/projects/yiss3.html, accessed on 24 April 2012.
195. The phenomenon of 'juvenoia' was described by David Finkelhor in a presentation entitled 'The Internet, Youth Deviance and the Problem of Juvenoia' at the EU Kids Online conference at the London School of Economics and Political Science in September 2011.
196. Hinduja, S. and Patchin, J.W. (2011) *Electronic Dating Violence: A Brief Guide for Educators and Parents*; (2010) *Cyberbullying: Identification, Prevention and Response*; (2011) *Cyberbullying Research Summary: Bullying, Cyberbullying and Sexual Orientation*.
197. Michelle Ybarra, president and research director of Internet Solutions for Kids.
198. http://cyber.law.harvard.edu/publications/2010/Kids_Data_Internet_Safety#cyberharassment

INDEX